PROBLEMS OF ADOLESCENCE IN THE SECONDARY SCHOOL

PROBLEMS OF ADOLESCENCE IN THE SECONDARY SCHOOL

Edited by Geoff Lindsay

CROOM HELM
London & Canberra

British Library Cataloguing in Publication Data

Problems of adolescence in the secondary school.
   1. Adolescence psychology
   I. Lindsay, Geoff
   155.5   BF724   0089845
   ISBN 0-7099-1621-3
   ISBN 0-7099-1643-4 Pbk

Filmset in English Times
by Pat and Anne Murphy Typesetters,
Highcliffe-on-Sea, Dorset

Printed and bound in Great Britain
by Billing & Sons Limited, Worcester.

CONTENTS

LIST OF FIGURES

LIST OF TABLES

To my wife, Margaret

INTRODUCTION

This book is concerned with the problems faced by young people as they develop through adolescence, and how these difficulties interact with the secondary school. Its focus is on educational and psychological problems, rather than those which are primarily medical.

In Britain we have recently (1 April 1983) witnessed the enactment of an important item of legislation: the 1981 Education Act. Derived from the recommendations of the Warnock Report of 1978, it is intended to improve the treatment of those children and young people with special educational needs. Despite its shortcomings it is likely to be an Act of major importance. Not only does it provide a new legislative framework for special education but, together with the accompanying circulars and regulations, it encapsulates the changed emphasis of our view of special needs and how they should be treated. Special education can no longer be seen as something to be ignored by the majority of teachers. Special education is now part of mainstream education and, as previously segregated children with special educational needs are integrated into ordinary schools, its impact will be felt by all teachers. If this reconceptualisation is to be more than mere philosophising, and the youngsters in question are to receive the education to which they are entitled, resources must be improved. But in addition teachers must become more knowledgeable of children with special needs, and in many cases attitudes must be examined and altered.

Schools, therefore, now have an increased responsibility towards children with special educational needs. But there are other pupils who also have special needs which are not *educational* in the strict sense. Adolescence is a difficult time for many young people and problems are faced which can often be alleviated by the action of the school. Teachers provide an excellent resource for helping pupils develop through adolescence in an optimal fashion, providing they have facilitating attitudes, appropriate knowledge and skill, and the organisation of the school encourages this.

The content of this book covers both of these special needs — educational and personal. Also, throughout the book reference will be made to the school's role as both a contributor to the causation of difficulties, and a major source of help. This is not to deny that some problems have their origins elsewhere, or to suggest that the school should try to cure all the ills of society. Rather the aim is to emphasise the true importance of the school in the lives of youngsters with special needs.

1 CHILDREN WITH SPECIAL EDUCATIONAL NEEDS — AN OVERVIEW

Geoff Lindsay

The publication in 1978 of the Warnock Report (Department of Education and Science, 1978) was a milestone in the development of thinking about children with special educational needs. Not only was this the first comprehensive examination of the issue of special education, the Report also presented a reconceptualisation of the subject. Although previous legislation and guidelines had assumed there to be a wide range of problems of development suffered by children and young people, particularly with respect to the education system, practice had been more rigid than such an appreciation would demand. For example, young people ascertained as having one or more of a number of handicaps would be placed in segregated special schools. In 1980 approximately 1.85 per cent of children were so placed, either in special schools or units within ordinary schools. Although the latter were intended to provide education which is less segregated, many units operated with little contact with the mainstream of the school. The Warnock Report emphasised that the actual number of youngsters with special educational needs was very much higher than the approximately 2 per cent in special schools and units. Drawing upon the evidence of large-scale epidemiological studies (Rutter, Tizard and Whitmore, 1970; Davie, Butler and Goldenstein, 1972) the Committee argued that about one in six children could be expected to have special needs at any one time, and that one in five would have these at some stage during their school lives. The Report also recommends moving away from a simplistic dichotomy where children are considered to be either handicapped or non-handicapped.

The Warnock Report has not gone uncriticised, but it certainly acted as a great stimulus to the education system. Many of the recommendations reflected good practice at that time, but this was often in a minority of schools or Local Education Authorities (LEAs). In others, facilities were poor or non-existent for some children with special needs. The Report brought parents into the centre-stage and their role as 'partners' rather than recipients and executors of professional advice was strongly advocated. Although

1

not going as far as some wanted, the Report did argue for a move towards an integrated educational system for children with special educational needs. Based largely upon the Report, and upon the comments made by professional associations, voluntary bodies, and other interested parties, a White Paper *Special Needs in Education* (DES, 1980) was produced, forming the basis for the 1980 Education Bill. This received a great deal of attention, and some amendments, before emerging as the 1981 Education Act. This Act came into operation on 1 April 1983 and lays down that children with special educational needs must be integrated within the normal school setting, except in certain circumstances (see Chapter 11).

These several documents have over the past five years helped to produce a greater awareness of the issue of special education. On the negative side, this was partly the result of some scare stories which gave the impression that within a matter of weeks the children then being educated in special schools would be transferred to (or 'dumped' in) an unprepared and unwilling ordinary school system. Given that in the late 1970s there were over 130,000 such children, a great deal of concern was expressed — to put it mildly. At times it was an unedifying spectacle.

But there were many positive aspects. During the past ten to fifteen years there have been major advances in the field of special education. Mentally handicapped youngsters became the responsibility of the LEA following the Education (Handicapped Children) Act of 1970. Research in special education has produced many useful findings, not least in the area of severe learning difficulties. In the late 1970s curriculum development in schools for children with moderate learning difficulties (ESN(M)) produced interesting results (e.g. Ainscow and Tweddle, 1979). Many special schools have begun to actively seek links with the community, including neighbouring normal schools. New technical equipment for some children with physical disabilities, including visual and hearing impairment, has facilitated a more flexible approach to teaching.

What are Special Educational Needs?

The introduction of new terms into the educational and psychological vocabulary is often met with justified resistance. Many appear to add little if anything to those they replace, while others seem particularly unhelpful merely adding to the amount of 'psychobabble'. A phrase which was used in the Warnock Report, and has subsequently been used in the 1981 Education Act, is 'special educational needs'. Although this term is not without criticism, its use does reflect a positive development. It encapsulates a change in emphasis from one of causality to that of action.

Traditionally we have tended to conceive many problems as residing within the child. In cases where there is an obvious and significant physical condition this approach may not seem unreasonable; an example would be severe or profound hearing loss. However, even with such an obvious organic causation of the problem, the person's development will be significantly affected by decisions on matters of teaching. Thus while the original locus of the problem for the hearing-impaired youngster is within him- or herself, in terms of action we must consider the interaction between the person and the learning environment.

Another tendency has been to locate problems within the family. For example, some children are considered to act as they do because of the intra-family dynamics, perhaps leading to excessive guilt, resentment, shame or other unhealthy reactions, which in turn produce some kind of maladjustment. A third problem-location is the community or subculture. Research on the effects of the peer group suggests that some problems can indeed be attributed to these loci, particularly that research into delinquency.

More recently a fourth, and for teachers a more threatening, location has been postulated by an increasing number of authors — the school. Studies including the classic by Hargreaves (1967) have indicated that the way the school operates can have a major effect on the way its pupils act. There are now a number of studies which support the idea that schools matter in many respects, and that given similar intakes of children and resources the processes within a school can produce different effects on a range of variables as different as examination results, attendance rates, and out-of-school delinquency (Gillham, 1981; Rutter *et al.*, 1979). However, this is an assertion which is more threatening to teachers. We expect schools to be an influence for good, but are often reluctant to accept that their impact can be negative.

There is now an increased awareness that there is a range of possible locations of problems. In reality various factors will be pertinent, although their relative contribution will differ from case to case. For some pupils a physical disability will be the main factor, for others it may be the family. But in all cases it is important to recognise the interaction between all the various factors, both in terms of the causation of the problem and its resolution or amelioration. In some instances a problem may be primarily caused by the family dynamics, yet the most appropriate focus of help might be the youngster in his or her school setting, or by individual counselling, rather than some form of family intervention which would seem the most logical approach (Lindsay, 1981a). The progress of a pupil with impaired vision may be more affected by the degree of support of parents and teachers than the degree of impairment. Youngsters who fail to learn adequately may have a specific problem with processing certain kinds of information, but the impact of the school will cause different rates of progress for similar within-child difficulties. This interaction effect is particularly well shown by studies of problem behaviour. Gillham (1981) suggests that, when transferring a pupil exhibiting problem behaviour from one school to another:

> Having prepared many detailed and careful reports on a child's maladjustment, a common experience for the writer has been to find that the receiving school did not recognise the child in my report. (p.13)

Increasingly the emphasis of assessment, at least by educational psychologists, has changed. No longer is it considered sufficient to investigate the child, and possibly the family, in a vacuum. Rather, the learning environment is also an important point of study. The child with a problem is investigated within a context, and at the end of the assessment process it may be determined that it is not the pupil who must change but some aspect of that context. Assessment is no longer to be confined to ascertainment, or categorising a pupil as educationally subnormal, maladjusted, or any other category of handicap. The good practice which has been developed over the past ten years has now been given the official stamp of approval.

A similar widening of the range of options has occured with intervention. The traditional method of treatment was at the level of the individual, particularly the child but often also the parents (in reality usually the mother). Individual psychotherapy for children with emotional problems, remedial teaching or educational therapy (often in a clinic rather than the child's school) for those with certain kinds of learning difficulties are some examples. However, with the increase in awareness that schools might be contributors to the causation of problems has come an interest in intervening at the level of the system rather than the individual. In this case it may be the school rather than the child that is the client. A number of teachers, advisers and educational psychologists have developed their practices to work at this level. A simple, yet interesting, example is provided by Hastings (1981), who is a head-teacher. He describes how the alteration of the arrangement of the school day reduced problem behaviour. Years 1 and 2 had five lessons in the morning while years 3, 4 and 5 had only four. During the time that the lower school was at lesson 5, the upper school was in lunch; similarly as the older pupils began lesson 5 the younger children started their lunchbreak. This organisation both reduced the number of pupils out of lessons during the lunch period at any given time, and also reduced the length of that period. The results appear positive, although evaluation is limited to Hastings' impressions:

> There has been less litter (less time in which to create it?), the school has been cleaner (fewer people moving in and out?), and there has been a negligible amount of vandalism (less time for boredom and greater awareness by the small groups of pupils of the presence of supervision?) (p. 122)

Other schools, for example that described by Eileen Gledhill in Chapter 3, have also tried such alterations with similar results.

If such simple changes can affect deviant behaviour, what greater possibilities for positive action must exist at the level of classroom practice. Although there are never any simple or comprehensive answers, mixed ability teaching and some curriculum modifications have been found to have a positive effect on behaviour, including learning. For example, Ball (1981) reports that there was an important reduction in the number of behaviour problems at Beachside Comprehensive when it changed from a banded to a mixed ability arrangement. Second year pupils in mixed ability classes recorded a total of 90 detentions, compared with a previous banded second year's total of 243 (0.30 compared with 0.85 detentions per pupil).

The development of our thinking about both causation and inter-vention has led to a much wider conceptualisation of special education needs. We still must investigate causes, as appropriate, but it is not enough to simply categorise and thereby 'explain' a problem. Intervention might still include traditional individual approaches (e.g. counselling) for personal problems, or systems intervention for school- or LEA-based problems. In some complex cases different contributing causes and methods of intervention might be indentified (Lindsay, 1981a).

Used appropriately the term 'special educational needs' reflects a positive development. There are, however, some difficulties. First, the use of the word 'educational' could lead to a reduced appreciation of other needs. An adolescent may have an emotional difficulty which, though not having an effect on schoolwork is causing personal distress. Teachers and psychologists would still consider such psychological problems as important. The second criticism is more difficult and relates to the way in which 'special' needs are defined. Many educationalists have pointed to the underachievement of working-class youngsters, and more recently to those from certain ethnic groups, particularly those of West Indian origin. This failure, it is argued, is not a result of intrinsic deficiencies or disabilities within the child, but of the inappropriateness of, or the antipathy (even hostility) within, the system to the needs of these pupils. In such circumstances to talk of the youngsters having special educational needs is inappropriate, not to say insulting. Now the general interpretation of the term does not necessarily imply deficiencies within the child. As was argued above, the emphasis is on what the pupils need rather than why they have special needs. But in some discussions there is a danger of subtle differences being ignored.

Changing Aspects of Adolescence

Adolescence has been the subject of many studies but, as Elder (1980) argues, these have varied in their main focus over the past 40 years. Investigations in the 1940s were characterised by a consideration of the physical changes during adolescence and their psychological correlates. Later, emphasis switched to social themes, with a focus on the relationships formed by adolescents and the impact upon them of society's expectations. For example Hollingshead's classic study *Elmstown's Youth* (1949) had as an underlying assumption that adolescent behaviour is far more dependent upon position in the social structure than upon age-related biopsychological phenomena. Social ambiguity and status contradiction were highlighted as two of the important aspects of adolescent development. The study found no support for the widely shared concepts regarding upper and lower age limits of adolescence. As in this country, behaviour is legitimised at different ages.

However, these two strands of research are not sufficient and a third theme has subsequently been considered. This concerns the historical time during which a young person is developing. It is immediately evident that today's youth inhabits a world very different from that of only 20 years ago. In the case of some factors, particularly unemployment, major changes have occurred during a period of only a few years. Alterations in the nature of society have happened at various levels, including society as a whole, youth culture and the education system.

It is commonly asserted that society has become more affluent. Indices of ownership of consumer durables (e.g. televisions, cars) have shown an upward trend; but this may now be going into reverse as families find they can no longer buy what were once called 'luxury goods'. Also more subtle trends must be examined. While a family may continue to own a car it may now delay its replacement.

A major characteristic of society is presently unemployment, with official figures reporting about three and a quarter million people being out of work, and the real number possibly being as high as four million, if those who do not register are included. School leavers in particular have been seriously affected. Despite initiatives such as the Youth Opportunities Scheme, 'real work' (as defined by the young people themselves) is a scarce commodity.

Attitudes to and legal constraints on some aspects of behaviour have also altered. Censorship has been relaxed and it is now possible for older adolescents to see films whose sexual or violent explicitness is far greater than those available in cinemas ten years ago. This trend has been accelerated by the greater availability of video recorders. A study in Sweden by Wall and Cederblad (1982) investigated the video-viewing habits of 10 to 16 year olds. Among those who watched video frequently (once a week or more) violent and pornographic films were the most popular. A small number (14 per cent) obtained the videos themselves, and about three-quarters acknowledged that their parents knew they watched violent, horror or pornographic films. Although there is a lack of evidence on the effects of such films, research on the effects of television, with less extreme presentations, and our knowledge of child development do suggest an *a priori* case for concern about films portraying explicit violence, especially when this is linked with sexual behaviour.

Divorce rates have risen dramatically following the Divorce Reform Act of 1969. In 1980 there were 148,000 decrees absolute and of these 88,000 involved children under 16 years. Immigration has been reduced by government action but there is now a new generation of young people who were born in this country of immigrant parents. Although British by birth they are often regarded as immigrants, particularly if they are black. The past ten years has seen a growth in the number and size of extreme racist groups, and racially-motivated attacks. In 1981 some cities, particularly Liverpool, were the scene of riots, mainly by young people.

Adolescent culture itself has also changed. Various subgroups have come, gone and reappeared. Appearance has been the subject of confrontations with pupils being sent home for having 'inappropriate' styles. Hair has been too long or too short, or the wrong colour. Some youngsters would currently be at risk of such treatment on all three criteria! Mobility has increased among the young and it is common for adolescents to visit towns hundreds of miles away, and even other countries, to follow their football team. Preferences for drugs have changed and tobacco, alcohol, amphetamines, cannabis, glue and many other substances have all found varying degrees of favour.

Thus when considering adolescence as a stage in development it is important to take note of these three separate, though related, factors:

(1) Life or developmental time — this includes biological aspects of aging relevant to this period.
(2) Social time — relationships with peers, adults and the effects of contemporary social norms and role expectations.
(3) Historical time — the year of birth defines location in the historical process, and membership of a cohort will be characterised by differences in composition (social, cultural and psychological), size and ecological setting.

Adolescence, therefore, is not a static concept. Evidence that was collected on adolescent experiences in the past may be of limited relevance today, particularly if the historical time dimension reveals significant changes. But it is against a background of general adolescent development that we must consider youngsters with special needs.

Of particular relevance to this issue is whether much can be done anyway with adolescents who have special educational needs. During recent years there has been a major emphasis on intervening with very young children, based upon an assumption that the earlier identification of special needs occurs, the sooner some action can take place, and the better for the child. There is much evidence to support the usefulness of these approaches, but it is increasingly being recognised that they are not enough. What is required is a life-span perspective, for two reasons. First there is now a good deal of research which shows that early gains in performance following intervention programmes can be 'washed out' when the intervention stops, if the children are simply returned to mainstream settings which are not designed to meet their needs. Second, recent evidence suggests that adolescence is a time when youngsters can be receptive to new approaches. If these are tried adolescence can be a time of an intellectual growth spurt beyond that predicted by earlier development (see Hobbs and Robinson, 1982). These authors argue that there should be a change in public policy, and that more money should be allocated to fund projects with adolescents. If this more positive view of adolescence is taken there would be implications for the treatment of many pupils in secondary schools — particularly those with mild and moderate learning difficulties. At present these are often considered to have problems which, because of their long-standing nature, are highly resistant to solution. The alternative perspective, argued by Hobbs and Robinson, would be that the pupil's developing cognitive abilities and increased emotional maturity, associated with adolescence, can be harnessed more productively to overcome the difficulties which the youngster has been experiencing.

Integration

Where a local education authority arranges special educational provision for a child for whom they maintain a statement under section 7 of this Act it shall be the duty of the authority, if the conditions mentioned in subsection (3) below are satisfied, to secure that he is educated in an ordinary school. (para 2(2))

This clause of the Education Act 1981 places a duty on LEAs to educate pupils with special educational needs in ordinary schools. There are of course exceptions made, in the following paragraph of the Act, but that clause reproduced here does contain a clear statement of principle. As such it corresponds to the legislation in the United States, the Education for All Handicapped Children Act, PL 94-142, passed in 1975, and reflects a general change within Western society concerning the way people with special needs should be treated. The traditional model was that of segregation: deviant adults and children were placed in institutions, often outside the main centres of population (e.g. Victorian asylums) or at least away from the mainstream of life (e.g. most special schools). This arrangement had a presumed positive aspect: expertise and resources could be concentrated to the advantage of the handicapped population, who would also be given the advantage of a protected environment. However, there was also the negative side. Segregated provision could enable society to function more satisfactorily by removing misfits who created extra demands and interrupted its smooth running. In the case of schools, the removal of children who pose problems by their behaviour or learning difficulties eases the task of the school, and facilitates the achievement of better results by the remaining pupils.

Experience and research have both shown that the positive aims of segregated provision have often not been realised. The Warnock Report states that only 22 per cent of teachers in special schools held an additional qualification in the teaching of handicapped children. Although teachers of children with sensory disabilities could usually be exempt from this finding, this very low percentage for special schools as a whole challenges the view that they are centres of expertise. Research on the efficacy of special schools has also produced disappointing results. Ghodsian and Calnan (1977) report that children ascertained as being educationally subnormal at the age of seven years made better progress if they remained in ordinary schools than if they transferred to ESN(M) schools at that age. Other studies of ESN(M) and maladjusted schools have also failed to show positive effects of such provisions (Galloway and Goodwin, 1979). Tomlinson (1981) has also studied the process whereby youngsters entered ESN(M) schools in one large urban LEA. She claims that the aim of this process is to remove pupils who are disturbing to the smooth running of the system, rather than to provide a positive resource for the children. She places this in a wider sociological context, pointing out that the vast majority of children entering ESN(M) schools are from working-class families who are reluctant to challenge the system. Despite some flaws in the study, the evidence she presents on this point is persuasive.

The arguments made by Tomlinson relate not only to the efficacy of special education but more particularly to the issue of children's rights. Proponents of this argument contend that segregated special schools (or at least how they have developed for many of the children concerned) are an inferior form of provision compared with ordinary schools in several important dimensions. As a matter of principle children should attend schools that are designed for all children, so that they might develop together, to the mutual benefit of those with special needs and ordinary children. Removing children from mainstream is seen as an infringement of their rights. This argument is quite separate from that concerning efficacy, although the two are related; unfortunately they are often confounded. It may be shown that children with certain disabilities currently make better progress in segregated special schools. This does not negate the argument based on rights whose advocates would stress that these children should still be educated in ordinary schools, and be provided with the facilities or teaching which enabled such good progress to be made in the special school. This is often a persuasive argument, especially where there is a lack of demonstrable effectiveness of the special school. But where such schools are of proven worth, and the likelihood of similar resources being available in the ordinary schools is remote, the issue is more problematic.

Furthermore, a move away from segregated provision does not necessarily imply fully integrated arrangements. The concept used in the United States 'least restrictive environment' is helpful in this context, despite its rather negative tone. If youngsters' needs are analysed in these terms a series of environments ranging from completely segregated schooling to total integration with no extra support can be proposed. A continuum of this kind has been described by Cope and Anderson (1977) and is shown in Table 1.1.

Some youngsters with profound mental and physical handicaps may require hospitalisation, while many less severely affected young people would benefit from varying degrees of assimilation into special or ordinary schools, or special units within normal schools. For example, some youngsters with Down's syndrome are now

Table 1.1: Range of Special Educational Provision

1. Ordinary class, no special help

2. Ordinary class and ancillary help on care side

3. Ordinary class as base and resource room part-time

4. Special class (base) part-time
   Ordinary class part-time

5. Special class full-time

6. Day special school formally linked (e.g. same campus) to ordinary school

7. Day special school, no such link

8. Residential special school

Source: Cope and Anderson (1977).

attending ordinary secondary schools, whereas perhaps 10 or 20 years ago they would have been deemed 'ineducable'. Many young people with severe and profound sensory and physical disabilities also attend ordinary schools with the support of peripatetic teachers, or a unit within the school. A number of examples of integration projects are described by Hegarty and Pocklington (1982).

But it is important to remember that this discussion should not be confined to the 1 or 2 per cent of moderately and severely affected youngsters, i.e. the percentage currently in special schools. The Warnock Report stressed that the figure was nearer 20 per cent, and that the bulk of these pupils have always been educated, for good or ill, within ordinary schools. It is more useful to talk less about integrating handicapped children and young people into ordinary schools, and to concentrate instead upon how children's special educational needs can be met within the normal school with the support of other agencies and resources, including special schools and units. Also, while it appears that most pressure groups and parents of children with special needs would prefer their children to be educated in ordinary schools, this opinion is not universal. Some worry whether the youngsters will in fact be better off, and indeed some have become vociferous proponents of segregated provision. This is particularly the case in the deaf community. While the hearing parents of deaf children usually seek placement in ordinary schools for hearing pupils, older deaf people often reject this arguing that this arrangement denies them their rights to their own language and community. They object to having to fit into the hearing world on its terms (Gill, 1982).

Secondary schools have always had a large number of pupils with special educational needs going under a variety of labels, including: slow learners, remedial, disaffected, behaviour problems and under-achievers. The results of recent legislation and public pressure should be to increase slightly the numbers of youngsters with more complex and long-term special educational needs, particularly that group of pupils previously called ESN(M), and now described as having moderate learning difficulties. Schools will be faced with rethinking their curricula and organisation. The parents' rights to demand an assessment of their child if they suspect him or her of having special educational needs will increase workload and accountability, as the draft Statement which details the professionals' assessments and the LEA's proposed provision will be available to the parents to challenge if they so wish.

Evidence from the United States (Brown, 1980) suggests that the first few years will be a difficult time. He reports that five years after passing PL 94-142 there was still confusion about implementation, including which special services must be provided pursuant to this legislation, and there had been an alarming increase in the amount of litigation against the schools. If we are to avoid some of the pitfalls experienced in that country it is clear that schools and LEAs must devise well-considered procedures for identifying youngsters' special needs, and be able to show that they have made a reasonable attempt to provide the resources to meet those needs.

As professionals we must strive to ensure that it is not only those with the loudest voices who gain resources for their children. Some pressure groups representing children with special needs have been highly successful. These are usually well supported by middle-class parents, often professionals themselves, who can find their way around the system. But children with mild and moderate learning difficulties, and most of those currently attending schools for the maladjusted, come from working-class families who are less skilled in this area, although events in the summer of 1982 at Croxteth School in Liverpool suggest that working-class parents can and will mobilise to fight the education system if they feel sufficiently strongly about an issue. The need to work with parents as partners is increasingly being recognised.

Secondary Education

In addition to changes in thinking and practice within the particular area of special education, there have been major developments in secondary education in general. Teachers in secondary schools have been required to adapt their teaching methods, and the content of what they teach, as schools have been reorganised to form comprehensives, new examinations have been introduced, and curriculum developments have taken place. These various alterations are still in process in some schools, while in others a new set of changes is being considered or even implemented. These macro changes of the system, dating mainly from the sixties and seventies, together with the new demands of the eighties, must be meshed with the more specific developments in special education derived from our rethinking, altered practices and the new legislation.

Most LEAs now have a system of secondary education which is comprehensive: that is, schools do not admit children selectively by ability. Some have had a reasonably well developed and fair comprehensive system for ten, twenty years or even longer, while others have changed more recently. Often the latter group had a system which included quasi-comprehensives: schools labelled 'comprehensive' and even intended to be such, but in fact admitting pupils from a restricted range of ability as grammar and other selective schools 'creamed off' the more able children. Currently there are some attempts to reverse the trend to a comprehensive school system, while other LEAs are extending the principle to the post-16 sector: sixth forms in schools and colleges of further education will be amalgamated to form comprehensive tertiary colleges.

All schools have, and have always had, pupils with special needs. These changes in organisation, however, have increased the number of teachers who must teach such youngsters. The 20 per cent of pupils considered to have special educational needs at some stage in their school lives includes a large number of youngsters who may be described as disaffected, often finding school work difficult, uninteresting, or both. One criticism of comprehensive schools is that while they have improved the educational opportunities of the majority of children, the position of the least able and least motivated pupils has worsened. In order to justify themselves on the traditional criteria, success in 'O' and 'A' level examinations, comprehensive schools have organised their resources and structured their curricula so as to maximise the chances of pupils likely to do well on these measures. Success in external examinations has been used as a motivating force for pupils, and generally seems to have been effective, as the increase in the number and percentage of youngsters taking and passing these examinations suggests. However GCE and CSE examinations are not intended for all children; for any one subject these should be suitable for a total of about 60 per cent of pupils. What of the other 40 per cent? Schools must either form non-examination classes, or try to incorporate the pupils into classes undertaking a curriculum which was not intended for them. In either case the pupils are placed in an inherently unsatisfactory position, despite the attempts of teachers to alleviate the problem. If they are in non-examination sets they are readily identified as 'failures', by themselves and their peers even if the staff would deny this. If they are members of examination classes they are faced with attempting work which is unsuitable.

The internal organisation of schools has also affected the number of teachers called upon to teach this group of pupils. In many schools, the common system was that the more senior staff taught the more able classes. Now many of these teachers are expected to teach pupils with a wide range of ability. This process has been taken further where classes are organised along mixed ability lines. This arrangement is often advocated as a means of avoiding the social stigma and reduced motivation associated with streamed organisations. However, teachers are often unenthusiastic about a change to mixed ability arrangements, and even among those who are keen academic considerations are often dominant. Ball (1981) studied one school's change from a banded to a mixed ability arrangement. He reports:

Those teachers who were ideologically committed to a mixed ability system represented only a handful of the total staff group. But cvcn among these ardent adherents justifications for the mixed ability system were sought in terms of the maintenance or improvement of academic standards. (p. 285)

But mixed ability teaching is more than an issue of organisation — what matters is how the children are actually taught. Pupils who find it difficult to learn effectively, particularly given the problems of curriculum match outlined above, are at an even greater disadvantage if they are a minority in a class of 20 or 30. There are ways in which these difficulties can be alleviated (see Chapter 4), but the fact remains that the youngsters' problems are largely determined, or at least aggravated by, factors outside themselves.

Secondary schools have recently been subjected to a number of reports urging a re-examination of the curriculum for all their pupils. The DES, Schools Council and the Inspectorate have all produced documents which have challenged schools' practices. To these can be added the books and pamphlets by educationalists and pressure groups, including political lobbyists. Together these present contradictory advice to schools. Should schools have a clearly defined core curriculum for all? Should youngsters be expected to reach certain minimum standards in the basic subjects before being allowed to leave? Should they be allowed to leave at 14 years? Or be encouraged to stay on beyond the present compulsory age of 16 years? Should there be a greater emphasis on the academic subjects, or should the balance of the curriculum be changed to include more community-oriented work? All of these decisions have implications for the education of youngsters with special needs.

The issue of sex differences and the curriculum, and school success, has also come to the fore. There is clear evidence that girls and boys have significantly different school careers in terms of the options they choose. For example, a recent publication by the Equal Opportunities Commission (1982) reveals that in 1979 girls obtained 98.2 per cent of the GCE 'O' level passes in cookery, but only 2.7 per cent of technical drawing passes. The trend over the past decade shows a slight change in the general imbalance of examination passes, but this is indeed small. It has been asserted that teachers' styles and degrees of interaction favours boys (Spender, 1981) although evidence presented for this is not totally convincing (see Pecherek, 1982). However, there have been demands for a reversal in the trend towards mixed education, and an increase in the number of single-sex schools, or at least separate lessons for girls in some subjects.

These and many more educational issues have been forced upon secondary schools for their consideration. In addition, the 1980 Education Act has required them to give more information about themselves to the community — examination results, the curriculum and organisation of the school will be more public. These various demands and suggestions are confusing in their number and conflicting requirements. They have taken up a great deal of time and energy as staffs have had to change their practice when they had no choice, while developing their own philosophy and ways of working. Into this melting pot must also go the issue of young people with special educational needs.

Conclusions

We are now entering a new era in the development of education for children with special educational needs, and the publication of the Warnock Report can be seen as a major milestone in this process. Although subject to many criticisms it did bring the issue of special education out of the area of marginal education and into the mainstream debate. All teachers and many parents have been affected by this. The Report acted as an impetus to the development of good practice and the criticism of less satisfactory procedures. There has been a re-examination of their roles by a number of special schools, often resulting in their becoming less cut off from the ordinary school community. LEAs have reconsidered their provision, and ordinary schools have had to rethink their practices. Of course not all of these changes can be attributed to a positive response to the Warnock Report. The threats of falling rolls and school closure, and the changing patterns of incidence of some disabling conditions, have also been powerful stimuli.

In general secondary schools have been less affected by these developments, for two main reasons. First, the integration of children with more complex educational needs has usually started with the younger age range — particularly in nursery and infant schools. Given present resources, many of these children can develop satisfactorily at this stage; the extra provision of a small amount of resources can often have a significant effect if the conditions are conducive (see Hegarty and Pocklington, 1981, for a discussion). Integration into secondary schools is for youngsters with more long-term and complex special needs a more difficult process. Curricular and organisational issues are of a different order. However, the momentum towards greater integration is there. Parents who have seen their children benefit from placements in ordinary primary schools will be reluctant to accept segregation at the secondary stage. There are increasing examples of good practice which both encourage parents to demand integration, and help schools to set about the process sensibly. There seems little doubt that the numbers of youngsters with complex special needs being educated in ordinary school will increase.

Second, there has been a very large number of other demands on the secondary school. In addition to debates on methods of organisation, curriculum and examination reform there are new worries. Unemployment among school leavers has reached a staggering level; the effects on these youngsters and the knock-on effects on those in their earlier secondary years are causing much concern. If those with good qualifications are unable to obtain 'real' work what chance is there for the less able, or those with various disabling conditions? Also, falling rolls are increasing insecurity among staffs.

The argument in this book is that we must no longer consider children with special educational needs as a distinct category for whom separate discussions must be held. Large numbers of youngsters have educational difficulties at some stage or continuously; many more have personal problems which, although not necessarily having significant educational implications, benefit from the help given by those within the educational system. Both causation and intervention are conceptualised as interactive in nature. Some problems can be seen as largely caused by a disability within the child or a failing within the family or school environment; but in all cases these factors interact. Similar considerations apply to intervention. Some youngsters may be best served by individualised help, including work programmes and counselling, while to help others we may need to make major alterations to the school system. But again the issue is one of emphasis. Given the large numbers of pupils disaffected from school, the main focus must be upon institutional solutions (Baird *et al.*, 1980), but this should not preclude individual approaches. Many teachers, advisers and educational psychologists have started to work at the systems level, with some success (e.g. Gillham, 1981), but this should not be taken to imply a rejection of an interest in the individual. Ultimately learning and behaviour in general are the result not only of the conditions but of the individual's intepretation of those conditions. Youngsters with special needs and their parents are becoming increasingly sensitive to the way they are treated, and more demanding of a fair deal.

For the future it is important that provision for youngsters with special educational needs should be considered together with that for ordinary pupils. Curriculum development projects should always include consideration of the requirements of children with learning or other relevant difficulties; and this consideration should be a central concern, not an afterthought. School building programmes should automatically be undertaken with the needs of the physically disabled in mind. Special education must be brought, screaming if necessary, into mainstream. Pupils must be provided with a least restrictive environment, to use the American jargon, or an opportunity for optimal development, to use my own. The 1981 Education Act demands of LEAs and schools that the special needs of children be assessed, and that suitable provision be made, usually in an ordinary school. This legislation ensures that special education must be a matter for all schools to consider.

But legislation is not enough: it must be made to work. Young people with special educational needs have the right to the best education possible; we have the duty of ensuring that they receive it.

2 IDENTIFYING PROBLEMS

Geoff Lindsay

When children enter secondary schools they will normally be 11 or 12 years old, and have attended schools for at least six years. It would seem reasonable to expect that most if not all problems would have been identified by this time. If this were the case there would be little need to talk about identification at the stage of secondary schooling. However, as all teachers in secondary schools know, difficulties do come to light during this period. Many of these, on investigation, appear to have origins in the pupil's early years and it is quite common for secondary teachers to question why such problems were not identified much sooner, with the corollary that something should have been done about it.

How realistic is such a view? Certainly there has been increasing concern to try to identify children's difficulties at as early a stage as possible. The Bullock Report (DES, 1975), for example, devoted a whole chapter to this issue and strongly recommended early identification of language problems, including reading. Many researchers and practitioners have developed instruments, including tests and rating scales, designed to do just that (e.g. Lindsay, 1981b). The results of a recent survey by the Division of Educational and Child Psychology reveals that 85 per cent of LEAs now have formal identification procedures in the infant school. However, the initial high expectations for such a venture have been questioned as the complexities of the issue have been revealed. In general, while profound handicapping conditions should be identifiable very early in a child's life, the mild to moderate learning difficulties are much more difficult to identify until the child is within the school system, and has had an opportunity to attempt the tasks with which difficulties are encountered. Results of assessments of pre-school development, and even that in the early infant school, have been shown to be far from perfect predictors of later problems (see Lindsay and Pearson, 1981).

However, by the time a child has entered the top of an infant or bottom end of a junior school, general difficulties with school subjects will be apparent, though the precise nature of such difficulties must be investigated in more detail. Hence, by the time a child enters secondary school, it is certainly reasonable to expect that learning difficulties will have been identified. This does not always happen, unfortunately, and it is not unknown for children, particularly those with specific learning difficulties, not to be identified until the secondary stage. This is a function both of the awareness of primary teachers, the availability of specialists such as educational psychologists, and the complexity of some of the problems in question.

The identification of behavioural and emotional problems is more difficult. Some children who cause concern in the secondary school have a long history of such difficulties often relating to family circumstances, but others' problems arise at later stages of their development as they react to the stress of different life events. A change of school, death of a loved one and the influence of a peer group, for example, can all have a profound effect on a young person's behaviour and emotional state. In addition, the construction put on different behaviours by different people will vary. To teacher A a pupil might be lively, intelligent, with a desire to challenge assertions; to teacher B the same child might be seen as argumentative, stroppy and a nuisance.

A study by Dowling (1980), for example, considered the transfer of 503 pupils from primary to secondary school. They were assessed in the Junior 4 and the Secondary 1 years on a number of measures, including teacher ratings of behaviour and the Rutter Behaviour Questionnaire. The correlation between measures over this one-year period was poor. For example, teacher prediction in J4 of behaviour in S1 correlated only 0.31 with the ratings of that behaviour by the S1 teachers. Dowling concludes: 'The variables that are easily measured in the primary school have only a weak relationship with various criteria of adjustment in the secondary school.'

A study by Pumfrey and Ward (1976) of 45 children over four years (from age 9−10 years to 14 years) using the Bristol Social Adjustment Guide (Stott, 1974) and other measures produced a similar finding. They report that 81 per cent of the children defined as 'maladjusted' by the BSAG at age 10 were no longer so defined at 14 years — i.e. that only about 20 per cent remained 'maladjusted'. Of the normal group, 2 of the 19 had now become maladjusted. A study by Cox (1978) over six years (age 6 through to 12 years) showed that at any one time 25 per cent of his sample (largely drawn from educational priority areas) showed emotional disturbance, but there was great variation in who these children were at different stages. Compare these findings with the results of, say, reading tests taken at the end of the last year in the junior school, and the start of the first year of secondary when results can be expected to show great similarity.

Who Can Identify Problems?

Without doubt the key people are teachers and parents. These are the people in greatest contact with the child and so have the best knowledge. Unfortunately we have traditionally relegated their significance. Screening programmes in schools have been, and often still are, conducted by outside professionals (e.g. remedial advisers, educational psychologists). This arrangement increases objectivity: it is not unknown for teachers to try to influence their pupils' marks. For example, a colleague reports entering a classroom to find the teacher coaching the class on the Burt Graded Word Reading Test, which was written on the blackboard.

This reliance on objectivity, however, has drawbacks. The validity of a particular pupil's score is not apparent: children have bad days or may copy. The result gives only limited information, perhaps a reading age score, which must still be interpreted and matched with the rate of development, and the provision available.

Perhaps worse still, the knowledge of parents has been sadly neglected. Although there are some parents who are reluctant to work with schools, perhaps are even openly hostile to them, most are keen to help but often feel reluctant or inhibited. Yet they might have a wealth of highly useful information. The past few years has seen a change in this situation, and more parents are being increasingly involved with professionals. They may wish to know what the doctor thinks is *really* wrong with their child, and what the side-effects of drugs are; similarly they may wish to have a clear statement of the educational provision available. Certainly in my own dealings with the parents of children who may attend special schools, I have been generally impressed, by their concern and willingness to help their child. Consequently there has been a rise in the involvement of parents, particularly of pre-school severely handicapped children, in both assessment and treatment and professionals have recognised the good that can come of such developments.

Any system of identification must, it is argued, make the best possible use of teachers and parents. In addition there is a need to involve others, including education welfare officers, clinical medical officers, and educational psychologists at appropriate stages.

The Process of Identification

There are several related but distinct aspects to the identification process. These, and their integration, will now be considered.

Survey

The use of a survey enables a school, or LEA, to judge the magnitude and nature of a problem. For example, a school might give all its first year pupils a reading test. The results will give an overall picture of reading ability and also enable decisions to be made about provision. For example, a school might discover that 30 per cent of its intake have reading ages below nine years. This would suggest the need for a large amount of basic literacy on the curriculum, and the organisation of the first year timetable should be arranged accordingly.

Screening

Unlike a survey, a screening process is not concerned with the general picture. Here the objective is to identify individual pupils, rather than absolute numbers or percentages, as a result of which the pupils can be allocated to appropriate educational provision. In a school, the same instrument might be used to provide both survey data and identify individual children. To be worthwhile, screening procedures must be quick, simple to use but accurate.

Assessment

Following screening it is necessary to examine in more detail the exact nature of a child's abilities and disabilities. To know that the reading age is 8.5 years gives some useful information but it is far from sufficient. It may be necessary to examine aspects of the reading process, level of motivation, medical factors and much more. Thus, at this level, the information required is more specific and extensive, and therefore requires more time and expertise to collect.

It can be seen from this description that there is an increase in the specificity of information required when screening and assessment are compared. The Warnock Report suggests that at any time about one in six children have special educational needs. In an average school, therefore, a screening programme would identify about 16−17 per cent of the pupils investigated. This group will then require a more intensive assessment in order to identify their particular needs. In a school of an annual intake of 200 pupils, this results in about 30−40 pupils requiring such detailed investigation. In addition, a smaller group of these 30−40 pupils may require assessment which is more specialised than the school can provide. In this sense the assessment stage can also be said to be a screening stage for more detailed assessment by outside professionals.

An Evaluation of Identification Methods

In order that information is useful it must be accurate, reliable valid and meaningful. To what degree do the currently available instruments meet these simple criteria?

Reading Tests

Pumfrey (1976) has provided a comprehensive review of reading tests available. When the tests favoured by teachers, as shown by a survey reported in the Bullock Report (DES, 1975) are examined in this monograph it is apparent that many of the most popular, while being simple to use, have major weaknesses. In many cases the standardisation of the test is either unknown (e.g. Daniels and Diack Standard Reading Tests) or dated (e.g. Burt and Schonell Graded Word Reading Tests). When such tests have been subject to restandardisations, the samples have often been restricted and their match with the national population unknown (e.g. Salford restandardisation of the Schonell GWRT). However, there are several reading tests which are suitable for children in the 11−12 year age range to provide a general assessment of reading that do appear well standardised and meet the accepted psychometric criteria of readability. These include the Wide-Span Reading Test (published by NFER-Nelson) and the Edinburgh Reading Tests (published by Hodder & Stoughton).

Whether such tests are true tests of *reading* is open to dispute. Many educationalists would question whether reading isolated words or even sentences is *reading*. However, this valid criticism notwithstanding, the better tests do give a helpful general appraisal of level of reading development. Some, including the Edinburgh Reading Tests, claim to give more specific information about different aspects of the child's strengths and weaknesses with the reading process. These tests are open to criticism on the grounds that the supposed different abilities measured are in fact highly intercorrelated — that is a child who does well in one sub-test will tend to do well on another. For example, the correlation coefficients for the sub-test of the Edinburgh Reading Test range from .433 to .795.

In general group tests are most suitable for the stage of screening, while individual tests such as the Neale Analysis of Reading Ability (published by Macmillan) are appropriate for individual assessment. The latter, despite now being over 25 years old, does enable an analysis of reading errors to be made, which may be useful in remediation.

Mathematics

The National Foundation for Educational Research has produced several tests of mathematical ability, appropriate to various age ranges. Many of these are now rather outmoded, and the standardisation of some is also questionable. A new test which appears to be well-standardised and to have modern mathematical content is the Profile of Mathematical Skills (published by NFER-Nelson). This would be suitable for screening children coming into a secondary school and indeed would claim to give more specific information to guide teaching. For example, the Profile of Mathematical Skills has different sub-tests including Addition, Multiplication, Operations, Diagrams. This and other tests, should be judged against criteria of ease of administration, relevance of content and standard of reliability and validity.

Intelligence

The topic of intelligence testing has become highly contentious. It is not unknown even now to find teachers who believe the score on an IQ test is non-changing and totally accurate. On the other hand, there are some teachers and psychologists who totally reject the usefulness of IQ tests, or declare that their use is invidious. The work of Kamin (1974) adds weight to their argument for he has traced the history of the interaction between intelligence testing with politics. The eugenics movement, the development of the tripartite system of education and the over-representation of black children in ESN(M) schools have all been influenced by the belief that IQ is a stable measure predicting future intellectual ability.

The position adopted here is that the use of measures of general cognitive ability is to be discouraged at the level of screening. However, individual assessments of children using intelligence tests can be of help in presenting a full picture of a pupil. Such assessment would normally be carried out by an educational psychologist as the tests are restricted to those with appropriate training. However, any results are of limited use unless discussed with the teachers concerned.

Behaviour

The most well-known screening instruments for pupils with behavioural problems are the Bristol Social Adjustment Guide (Stott, 1974) and the Rutter Behaviour Questionnaire (Rutter, 1967). These two are both simple to complete but are based on very different premises. For school use the Rutter is probably simpler to use and provides information which is easier to handle. It was used in the Isle of Wight study (Rutter, Tizard and Whitmore, 1970), and subsequent research has suggested it is a useful screening instrument. It comprises 26 descriptions of behaviour and the teacher has to judge whether each one 'does not apply', 'applies somewhat' or 'definitely applies'. The items provide scores on two scales: neurotic and antisocial.

The BSAG comprises 110 brief statements drawn originally from terminology used by teachers describing children's adjustment difficulties and these therefore require little interpretation. Several mutually exclusive and homogeneous groups of behaviours are defined, which are themselves grouped into two scales: Over-reactive and Under-reactive, generally similar to Rutter's neurotic and antisocial scales. A high score on either scale is deemed to be indicative of 'maladjustment'. An analysis by McDermott (1980) of the data on the 2,527 children in the standardisation sample provides support for these two dimensions.

There are other checklists which are designed more to identify emotional problems, often making use of the pupil's self-reports. The Mooney Problem Checklist, for example, comprises a series of 'problems': pupils underline those that apply to themselves. These self-report forms, however, are generally not suitable as a screening device as they require interpretation, so increasing the complexity of the process.

A recent British scale which is well standardised and the subject of a number of evaluative studies is the Lewis Counselling Inventory (Lewis and Pumfrey, 1978). This is an easily completed instrument which requires only that the pupil agrees or disagrees with each of 46 statements, e.g. 'I often lose my temper for no reason at all'. A reading age of about 10½ years is required, and time for administration is about 10–15 minutes. The purpose of the Inventory is to identify those pupils who are in need of counselling and initial evaluation of the construct validity and reliability of the Inventory are encouraging (Pumfrey, 1981). However Carrick-Smith (personal communication) reports that in his small-scale study the degree of overlap between pupils identified by the Inventory, and those by their teachers, was low. This, of course, raises the interesting issue of external validation. Perhaps the Inventory wrongly identified pupils 'needing' counselling, or perhaps the teachers were insensitive to their needs. Conversely, the Inventory might have missed genuine cases needing help, or the teachers were being oversensitive. In short, the evaluation of such instruments is extremely difficult and will require a number of studies, particularly controlled follow-up evaluations, before effectiveness can be assessed.

Programme of Identification

Having considered a number of examples of instruments used for screening, it is necessary to combine this information into a programme which a secondary school might wish to carry out. In this context a screening process will be developed which encompasses more than simply administering tests or other instruments. The total system of information-gathering, resource allocation and helping pupils will be considered.

What Resources are Available?

In many ways this is not the most appropriate first question. We should be trying to identify special needs, and then doing something to meet those needs. However, in reality, this question is a very important first step as schools vary greatly in their numbers of remedial teachers and other resources. In these days of falling rolls and cutbacks, a remedial department could be halved or even removed by one person leaving and not being replaced. Hence it is important to have some idea of the probable resources available before trying to identify special needs. One year tutor when asked to try out the Lewis Counselling Inventory to identify pupils in need of counselling replied: 'I haven't got time to deal with the one I *do* know about, let alone any that might be revealed by this'.

Timing

The model of identification suggested here is based upon the idea that children and young people are changeable, hence it is inappropriate to consider only one time for the identification of special needs. However, to face reality once more, decisions do need to be made at particular times in order for an organisation as complex as a school to operate. The most important time for identifying special needs is around entry to the school. At this point decisions will be necessary on allocation to classes or groups. The exact nature of such decisions will depend on the organisation of the school, and its relative use of mixed ability or other form of groupings. The period of identification should be seen as ranging from the top of the junior school, particularly the last term, to about half-term in the first secondary year. This would enable information on the pupils' abilities and behaviour in the primary school to be gathered, and allow an assessment of this to be made by the secondary staff. Gross decisions on the allocation of provision to meet the special needs can then be made prior to the pupils arriving. During the first half-term of the secondary school these assessments and placements can be evaluated, to allow changes to be made, if necessary, before the child is too far into the school year.

Subsequently decisions of a general nature should be made once a year, when pupils' progress is reappraised, but this should be complemented by more frequent assessments of the pupils identified as having special needs. This allows decisions to be made regarding both gross provisions (e.g. placement in a remedial class) and more specific curriculum choices (e.g. a change of teaching method for reading).

This system, however, does not fully take account of those pupils who, on entry, appear satisfactory but who later may be identified as having special needs. It is advocated that in addition to regular appraisals of development there should be attempts consciously to seek out children with special needs, a system which allows teachers' concern about individuals to be investigated and discussed. Regular meetings of pastoral care staff, possibly involving outside professionals, are a useful forum for sharing worries and identifying incipient problems at an early stage.

A particular need is to ensure that attention is paid to those who pose no problem to the school, yet may have significant personal difficulties. Quiet, withdrawn pupils are often ignored, yet on investigation are found to have problems of adjustment.

What Special Needs Should be Identified?

This question can only be answered with reference to the aims and nature of each school. For example, schools may vary in the extent to which they consider pastoral care to be part of their responsibility. Marland (1974) argues that 'there can be no pastoral/academic split' and suggests that schools have always recognised a pastoral, as well as academic, responsibility. However, while this is no doubt true, schools would certainly seem to vary in their relative attention to pastoral and academic matters. Similarly, teachers within schools will admit to a range of attitudes from those who see themselves as subject specialists to those who adopt an interest in other aspects of their pupils' development. A study of the aims of primary school teachers (Ashton *et al.*, 1975) revealed a general opinion that the aim of schooling should include the development of socialisation. It would be interesting to compare a study of secondary teachers' aims — would they, as is commonly asserted, be more academically biased?

The aims of education can also be seen to be related to the organisation of the school. Historically, major decisions in education have usually been based upon two types of philosophy — the educational and the ideological. Thus comprehensive schooling was advocated as a means of improving the quality of education for more children, and also as a means of producing an egalitarian society. Similarly, the integration of children with special educational needs is justified on the grounds that it will help the development of these children (and the ordinary children with whom they are integrated), and also that these children have rights which are denied by segregated provision. Unfortunately the reasons for change in education are often confounded.

In the present context it is important to consider the aims of the school with regard to children with special needs. Does the school consider it should be fully comprehensive, and cater for all children in its catchment area unless such placement would be impossible? Or does it prefer to focus attention on a restricted range of pupils, with others either being referred to special school, or absenting themselves? The identification of special needs will depend upon these considerations. There is little point in identifying children who need counselling if the school does not consider this part of its role. Similarly, the identification of children with learning difficulties of the kind described in Chapter 4 will be unnecessary unless there is a willingness to differentiate between the different needs of pupils who have problems with academic subjects. Thus the position presented here, of necessity, assumes a positive inclination on the part of the school.

Identification of children's needs can be considered in two main ways. The traditional method is to delineate *problems*. More recently the emphasis has changed to a statement of *needs*. Although these two approaches are complementary they do represent different perspectives. For example, it is not uncommon for a child to have a problem which requires little extra provision in the primary school over and above the class teacher's awareness and ability to tailor the curriculum; yet when that child transfers to a secondary school, perhaps with over 12 different teachers each week, a need for a special class placement becomes evident.

For present purposes, problems and needs will be divided into two major domains: academic and pastoral, and two main stages of identification will be considered: screening and assessment.

Stages of Identifying Special Needs

Pupils enter secondary schools not from a vacuum but from a prior stage of schooling — junior or middle schools. Unfortunately it can be the case that this fact is not always noted, and valuable information from the primary stage is not used by the secondary school. The system of identification proposed here uses a sequential model which starts with the primary stage, particularly the last 1 to 2 terms of the top year. The model is sequential in that different stages of investigation are suggested, and these are designed to build upon each other to give more and better information about the pupils. Also, identification of need is divided into two major domains — the academic (i.e. learning difficulties and particular academic strengths) and the pastoral (emotional and behavioural problems).

It is not possible to investigate all matters in detail at the same time. However, some systems of identification appear to be designed in defiance of this truism. Information must be collected efficiently and in a form which is usable. There is little point in passing on great piles of children's work and expecting the next teacher to absorb the implications before meeting the class. Test scores are only worthwhile if used properly. Screening is only a first stage and subsequently more refined methods of assessment are required to specify children's special needs.

Records

Before discussing the actual stages of identification it is necessary to consider the general issue of records. The system advocated here requires detailed, careful monitoring of pupils' progress. For this to happen in a large secondary school requires both the recording of information, and the involvement of several, or more, teachers. Making records of pupils' development should be a helpful process, designed to ensure optimal progress; but it has a negative side. Over recent years many people have complained about the number of records kept on them, and their content. School records have often been cited in this context, and the magazine *Where*, published by the Advisory Centre for Education, has carried several critical articles.

There is, therefore, a general ethical issue to be considered concerning records. This has two major components: content and access. Some records, reprinted in the articles mentioned above, contain comments about youngsters which are far from sensitive, professional reports expected of teachers. In general such criticisms have been levelled at judgemental comments. These, presented with no supporting evidence, and in a particular style, can be unhelpful at best, and highly prejudicial at worst. However, although they cause great concern when discovered, they are probably not very common. A more pervasive problem is the general quality and standardisation of reports.

A recent study by Clift *et al.* (1981) revealed major differences in the use of record cards by the 66 LEAs investigated. For example, the number of categories varied from 10 to 70 and some 120 categories were identified in total. Only 34 per cent gave reading test results and as few as 6 per cent indicated that remedial help was required. This can be compared with the results of the study's survey of primary teachers which revealed that 96 per cent considered a statement on the stage of reading reached was either desirable or essential, and 90 per cent who thought that reading test results should be recorded. Similarly worrying results were found for other aspects of the cards.

The second concern is that of access. Cohen (1982) reports that only 4 LEAs allow parents to see school records — she contrasts this with an educational guidance centre where the youngsters (aged 9–15) are allowed free access. If the spirit of the advice offered by the DES Green Paper of 1977 were followed the first problem would be overcome, and perhaps teachers and administrators would be more willing to allow freer access to records by the parents.

However, this is not a simple issue: improving professionalism in terms of record-keeping is only part of the problem. Some information is given in confidence. For example, a parent may confide personal details to a headteacher, but not wish this to be passed on without permission. Given the failings of human memory, what does the headteacher do with those data? Another problem arises when parents are separated and one (or both) may confide information which they would not wish the other to know. Furthermore, information can be usefully shared at one stage, while at another it could prove counter-productive. These issues are particularly acute in relationships that parents and youngsters have with other professionals such as educational psychologists. It cannot be assumed that a simplistic free-access model is always appropriate.

A suitable starting place for considering this issue is the needs of the pupil. Will this youngster's development be helped or harmed by keeping and then passing on this information? In most cases factual information about educational progress and relevant medical conditions should both be recorded and passed on. For a secondary school to rediscover a pupil has a significant hearing loss, or is retarded in reading, is not in the pupil's interests. The time prior to such discoveries can be unpleasant and even traumatic for the youngster. More personal information should not necessarily be passed on. Comments about past behavioural or emotional problems are probably best *not* transmitted unless there is a clear need to do so. In such cases it is often advisable to limit knowledge of such information to senior staff.

Andrew was causing his primary teachers concern to the degree that they sought a transfer to a school for maladjusted pupils. The educational psychologist, however, considered that his needs would not be best met in such a school and that as a transfer to secondary school was due to occur in only a term, a decision should be deferred. The headteacher and first year tutor of the secondary school were both informed and were agreeable. In the event he transferred with no difficulty and caused no problems. How would his teachers have reacted to the idea of teaching a child destined for a school for maladjusted pupils?

The involvement of parents in decisions about record-keeping and the transmission of information should be seriously considered. Where schools and other professionals have tried this, their fears have usually been found groundless. Many educational psychologists either give copies of their reports to parents or inform them that they may have one if they wish. Cohen (1982) reports several case studies where people are given access to records, including their own medical records, with beneficial results. In the case of educational records parents' own views can form a major contribution, and they are to be made a required component of the Statement issued under Section 7 of the 1981 Education Act (see Chapter 11).

Stage 1 — Transition: Junior 4 to Secondary

The general issues concerning records have been discussed above. In this section the emphasis will be on the process of attaining information at the end of the primary school, and how this might be passed on to the receiving secondary. There are three main aspects: the content of records, liaison and the use of standardised tests.

Records. Many schools supplement the official record card with information they consider important. This could be very specific and useful to the present teacher, but in its raw form can be meaningless to a teacher in another school, unless written in a way which is unambiguous. Also, large quantities of information are not useful in the first place on transition to secondary where perhaps 200–300 children are transferring schools. What is necessary is a summary of important points, with access to some detailed records at a later stage.

Liaison. Second, there is the issue of liaison between secondary and primary schools. Where parental choice of secondary school is great, the school could have pupils transferring from a dozen or more primaries. In this situation most pre-entry information must be in written form, so necessitating clear well-documented records, devised at LEA level. However, where a secondary school accepts children mostly from a few primaries, it is possible to organise visits to the feeder schools to discuss the pupils. These can very usefully supplement the written records by allowing secondary staff to see the children in action and the children to meet the staff. Children considered by the primary school to have special needs can then be discussed face-to-face and the secondary teachers can gain first-hand knowledge of their future needs. In addition, primary staff can visit the secondary school. When such a system works well it not only encourages dialogue about individuals, but also about continuity of curriculum.

Such a system is found to help alleviate the worry that teachers have about passing on sensitive information. A study in Sheffield among primary teachers found that they were quite happy to pass on records of academic progress, but very reluctant to do so for many aspects of behaviour (Lindsay, 1980). Exposés of some school record cards have shown these fears to be well-founded. However, face-to-face discussion can help alleviate these problems by engendering trust and avoiding the commitment of some concerns to official records.

Tests. Third, many if not most primary schools also use standardised tests, particularly of reading and mathematics, which can provide useful information for the secondary school. However, problems will occur unless the schools are using a common instrument as children's scores will vary depending on the test given. A sample of 15 Sheffield schools involved in follow-up research on the Infant Rating Scale used 8 reading and 6 maths tests between them. In this situation it is unsafe to regard the standard scores from different tests as comparable, so reducing the usefulness of collecting these data.

On the basis of the range of information detailed above it is possible to make general decisions about pupils at the stage of transition. When the information is of high quality and reliable, it is possible to judge those pupils who are *likely* to have special needs. This caveat is necessary given the evidence on situation-specificity of many forms of behaviour and of the reliability of teacher perception discussed above. Any judgement, therefore, should be regarded as a preliminary rather than a final decision.

Stage 2 — First Half-term

Academic. Once the pupils have transferred to secondary school there are conflicting factors both aiding and hindering the identification of special needs. On the positive side, it is now possible to examine the total population in question, in the relevant setting. On the negative side, there is initially a need to allow the children to adjust to their new school, and immediately facing them with a battery of tests is perhaps not conducive to that.

What is advocated, therefore, is that during the first month there should be a screening of all first year pupils on maths and reading using a standardised test. For this purpose it is necessary to use a test which is simple to administer and interpret. Tests with a variety of sub-scales purporting to measure different aspects of reading or maths are not necessarily better. Apart from the fact that the sub-scales may not be as discrete as is implied, it is questionable whether such detailed information, even assuming it is valid, is helpful for this purpose. This should not be necessary when there is very good liaison with feeder primaries, and especially if they all use the same instruments, but otherwise this simple procedure allows reasonable identification of those children requiring special help in these basic subjects. During this period, subject teachers should also be encouraged to start to monitor the children's reaction to curriculum demands in terms of reading and writing. The children identified by these two methods should then be allocated to the special provision necessary to alleviate their difficulties (see Chapter 4).

During the rest of the first term the pupils' academic progress should be monitored in all subjects. The demands on the teachers of getting to know their pupils and organising lessons will mean that this monitoring will, of necessity, be limited. Pupils who are receiving specialist help, however, should be assessed in detail during this period to allow optimal curriculum provision.

Pastoral. During the first half-term there is also a need for pastoral monitoring. This would be done primarily by the form tutor and would have three main aims. First, there is the general aim of ensuring that the pupils adjust to their new school with as few upsets as possible. Second, there is a need to take special note of the children who were identified at primary level as likely to have special needs in the secondary school. Third, form tutors should be aware of other pupils who are showing signs of particular problems, not necessarily related to settling in.

By half-term the first year pastoral team should review the adjustment of new entrants and identify those pupils who appear to have special needs requiring counselling or referral to other agencies. This method of screening, by the careful monitoring of sensitive teachers, is probably sufficient for most needs. However, if a school wishes to make use of more objective measures, it would be appropriate to use these at this time.

Stage 3 — Second Half-term

Academic. An aspect of academic development not yet screened is spelling. There is probably no necessity to carry out a screening of this on entry as the main decisions concern children's special needs in maths and reading, or general curriculum placements. Most schools do not systematically assess spelling, leaving it to subject teachers to mark and teach as required. However, there are children who have significant problems with spelling and they should be identified early in their secondary school life. By about half-term, therefore, the whole year group could be given a spelling test as a screening measure. As with reading and maths, the test results should be supplemented by teacher monitoring. The same applies to handwriting. A simple method of identification is to ask all teachers of first year pupils to identify those who are causing concern in either or both these areas. Those identified by these two methods will, of course, require provision to meet their special needs.

For the rest of this term the main emphasis will be on subject teachers monitoring their pupils' progress on the curriculum provided, and on the specialist remedial teacher making more detailed assessments of the children's capabilities. During this period referral to outside agencies such as support teachers and educational psychologists will also be considered and negotiated. This should preferably follow staff discussion of pupils causing particular concern preferably with the psychologist or other specialist present. By the end of this term it should be possible to identify any child whose special needs with repect to learning are such that a school transfer is at issue.

Pastoral. If a screening instrument for identifying special needs has been administered, its results should be considered against the views of the pastoral staff involved. It may be apparent that there is a mismatch between children identified by such instruments, and teacher perceptions. This is not to say one is right, the other wrong, but that this disparity requires investigation.

Staff discussions of children identified as having special needs should be held preferably with outside specialists such as the educational psychologist to try to identify the exact nature of these needs. In some cases a more thorough appraisal of the child's needs by a psychologist, welfare officer or other professional may be necessary.

Stage 4 — Second and Third Terms

Academic. By this stage all children with special needs should have been identified. For those with special needs this period will be taken up with a more detailed assessment of those needs, and a monitoring of the effectiveness of the measures taken to help the child. In mainstream lessons subject teachers should still be encouraged occasionally to appraise their pupils' progress in a general way as it is possible that one or two might have slipped through the net.

At the end of the year, all children with special needs should have their progress reappraised. The nature of this will depend upon the curriculum. Where finely graded objectives-linked curricula have been used, assessment is built in. Otherwise, a reassessment using standardised tests will be required.

Pastoral. Unlike the academic domain it cannot be expected that special needs in this area can be largely identified by the end of the first term. Adolescence is a time of many problems and special needs can arise at any time, although some will certainly be identified at this stage. There is a need for a more careful monitoring of pupils with a purpose of identifying needs rather than just monitoring the reaction to intervention. Frequent meetings of teachers, ranging from senior pastoral care staff to all those teaching particular children, are necessary. Where this has beeen tried it is found that teachers are often initially defensive as it is not easy to admit that a child presents a problem — the teacher may be seen as to blame. However, when led sensitively, and particularly if senior staff admit their own problems with particular pupils, such meetings can be highly productive. Patterns of problems can be revealed which help to isolate the child's needs.

During this period it is also important for staff to discuss the pupils causing concern with outside agencies. Education welfare officers and educational psychologists are the most relevant here, but others, including psychiatrists and social workers, should be involved as necessary. Children receiving help in school, or from outside professionals, should also be monitored to judge the effectiveness of this involvement.

Stage 5 — Second Year Onwards

Academic. It was argued above that learning difficulties should be identified very early in a pupil's secondary school career. Methods of doing this are available, provided they are used sensitively and with competence. Identification of children with special needs, therefore, should not be an issue after the first year, other than with children transferring to the school from outside. However, there will continue to be a need to specify the exact nature of those needs as the children mature, and their problems alter.

Pastoral. As stated in the previous section, special needs in this domain can occur at any time in a child's school life. It is necessary, therefore, to have a system which allows for a continuous system of detection. This must be simple and easy to operate to be effective. The form tutor and year tutor or head of house, are of key relevance here. The exact responsibilities of the pastoral staff are beyond this discussion (see Marland, 1974) but together the staff must produce a coherent system which enables adolescents' emotional and behavioural problems to be both identified and then more fully explored. Contact with outside agencies, and of course parents, is a key component of this.

Conclusion

Children's special educational needs should be identified at the earliest opportunity in order that help can be provided to meet those needs. It is important, therefore, that schools have a coherent system of identification and provision. Even in the current climate of cutbacks and restraint it is still necessary in order that best use be made of resources available. But the process of identification is not easy, either at the theoretical or practical level. Research has shown that prediction of later problems is difficult, and often quite unreliable, particularly in the area of behaviour. Consequently a system of identification must be devised which is based upon a concept of youngsters who are developing and changing. This has implications for practice, certainly making the process more complex than simple 'one-off' screenings. But it also fits into the developing philosophies in secondary schools concerning a move from streaming to mixed ability organisations, and a more general review of assessment procedures in school, for all children, as the following chapter exemplifies.

3 INTRODUCING A NEW ASSESSMENT SYSTEM TO A COMPREHENSIVE SCHOOL

Eileen Gledhill

What is Assessment?

Assessment is any attempt made by a school to describe the state of a pupil's progress. All schools monitor the progress of their pupils. Newly qualified teachers embark upon their careers accepting the fact that a high proportion of their time will be spent on testing and examining their pupils, and marking pupils' work. From the series of marks or grades so accumulated they will assess the pupils' 'worth', and report on the youngster in the light of that assessment. They themselves have come through an education system in which they grew used to their work being marked, and receiving reports, rewards, awards and even qualifications, based on those marks.

The individual teacher assesses a pupil's progress by a number of different methods. Apart from the obvious examinations and tests, there is also classwork and homework to be considered, while observation of the pupil, and talking with the pupil, add other dimensions. The interaction of pupils and their aural participation prove valuable too.

Such assessments are then documented to provide a cumulative picture of each pupil's performance throughout his school life. How these records are made up and the use made of them differs from school to school, according to the attitude of the school concerned to the information, and the needs to be fulfilled.

Why do we Assess?

The obvious need, as stated above, is the monitoring of progress. This also gives us much-needed information for school records. The implications do not end there however, as these two are closely interwoven, giving implications for reports between teachers, between subject departments, and in reports to parents. Also in recommendations to future employers and further education and higher education establishments.

However, assessment may be used as an even more valuable tool. It can be used to evaluate teaching material, teaching skills and teaching techniques. These in turn can have a direct influence on the curricula of subject areas and ultimately on the curriculum of the school. Further, it helps teachers, if used diagnostically, to understand more fully the nature of the learning process of the individual pupil, and how best to take remedial or therapeutic measures where needed. The teaching practices and learning processes should be reflected in the assessment procedures, thus reinforcing the aims and objectives which have arisen from the general philosophy of the school.

What was our Assessment Problem?

We were becoming increasingly aware that too many differing methods of assessment were being used and that there was no consensus of understanding or opinion on how and why these were being used. Grades used even within a department often reflected widely disparate views of a pupil's ability, leaving untapped a large area of knowledge about pupils, which as teachers we should be using to enhance the opportunities we offer to pupils.

The senior staff, through their own discussion, researches and attendance at courses, were committed to tackling the problem. They had their assessment 'sights' set, but early discussions with staff (often informal) showed that there was a great knowledge gap among the staff as a whole concerning up-to-date methods of assessment and the philosophy behind them.

There was a noticeable gap between what the school wanted to do and how to set about doing it. The problem was there and we had to tackle it.

Setting up a School-based Assessment Procedure

Setting up a new assessment system in a school is a complex business. Particularly where individual departments, parts of departments, or even individual teachers, have been allowed 'to plough their own furrow' as far as assessment is concerned, in some cases failing to see that a school-based procedure is needed at all.

The method of introducing new ideas for discussion, when they are discussed and how they are discussed, is crucial. An early attempt on our part to introduce new ideas on assessment made no impact at all. Having just set up our own in-service programme in school, we invited a senior adviser from the local authority to lecture the staff on methods of assessment. This fell upon deaf, and in some cases hostile, ears. We realised soon afterwards that the climate of opinion had to be right, and that every member of the staff would need to feel deeply and personally involved in the discussion and implementation, for a realistic situation to emerge.

The in-service situation by this time was no longer new to us. An assistant head had been appointed 18 months previously, with responsibility for staff development. He had gently wooed the staff, for over 12 months, into accepting that in-service was necessary for all, and that there was something in it for every one of them. Nevertheless, we felt from our recent past experience that the introduction of a new assessment procedure to a large group staff meeting was not viable. Particularly as every teacher would view it from their own subject angle first, with year tutors adding the social assessment arguments. Few except the senior management team, would see an 'across the board', whole school-based assessment instrument as being immediately viable. As a result it was tackled in departments.

At the time it was our practice to hold regular, monthly head of department meetings to discuss new ideas, or put initiatives forward, prior to involving the whole staff. Each department head was then expected to take the discussion forward to their own department and to report back the feeling of the majority of the department. However, we were well aware that although this did happen in many cases there were others where no formal consultation had taken place; or people had been approached individually by their head of department who obviously used this method of influencing individuals towards his or her own private opinion. Thus 'reporting back' became suspect and was not guaranteed to reflect majority feeling. It was distinctly important that the new assessment procedure discussions did give us the majority feedback through a majority involvement.

For some time the assistant head responsible for staff development, and the senior teacher, had been involved in a series of meetings, organised by the LEA, concerning assessment. They were to be our 'anchor men'. For the first departmental meetings they prepared a discussion paper 'Proposals for Action on Assessment'.

Proposals for Action on Assessment

Needs

Improvement of the school's diagnostic abilities.

Objectives

To improve accurate diagnosis of pupils' limitations.

Criteria for achievement of objectives

To judge, by monitoring pupils' progress, whether individual remedial programmes, both long and short term, have been economically facilitated and have been successful.

Action

a. Increase awareness of staff through departmental discussions.
b. Develop profiles of assessment in cognitive/affective domains — an element of criteria common to all departments and others specific to individual departments or groups of departments.
c. Develop an efficient and cost-effective system of records and retrieval.
d. Identify areas of difficulty which can be remedied by inter-department curricula co-operation.
e. Ongoing in-service training on defining problems and identifying cause for individual pupils.
f. To look for appropriate ways of undertaking remedial action.

Resources

To be decided.

Timing

Started Easter 1980. To be developed and refined during 1980/1. Implementation of final plan 1981/2.

So, having introduced the idea of a new look at assessment to heads of department, the senior management team met every department separately, using the same guidelines for discussion. First we looked at the subject area and asked the following questions.

What are we teaching?
Why are we teaching it?
How are we teaching it?

Are we teaching it effectively?

What do we hope to have achieved with/for pupils by the time they leave school:

    (i) In the broad educational sense?

    (ii) Through the subject we teach?

How do we measure what we have achieved?

What resources do we have, what resources do we need, to help this achievement?

We then considered a few points that might help us to decide what to assess. For ease of discussion we divided them into personal development (the development of a mature, well adjusted person) and academic/intellectual development (the development, through effort and attitude, of competence in both mental and physical skills). This was a slightly false way of starting the discussion as no one present subscribed to these artificial distinctions, being very aware that the personal and academic development were so intermingled that in any assessment procedure all teachers should be involved in assessing both facets.

Under personal development we looked at: awareness; self-reliance; flexibility; responsibility; ability to cope with a changing society; self-discipline; self-motivation; perception about, and understanding of, other people; good relationships; tolerant and sympathetic attitudes; adherence to an accepted ethical/moral code; ability to communicate; ability to discriminate; ability to make decisions and act on them; ability to use initiative; powers of self examination and self criticism.

Under the title academic/intellectual development we looked at: powers of observation, retention, interpretation, understanding; reconstruction, reporting; technical ability — neatness, presentation, creativity, aesthetic powers; manual, physical skills; the development of a spirit of enquiry, discovery and endeavour; the understanding of human development; appreciation of our cultural heritage.

After several departments had attended these inaugural meetings a pattern of opinion started to emerge, which became more distinctly etched as we completed the round of meetings. Firstly, that all departments had points in common that they wished to assess, and a number of others that differed widely from department to department. The time element also was of great concern to all, resulting in the resolve that the assessment procedure must be simple, easy to cope with and easy of interpretation, consuming as little time as possible. Therefore each department would choose six or seven subject-specific criteria for assessment plus five or six that they felt all departments would have in common.

At this point the departments continued the discussion in a number of meetings convened by themselves and without members of the senior management team present, except where that member taught that subject. Heads of departments had been given a deadline by which to produce their department's assessment criteria. Another important issue had arisen, and that was how these criteria would be handled, i.e. recorded, reported on and made use of. There was a large census of opinion emerging that a 'profile' was the most viable way of doing this.

Much discussion took place about whether every department should contain in their profile subject-specific categories plus those they felt were common to all departments, or whether two distinct profiles be produced — one containing subject-based criteria, and a second containing school-based criteria. Both were to give us much food for thought. The subject-criteria discussions were to give rise to a reappraisal of not only school curricula, but also the part played by every teacher in the school management/decision-making process: a move giving us an in-service programme that lasted initially a school year. The school-based profile was to remain a bone of contention for some time. Was it really necessary? Which elements of each of the subject profiles should it contain? Without care it could become unwieldy!

Teachers soon decided that it was impossible to decide upon criteria for their subject profiles until they had looked, in detail, at what they were already teaching, why they were doing so and how they were doing it. They looked at changes they needed to make in attitude, practice and technique. Also at the implications for resources — financial, manpower and space (rooming in particular).

In many departments the question of how pupils were examined, and when, became of prime importance. Anomalies in practice became more apparent. For example, why examine junior forms annually, in a formal way, in subjects that at fourth and fifth year public examinations level depended upon continuous assessment? If a department really believed in continuous assessment for a 16 + course why not employ it, in that subject, throughout the whole of the school course. This, however, made the good profile even more essential than ever to ensure that all skills, abilities and attitudes would be monitored.

Departments differed widely in their approach to the assessment 'problem' and the way in which they set about remedial action. The History department had already started to look critically at their syllabus and their teaching approach. This would ultimately have led onto a discussion concerning assessment in any case. A new head of English was already causing his department to look critically at many aspects of the department's work, including assessment. This was a department where continuous assessment for 16+ was well established, and where there was already considerable expertise in assessing.

These departments led the way and within a short time had their assessment instrument ready, alongside a written appraisal of what their departments were intending to do in further development. The History department clearly defined their aims and then looked at 'ways of testing them to assess how successfully the children have learned and how successfully we have taught (a factor often forgotten!).' Their attitude to public examinations crystallised too: 'In the future we hope to break out of the "strait jacket" of the 'O' level situation by adopting the Scheme II approach (60 per cent external examinations and 40 per cent internal assessment).'

The prime consideration in the English department revolved round their attitude to continuous assessment. The following is a statement from the head of department:

> Having thought carefully about what we should be teaching pupils in each year and realising the sense in having a sequential development of language, with each year building on that preceding, then there would seem to be somewhat of an anomaly in our method of assessing pupils' ability in that we rely on a large element of 'traditional' examination in years 1 to 3 and then go completely onto continuous assessment for years 4 and 5, except of course for the 'O' level Literature course.
>
> This desire for continuity of approach and sequencing of language development has prompted the department to seek a move towards continuous assessment in all of the first five years.
>
> However, this is not to say that continuity of approach is our only reason for favouring continuous assessment of work. The following would all seem to be significant reasons for movement towards continuous assessment of courses.

1. The difficulty in assessing ability in English, other than grammatical/technical in the examination situation.

2. Assessment seems a much more appropriate method of evaluation for pupils following individual programmes of work, and the department has begun to move increasingly this way.

3. Continuous assessment places increased value and worth on each individual piece of work.

4. Continuous assessment allows for constant reviewing of work by both pupil and teacher and encourages careful planning and redrafting. It must be understood however, that redrafting is *not* the teacher marking the work and then the pupil rewriting it, but discussion between teacher and pupil during the rough planning stages before a final neat version is attempted.

5. We feel that continuous assessment will provide a more accurate selection of pupils for banded groups or 'O' level literature groups rather than a single examination performance.

The English department has a long tradition of continuous assessment in years 4 and 5 and has built up a considerable expertise here when assessing work alongside syllabus requirements or guidelines. It would seem sensible to harness this expertise at all levels.

The profile produced by the English department is reproduced here as Figure 3.1.

There arose the problem as to whether to allow departments such as English and History to forge ahead, or to delay the use of profiles until all departments were ready, and implementation throughout the school could happen simultaneously. Some delay was caused, as some departments took longer to adjust themselves to their part in the decision-making situation, or in making their minds up as to just what criteria to use, how to use them to best advantage, and how to record.

A special plea arose from a number of departments on several occasions. They wanted the senior management team to give them a sample of the type of profile we wished them to adopt. Whilst we felt sympathetic to the pleas we resisted the temptation, particularly with the slower moving departments, to give them a ready-made profile. The temptation for them would be simply to adopt it,

Figure 3.1: Pupil Profile in English

NAME:

	Form	Set	Teacher
Year 1			
Year 2			
Year 3			
Year 4			
Year 5			

READING	Test	Date	Score
Year 1 Term 1			
Year 1 Term 3			

COMPETENCE	Good	Average	Poor	Special help required
Year 1				
Year 2				
Year 3				

ATTITUDE	Good	Average	Poor
Year 1			
Year 2			
Year 3			

COMPREHENSION	Good	Average	Poor
Year 1			
Year 2			
Year 3			

WRITING SKILLS HANDWRITING	Competent	Inaccurate	Poor	Special help required
Year 1				
Year 2				
Year 3				

SENTENCE STRUCTURE	Competent	Inaccurate	Poor	Special help required
Year 1				
Year 2				
Year 3				

SPELLING	Test	Date	Score
Year 1			
Year 2			
Year 3			

Figure 3.1: Pupil Profile in English — *continued*

COMPETENCE	Good	Average	Poor	Special help required
Year 1				
Year 2				
Year 3				

PUNCTUATION	Competent	Inaccurate	Poor	Special help required
Year 1				
Year 2				
Year 3				

VOCABULARY	Good	Average	Poor
Year 1			
Year 2			
Year 3			

CREATIVE ABILITY	Good	Average	Poor
Year 1			
Year 2			
Year 3			

REASONING ABILITY	Good	Average	Poor
Year 1			
Year 2			
Year 3			

ORAL ABILITY	Good	Average	Poor
Year 1			
Year 2			
Year 3			

ATTITUDE TO CLASSWORK	Good	Average	Poor
Year 1			
Year 2			
Year 3			

ATTITUDE TO HOMEWORK	Good	Average	Poor
Year 1			
Year 2			
Year 3			

Figure 3.1: Pupil Profile in English — *continued*

SPECIAL NOTES
Year 1

Year 2

Year 3

Year 4

Year 5

whether it contained the essentials for their department or not. The senior management team felt strongly that what each department arrived at had to be as a result of their researches, discussions and feelings. Two members of the senior management team, previously mentioned as our 'anchor men' on assessment, were available to give help and assistance, but in no way directly to implement.

After a little while we gave the go-ahead to those departments who were ready to proceed. Their profiles had already been vetted and 'passed' by the senior management team. We agreed that the first year of use of profiles would be essentially a pilot scheme, and that certain further developments would be delayed until any necessary adjustments that became apparent were made.

Feedback from departmental discussions clarified other areas in which we would have to take immediate action. The awareness of teachers concerning the deeper philosophies behind their teaching became greater. How did their aims, teaching techniques and syllabi fit in with those of other departments, and those of the school as a whole? What part did they play in what was decided for their department, and for the school in general? How did they make their influence felt? How were they, in turn, influenced towards initiatives? The consequent curriculum review became the subject of an in-service course. On an average these sessions were held every three weeks, spread over three terms. Attendance was voluntary, but such was the interest that 40 out of 54 staff attended regularly, the number often being higher. They looked at aims and objectives, teaching techniques, teaching materials, interaction of departments, initiatives and school ethos. Much of the work was done in small groups, not based upon departments so much as friendship groups, so bias towards departmentalised thinking was lessened. Due to the length and intensity of the course it is mentioned only in passing here, as a direct result of our assessment discussions. However, the results were far-reaching and are ongoing.

For example, when we decided to join the History, Geography, RE, European Studies and Economics together in a 'subject area' under the head of History as 'area chairman' a further development took place. Each subject area still retained its input in years 1–7, but as an addition in year 1 a Humanities course based on the MACOS materials (Man, A Course of Study) was instituted. This course being very dependent upon video materials had implications for the Resources department.

A new decision-making structure emerged based upon seven 'areas' — Language and Communications, Maths, Science, Design, Guidance, Humanities, PE — each with an area chairman. The area chairman plus senior management team made up the joint consultative committee whose job it was to discuss suggestions for new moves and take the discussion back to their 'areas'. This area discussion was followed by a curriculum management team meeting made up of representatives from all areas, who would report back the consensus of opinion from their areas to senior management, thus involving all members of staff in the decisions ultimately made. This decision-making process we ran for a year.

After that time we decided that the 'germ' of the idea was still good — but the process of using it unwieldy as it slowed down final decision-making. So we joined the joint consultative committee and the curriculum management team together for consultation, with a meeting approximately every half-term, though on occasions the senior management team would meet the joint consultative committee on its own. By the time this second phase was introduced we had regularised the position of the chairman of areas into Scale 4 heads of faculties, and, as an addition, in three faculties, teachers specifically in charge of curriculum development in certain subjects had been appointed.

Whilst the curriculum review was progressing a couple of departments were already using their profiles; others were still struggling with criteria, though the discussions on curricula helped them to crystallise their thoughts on these.

The main discussion revolved round how much of the social aspect of a child's education should be included in the profile at all. Some departments ended up with profiles concerned mostly with levels of achievement based on the material content to be learned; while others were arguing out the possibilities of a self-assessment space on the profile for both teachers and pupils.

Assessment Profile 1982 — Art Department

Art and design is primarily concerned with visual and tactile modes of expression. An understanding of the subject is built up through the exercise of practical skills, relevant theory and conscious decisions based on intuitive, analytical and synthesising processes. A typical art lesson then would deal first of all with the idea, the initial conception; secondly the method of working — the technique — be it clay, printing paper etc.; and finally the interchange between the two, the way that one affects the other, the synthesis (see Figure 3.2).

Figure 3.2: Elements of an Art Lesson

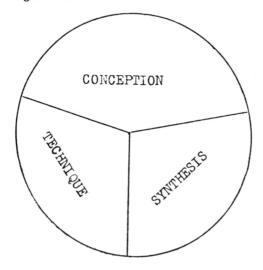

The department aims, therefore, for the whole pupil range, are to encourage:

a. the ability to perceive, understand and express concepts and feelings;
b. the ability to form, compose and communicate;
c. the acquisition of technical competence and manipulative skills which will enable individuals to realise their creative intentions;
d. intuitive, imaginative and analytical abilities;
e. the ability to identify and solve problems;
f. an understanding and appreciation of historical, cultural and environmental aspects of art and design;
g. the acquisition of a working vocabulary relevant to the subject;
h. the individual pupil's special aptitudes and interests.

Depending on the particular exercise or project involved, pupils may be expected to demonstrate their ability to:

a. show a personal response to an idea, theme, subject or other stimuli;
b. sustain a chosen study from its conception to the realisation;
c. work independently in realising their intentions;
d. analyse an idea, theme, subject or concept and to select, research and communicate relevant information;
e. select and control materials and processes appropriate to intention;
f. use and compose elements of visual form, e.g. line, tone, colour, texture, pattern, shape, space;
g. show some awareness of the relationship between art and design and the individual within a culture, society or environment.

Any assessment profile based on some kind of card system has to fall in one or other of two camps. Either it becomes all-encompassing and while certainly providing a complete profile makes too many demands of members of staff's time (I'm also of the belief that the more there is to fill in, the less thought and accuracy goes into what is actually written); or one adopts a more general system which acts as a summary and serves to reinforce, confirm or add to one's previous knowledge of a particular pupil. At the same time, bearing in mind the very wide variety of materials, techniques and projects involved in our subject, we feel that the card should also act as a permanent record of the areas that the pupil has actually tackled.

The system that the department would like to adopt then is as follows: As well as the date, space should be left for a short description of the project the child has just completed, and/or any relevant comments; followed by three columns marked Attitude/Progress/Attainment (see Figure 3.3).

Attitude

Is the pupil on time for lessons; does he display a keen and enthusiastic approach or a commitment over and above that normally expected; does he take part in any verbal discussion of the lesson; does he ask questions; does he hand his homework in punctually; does he appear to enjoy the subject?

A — yes, to all or most of the above questions.

B — yes, to some of them, or most of them some of the time.

C — no, to any of the questions.

Progress

This covers the pupil's own personal progress compared only with his previous results.

A — definite and real progress since his last piece of work.

B — no real improvement, but existing standards maintained.

C — a noticeable deterioration in standards.

Attainment

How does the pupil's work compare with that of the rest of the group?

A — above average results, top 30 per cent.

B — average results, middle 40 per cent.

C — below average results, bottom 30 per cent.

Figure 3.3: Art Department Record

Date	Pupil's name and form	Attitude	Progress	Attainment
	Description of completed project and/or relevant comments			

It is our habit to meet heads of feeder primaries regularly and for us to discuss matters of mutual concern and convenience. Other liaison is done by the senior tutor and the year 1 tutor. As both of these, at the time, were members of the English department, in consultation with their department head an English profile for use in primary schools was created, aimed at giving precise and up-to-date information not only on the standard achieved but also just what each child had learned, likewise pointing out the gaps in their knowledge, or the weak areas needing still to be worked on. After some deep discussion all the 'feeder' heads except one accepted the profile (see Figure 3.4) and used it for the first time in the summer of 1981. In due course a maths profile will be useful too.

Where Had we Arrived in September 1982?

All teaching staff, except those recently appointed, have been involved in ongoing discussions concerning assessment, assessment procedures and especially pupil profiles. Some departments are already using their profiles. All departments adopted a profile system in January 1982, slightly later than we hoped but near enough to the implementation plan originally set out.

The Sheffield-based in-service course on assessment, which senior staff had previously attended, is being presented again. Heads of departments are being encouraged to attend. What they learn will help to put their own initiatives into perspective, and they will bring their own viewpoints of what they hear back into the school. They will probably be most critical of the final session which in the last two years has comprised some of our staff talking about their assessment instruments!

Where do we Go from Here?

The assessment discussions will still continue and modifications will be made in the light of working experience. The school profile will emerge also, in the light of that experience. We will be observing, noting and assessing more about each individual child than we have ever done before. Used diagnostically this is having implications for our Remedial department, both in structure, teaching techniques and deployment of staff.

Figure 3.4: Transfer Profile in English

NAME OF PUPIL:

READING	Test	Date	Score	Reading age
Competence	Good	Average	Poor	Special help needed
Attitude	Good	Average	Poor	
COMPREHENSION				
Written	Good	Average	Poor	
Oral	Good	Average	Poor	
WRITING SKILLS	Competent	Inaccurate	Poor	Special help needed
Handwriting				
Sentence Structure				
USE OF Punctuation				Not taught
Spelling				
SPELLING	Test	Date	Score	Spelling age
VOCABULARY	Good	Average	Poor	
CREATIVE ABILITY	Good	Average	Poor	
ORAL ABILITY	Good	Average	Poor	
ATTITUDE TO WORK	Good	Average	Poor	
SPECIAL NOTES				

The head of Remedial receives pupils into the department at the request of other teachers. Apart from the tests she applies to establish the particular difficulty of the child concerned she will gather important details of weaknesses, missed work, etc., from the profiles, thus enabling her to set out a detailed programme of remedial or therapeutic work tailored to the individual need. This work may be carried out within the Remedial department or within a subject department — the head of Remedial department always being available as a consultant to other staff. An enormous benefit is the more detailed information on progress that we can supply to local hospitals, assessment units, psychologists, etc., on individual pupils.

Central to the school's philosophy is emphasis on the development of the individual pupil. Our reappraisal of the curriculum, the consequent curriculum development, and the setting up of new assessment procedures, were all geared to enhancing the educational provision for the individual. Thus pupil self-assessment becomes an issue. At present one member of staff who is particularly interested in this area is investigating the possibilities, alongside the idea of supported self-study for years 4 and 5 at least.

How about teacher assessment? This happens already in an informal way through critical interchange of ideas between colleagues in a department or faculty. The in-service programme for 1982–3 is entitled 'Good Classroom Practice' and will be used not only on a staff-wide basis but through individual departments also. Here again the self-assessment will be used to aid further curriculum development, towards better classroom practice and teaching techniques, and a furthering of the assessment procedures. Meanwhile we hope this will also give rise to the cross-fertilisation of ideas and sharing of resources.

Other developments are inevitable. Having filled in our profiles and used them for diagnostic purposes, how do we report to the parents? Our present system of subject report slips containing grades and comments are adequate for the present. Staff already work hard on them and the comments made are 'in depth'. The form of report may need to be different. For instance, should that be in profile form, and, if so, will parents understand it, or appreciate everything we are trying to say? It may well prove that there is a need to educate parents directly, concerning assessment procedures, and the value of this approach to their child's education. The implications towards new forms of parent consultation evenings are there too.

Already the pattern of exams/tests/assessments has been changed, alongside when we report to parents and the pattern of parents evenings. Previously an exam has been followed by a written report followed by a parents evening. In the future parents will receive one report per year; at other times of the year there will be the opportunity for parents to meet form teachers and, on a separate occasion, subject teachers. This virtually means a 'reporting back' of at least three times a year. The 'profiles' will certainly make this easier to do.

Spot checks on pupils' progress will also be easier, especially in reporting to parents on the occasions when they come into school to talk about specific problems.

It would be easy to say that we tackled the problem by putting the cart before the horse. Why did we look at assessment problems before looking at curriculum? It would seem more logical to tackle assessment as an offshoot of curriculum review and development. If we were beginning the process now, at this precise point in time, we might well use the more logical progression — but that is because the 'climate' is right. However, the climate is right only because we engendered it through a discussion on a sore problem — 'assessment'. To have coldly approached the staff from the outset with the idea of a curriculum review, and possible curriculum development, would not have achieved as much, and without as much willing participation.

The curriculum catalyst for all departments has been used, and the review and development situation will continue, stimulating established teachers and providing support and training for new teachers. Motivation is of supreme importance. Where motivation is high, success, through involvement, becomes apparent.

Acknowledgement

The author is indebted to all the staff of Bradfield School for their dedication and hard work on this and many other topics, but especially to the senior management team for their enthusiastic and continuing support.

Appendix A: Extract form Mathematics Profile (Fractions Profile)

SET P   1. Able to shade in factions of different shapes ½, ¼, ⅔, ⅝ (and combinations of these) and so understand the meaning of both numerator and denominator.

      2. Able to add fractions with same denominator (including mixed fractions).

      3. Able to subtract fractions with same denominator (including mixed fractions).

SET Q 1. Able to produce equivalent factions.

        2. Able to reduce fractions to lowest terms by cancelling.

        3. Able to multiply fractions by whole numbers.

SET R 1. Able to multiply fractions by fractions.

        2. Able to divide fractions by whole numbers.

SET S 1. Able to divide fractions by fractions.

SET T 1. Able to divide fractions by fractions.

        2. Able to divide using mixed numbers.

        3. Able to do mixed operations involving fractions.

Appendix B: Summary of Humanities Profile

This document is not in a finished form, but represents an interim stage in the development of the profile.

FULL NAME		
YEAR TEACHER		
1		
2		
3		
4		) Course
5		)

a. *Personal and Social Development*

Staff are invited to make a comment upon such things as relationships with peers; relations with staff; working with others; and self-image.

Possible Continuations

b. *General Educational Abilities (Title?)*
Boxes/ticks? *or* staff are invited to make a comment upon such things as . . .

c. *Departmental Criteria*
To be decided by individual departments — this part will be different presumably for each department.

d. *Special Notes*
Space left for each year for comment.

e. *Teacher Assessment of His or Her Success (Optional)*
Space left for each year for comment.

f. *Sixth Form Potential*
Space left for comment by fifth year teacher.

g. *External Exam Results*

Appendix C: Physical Education Department

A.   NAME   _____
B.   FORM   _____
C.   TEACHER(S) I/C   _____

Part One

	Term 1	Term 2	Term 3
Activities Covered			
Comments	To cover (1) Practical work in lessons (2) Effort, concentration and willingness to learn (3) General behaviour and appearance		
Term 1			
Term 2			
Term 3			

Part Two

Self-discipline	Overall achievement grade
Responsibility	Comments
Motivation	
Reliance	
Relationships	
Observation	
Decision-making	Performances for form/school/representative teams
Self-examination	

4 LEARNING DIFFICULTIES

Geoff Lindsay

Within most comprehensive schools there should be children of all ranges of ability, from the very able to those who find learning in school a difficult process. In practice, the degree to which a total range of ability is found will vary depending upon other provisions and the type of catchment area. A Local Education Authority (LEA) which has a large number of private schools within its boundaries may well find that 'Comprehensive' is a misnomer for some of its schools, as many of the more able children are 'creamed' off.

At the other extreme, separate provision for youngsters with learning difficulties will also affect the degree to which a school is comprehensive. Thus while in 1977, 1.8 per cent of the school population were receiving special education outside ordinary LEA schools, the relative incidence varied considerably from one LEA to another, from 120 to 300 per 10,000 of the school population (DES, 1978).

While the spread of ability and attainment will vary from school to school, it seems to be the case that in all schools there are some pupils who can be said to have learning problems in that they find difficulty in coping with the normal school curriculum. Thus all schools must take note of the abilities of all children under their care if optimal learning is to occur. Many schools try to overcome the problems posed by those considered to have learning difficulties by forming special classes or remedial units; withdrawing pupils from certain lessons for extra help in basic attainments, providing remedial education across the curriculum; or referring the pupils for special schooling.

But who are these children with learning difficulties — how many are there, what are they like, how do they fit in?

Case 1: Jean

Jean transferred to a comprehensive school of about 1,000 pupils from a small junior and infant school. Since school entry she had been recognised as having obvious learning problems. She entered the infant department at five years unable to perform any of the types of tasks common among children of that age, and continued to make extremely slow, though steady, progress throughout her primary schooling. At the age of 6 years she was given a Stanford Binet Intelligence Test which suggested that her general cognitive ability was in the lowest 1−2 per cent of her age group.

In addition to her learning difficulties, Jean also had a number of physical problems. As a 5-year-old she was exceedingly frail and could easily be knocked over in the normal rough and tumble of school life. Her articulation was impaired and her language usage was poor. By the time she entered secondary school she was physically tougher, though still thin, and her speech was generally clear except when she was anxious or excited, at which time she stammered. Her reading ability had improved to that of an average 7-year-old, but her mathematical ability was lower. Jean found difficulties in adjusting to her new school for three-quarters of a term, but then seemed to settle happily. She attended half the normal timetable, and spent the rest of the time in a small withdrawal class.

Case 2: John

John transferred with Jean to the same secondary school. His level of attainment in the basic skills of reading and maths were comparable, but the picture he presented over the years had been different in many ways from that given by Jean. John had been under surveillance during the pre-school period and concern had been expressed about his lack of speech. Investigations were carried out at this time and it was concluded that this problem had an emotional causation.

In view of his language problems, and his problems with bladder and bowel control, it was decided that rather than go to his local infant school he should attend a school for children with learning difficulties. Most children who attended this school stayed for up to two years and then went back to mainstream schools.

As time went on it became very obvious that John's problem with talking was not caused by an emotional difficulty, but that there was a primary language disorder. His sentence structure was deviant, not simply immature, and he produced very little speech. However, his drawing and manipulative skills were very good. At the age of 10 years it was found on a test of non-verbal cognitive ability (one requiring no speech from him, and very few verbal instructions) that John scored at about the 85th percentile, i.e. only 15 per cent of his age group would be expected to gain a better score. He was highly competent on non-verbal puzzles, drawing and model making, showing a well developed sense of perspective and form.

Entry to secondary school was considered problematic as he continued to have a problem with bowel control. However, this was overcome by the time he transferred and he settled well into his new school. He continued to have difficulties related to his poor attainments and his language disorder, but was happy and progressed satisfactorily.

Case 3: Martin

Martin was referred to an educational psychologist when he was 13 years. He was a very able boy, recording a score on a test of general cognitive ability above the 98th percentile, i.e. a score bettered by only 1−2 per cent of his age group. His reading was excellent, but his spelling was appalling, being at a 6-year level. Handwriting itself was also very poor, and coupled with his spelling difficulties, resulted in written work which was barely legible at best and often unreadable. His teachers needed to be informed that his current written work was not indicative of his level of knowledge, and specific work and teaching was necessary to help him overcome these disabilities.

These three pupils all experienced learning difficulties which affected their ability to cope with a normal school, but it is readily apparent that they are three different children, with three very different problems, or clusters of problems. Further examples could easily be given to emphasise this point. Yet all three youngsters were in ordinary secondary schools, where they received a mixture of normal lessons and special provision. What are these pupils' special educational needs? How does a school decide how best to cater for most children's needs? What causes their learning difficulties?

Causes of Learning Difficulties

The three case studies illustrate the problems involved with trying to define children with learning difficulties. Different researchers at different times have emphasised different reasons why children and young people have problems in learning in school (in many cases they seem to learn perfectly adequately in their natural environment, see below). Investigations of reasons for difficulties is justified by the belief that in order to treat a problem it is important to know the cause. This is often true in the field of physical health, but is it true in education?

Causes for learning difficulties which have been investigated can be divided into several categories, and there can be seen to be an historical progression.

General Intelligence

At the beginning of this century the research of Binet and Simon, and later Terman and Burt, laid the foundations for the development of the mental testing movement. Many research studies demonstrated that for large samples of children, the results obtained on a test of attainment (e.g. reading) correlated with tests of mental ability (intelligence). The correlation was not perfect, but was statistically significant. Rutter (1975) for example suggests that the correlation between reading and an intelligence quotient (IQ) is about 0.6. Hence, in general, children recording low scores on intelligence tests tended to have low scores on tests of attainment. As the idea that a child's IQ was a relatively stable measure took hold, the use of intelligence tests as *predictors* of academic performance increased. The eleven plus system was founded, in part, upon such a practice.

At the same time, the use of measured intelligence as an *explanation* became increasingly popular. Low attainments were, it was argued, *caused by* low intelligence. This explanation was not thought to be the only one: the effects of prolonged absence from school, poor nutrition and some physical problems were recognised, but low general intelligence was regarded as the major cause for most children with low attainments. Hence IQ tests were used to determine which children needed to be transferred to schools for the educationally subnormal or ESN(M) — now called children with moderate learning difficulties.

This explanation of learning difficulties called for long-term intervention to deal with what was viewed as a long-term problem: part of the child's basic nature. Hence streaming in schools, with children of low IQ in lower streams, was advocated. The institution of separate grammar and modern schools, using the eleven plus as a classifying instrument, was an extension of this idea. Finally separate schools for educationally subnormal children were set up and increased greatly in number (see Galloway and Goodwin, 1979; Tomlinson, 1981).

Criticisms of this view of the causation of learning difficulties are various. IQ tests have been shown to give results which are not unchanging (e.g. Hindley and Owen, 1978); The eleven plus was shown to misclassify a small, but significant, number of children. Streaming in both primary and secondary schools has been shown to have problems associated with reduced opportunities for some pupils, and the generation of deviant subcultures (e.g. Hargreaves, 1967). In short, criticisms have been made both of the instruments used to define the learning difficulties, and of the provisions made to cater for the children identified. Evidence has accumulated to show that children's abilities or potentials are not fixed (Clarke, 1978). Accordingly, systems which have been produced based upon a belief in fixed potential have been found wanting.

Emotional Difficulties

As child guidance clinics increased in number, from a handful in 1935 to 95 by 1945 (Sampson, 1980), another possible reason for low attainment increased in favour. Many of the children seen in such clinics were found to have low attainments, but an average or above average IQ. Investigation by the staff, comprising an educational psychologist, psychiatric social worker and child psychiatrist, revealed that many of these children seemed to be suffering from emotional difficulties, often as a result of the intra-family dynamics (for an interesting case study of such a child see Axline, 1971). Hence another causal factor was postulated: these children were failing at schools owing to an emotional disturbance. The treatment prescribed would include therapy, often both for the parents (though usually only the mother) and the child. It was hoped that by these means the child's disturbance might be alleviated or removed, and normal learning could then start or resume. In some cases, placement in residential or day schools for maladjusted children would be considered necessary, with a similar aim of reducing emotional disturbance.

A number of case studies have been published showing that with some children these approaches are effective (see Axline, 1971; and Sampson, 1980, for a review). However, Tizard (1973) has argued that: 'the child guidance clinic, linchpin of the child guidance service is an expensive, ineffective and wrongly conceived institution.' Many of the children and families referred either never presented themselves, or dropped out of treatment. Of the children who successfully completed treatment, only about half were thought to be improved, and the results of the study by Shepherd, Oppenheim and Mitchell (1971) suggested that children were as likely to improve without treatment (spontaneous remission).

Constitutional Factors

A third strand in the development of concept of learning difficulties concerns hypothesised brain dysfunctions. A wide variety of terms has been used within this context, often overlapping each other, but some intended to be more specific. These include minimal cerebral dysfunction, minimal brain damage, minimal brain dysfunction, dyslexia, word blindness, dyscalculia, and many more. The origins of this approach can be traced back to the work of doctors dealing with people considered to be wordblind as a result of brain injury. Interest in this area by psychologists and educationalists mainly began in the 1940s with the work of Strauss, Werner and Lehtinen (see Hallahan and Cruikshank, 1973, for review) and then increased during the 1950s until, during the 1960s, it accelerated dramatically, particularly in the United States. As with the earlier focus on emotional disturbance as a causation of learning difficulties, this development can also be seen to be a result of an uneasiness felt by practitioners with the then current standard explanations.

Work with adults with brain injuries, whose characteristics were known, had shown that various faculties could be lost depending upon the location of the lesion. The work of Strauss and Lehtinen suggested that children who were mentally retarded could be divided into those whose retardation was due to familial factors (endogenous) and those for whom a neurological impairment seemed a likely cause (exogenous). The latter group of children had no familial history of retardation, but their case histories indicated a prenatal, natal or post-natal disease or injury to the brain. Evidence on tasks such as a marble board, requiring the reproduction of a pattern by putting marbles into holes, suggested that the exogenous children were significantly less competent than their endogenous peers, who in such tasks could perform at a level comparable to normal children of similar mental age. The exogenous children seemed to go about their task in a different, strange manner. Work with children of known brain damage, such as cerebral palsied children, reinforced the idea that certain types of brain damage could cause learning difficulties. However, later work (e.g. Wedell, 1960) showed that even with overtly brain-damaged children such links were not straightforward.

What was more problematic, however, was the question of whether children with learning difficulties were necessarily brain-damaged. Support for this view came from studies which showed that some children's learning difficulties were of a similar type to those displayed by children with known brain damage. However, further research has revealed a far from straightforward link between learning difficulties and brain injury or dysfunction (see Wedell, 1973). Also it is not possible to prove brain damage unless an autopsy is performed and while some children with known learning difficulties who have unfortunately died in childhood have been shown to have brain damage, not all children with learning problems can be assumed to have brain damage.

To complicate matters still further, a series of fascinating studies carried out by Lonton at the Sheffield Children's Hospital on the largest sample of patients with spina bifida and hydrocephalus, had posed serious questions of traditional conceptualisation of the brain/behaviour relationship. Children with hydrocephalus suffer an accumulation of fluid in the ventricles inside the brain. Resulting pressure in a young child's head causes an enlargement of the skull, and a special valve needs to be inserted to reduce this pressure. However, longitudinal research with brain scans has demonstrated that in some people there is a truly massive proportion of the skull which is full of fluid, causing the cortex to be extremely thin. Lonton has followed up a series of patients with very high ventricle to brain volume ratios, and measured their performance on a variety of psychological tests. In a study of 449 patients, he showed that dramatically enlarged ventricles are not associated with dramatically lowered IQ (Lonton, 1979). An extreme case is that of a young man with a 95 per cent ventricle to brain ratio who achieved a first class honours degree in mathematics!

To summarise, while there is support for the belief that some children have learning difficulties which are constitutional in origin, and not a result of emotional disturbance or generally low intellectual ability, the relationship between brain function and behaviour is complex.

Environmental Factors

Research such as the National Child Development Study (Davie *et al.*, 1972) has dramatically demonstrated the relationship between social factors and attainment in school, and intellectual functioning. A series of startling relationships was summarised in a booklet entitled *Born to Fail?* (Wedge and Prosser, 1973). Disadvantage was shown to be related to a variety of factors, including shortage of living space, lack of hot water and inside sanitation, and sharing a bed. These and many more are all aspects of general poverty. Evidence from this and other studies has shown that the factors identified operate in different ways.

First, some have a direct practical influence. A lack of money may result in a child being kept off school for having no uniform or shoes (despite grants this still happens). Second, poor living conditions can cause secondary medical problems, including chest and ear infections. Children might then be kept away from school, or if they attend their performance may be impaired. In this context, ear infections and catarrhal disorders leading to hearing loss can produce a major impairment to a child's learning.

Third, there are complex interactions. Children of low birth weight, particularly those who are 'small for dates' and have not grown satisfactorily during their time *in utero*, tend to have learning difficulties at a later stage. But such problems are more likely if the child is born into a Social Class 5 family. Furthermore, low birth weight babies are more likely to be born to disadvantaged mothers. These mothers are less likely to have used ante-natal facilities, to have smoked more heavily, and to have not made arrangements for the birth of the baby. Hence many factors of material disadvantage can be seen to interact and to result in some children themselves being disadvantaged physically and educationally.

A more contentious idea is that of cultural deprivation. There is often an assumption that materially deprived children are also culturally deprived, but research and anecdotal evidence again suggest a more complex situation. Biographies of people born into materially poor homes often reveal a rich cultural influence. Robert

Burns, the poet, for example, was born into poverty in a farming community; see also the account by Roberts (1976) of his childhood in a Salford slum. Furthermore, as Keddie (1973) and others have agreed, cultural deprivation may be a myth produced by the middle class about the working class: culturally different is not necessarily culturally deprived.

However, there is evidence that a significant minority of children do suffer linguistic deprivation, restriction of play activities and reduced opportunities to form social relationships (e.g. see Chazan *et al.*, 1977). While not all materially poor children are intellectually deprived, there are still many children who do suffer this problem and who benefit from enhanced opportunities at an early age.

But schools also make a difference, and indeed are different themselves. The Coleman Report and the Plowden Report argued that school factors were of relatively modest importance in educational achievement compared with home (and child) factors. However, Byrne *et al.* (1975) argue that differential rates of attainment are largely a function of differential educational provision. Results of the study by Rutter and his colleagues on London schools, although subject to various criticisms, provide evidence that schools do have an effect on their pupils' development, even if that effect is rather less than that due to other factors. Gray (1981) has also provided evidence for this view from his analysis of school effectiveness studies.

Causes of Learning Difficulties — a Summary

The purpose of the preceding review was twofold: first, to trace the development of concepts of learning difficulties and second, to demonstrate the complexity of the isssue. Over this century there has been a gradual expansion of the generally perceived number of causes of learning difficulties. At each point a small group of exceptions to the rule has been shown to be more numerous. At this time there is a broad view of the causes of learning difficulties encompassing a general deficit in cognitive ability; specific deficits in cognitive ability; emotional disorders either reducing motivation or interfering directly with cognitive ability; environmental conditions leading to impaired development, both directly and indirectly; and schools themselves differentially alleviating or causing learning problems. Finally, some learning difficulties can be seen as the result of the direct or indirect influence of a physical disorder.

Helping Pupils with Learning Difficulties

It has been argued that learning difficulties can have a large number of different causes. It will similarly be suggested that a number of different ways of meeting the special needs of these pupils is necessary. These can be divided into two main groups. First, at the school level, there are questions of organisation of provision. How many teachers are available? How should teaching time be provided? Second, at the level of the particular child, there are issues of teaching method and curriculum materials.

The two most common types of provision for pupils with learning difficulties within a secondary school have been the special class and a system of withdrawal from certain lessons. The survey by the Schools Council in the early 1970s (Brennan, 1979) found that 62 per cent of secondary schools had organised separate classes, and that withdrawal teaching was organised in 54 per cent of the schools. Some schools operated both systems, in which case the separate classes were regarded as being for 'dull' pupils, while withdrawal was for those with more ability but reading difficulties. In some mixed-ability settings no remedial provision, other than that provided by the class teacher, was available. These findings confirmed an earlier study by Sampson and Pumfrey (1970), which also found that the average size of special classes was 19 in comprehensive schools and 17 in secondary modern schools. Withdrawal groups, however, had an average size of 7 but only one-third of schools had remedial provision for at least four years.

A number of problems with the provision of facilities have been identified by various studies. The number of teachers with special qualifications is low. A study by the Department of Education and Science in 1971 found only one in four teachers had received special training; a similar figure (28 per cent) is reported by Brennan (1979). Facilities are often poor. The DES survey reported that specialised accommodation was rare and that 12 per cent of the teachers were using accommodation such as stock rooms, dressing rooms, landings and medical rooms. Brennan's survey, however, did find that the pupils in a secondary school often had access to other specialised facilities.

There is also a problem with regard to admission to the group(s). A study by the present author in one secondary school found that a separate class in the fourth year comprised three distinct groups of pupils. Two pupils had very poor attainments (reading ages below 8 years). The main body of the class had reading ages of around $9\frac{1}{2}-11$ years, while a third group of two pupils had reading ages almost at their age level, and whose written work could match this. Discussion with these pupils revealed that they had been placed in the class because of behavioural problems the previous year, a view confirmed by staff. Finally, comparison with the bottom English set revealed that, in that subject at least, there could be a significant transfer of pupils from one class to another if level of attainment was the criterion. This finding of heterogeneity within a separate, special class, and comparability with other classes, replicates other studies.

The research which has evaluated the effectiveness of remedial provision is also less than encouraging (for reviews see Galloway and Goodwin, 1979; Moseley, 1975). Short-term gains are often reported but the findings for long-term improvement are contradictory. In addition, the assumption that greater gains will be made by pupils with higher levels of general cognitive ability has not been confirmed (Yule, 1973).

Provision in ordinary schools for children with learning difficulties, therefore, has not been shown to be effective. However, much of this research is old, dating from the 1950s and 1960s, and most was based upon younger children. More studies of children in today's schools would be helpful, but on the available evidence, together with personal experience, there is justification to be concerned about the provision in secondary schools for pupils with learning difficulties.

This view has also been declared by some of the teachers themselves and the role of the remedial teacher has been re-examined. In many cases the teachers concerned (usually called remedial teachers) have a relatively lowly place in the school hierarchy. The DES survey (1971) remarked that in the great majority of schools the head of remedial 'ranks in status well below that of the academic department'. A later study of all schools in Wales (Athey, 1978) suggests that this position has improved, but his comparison of the percentage of teachers on each salary scale suggests that remedial teachers as a group are still worse off compared with other teachers. Gains (1980) suggests that they are usually not involved in institutional decision-making, and that they accept this exclusion. Galletley (1976) asserts that 'in many schools you cannot get much further down the capitation pecking order than remedial'.

Thus while there is some evidence of an improvement in status, remedial education does seem generally to be a relatively low-status job. Taken with the evidence considered above that remedial education had not been shown to be effective, the picture is far from healthy.

A Way Forward

These concerns for the direction and status of education for children with learning difficulties, have led to several suggestions for a way forward. These can be grouped under two headings: organisation and the curriculum content.

Organisation

Recent developments have moved away from a use of special classes and withdrawal groups, to an input into the normal class-work of the children. This has been brought about in part by the criticisms outlined above, but also by the results of changes in school organisation to a mixed ability arrangement. Such an arrangement, when it is based upon a strong philosophical view of the educational needs of children, is difficult to reconcile with segregation of pupils. However, special needs must be recognised, and such schools, even the most ardent and convinced advocates of mixed ability teaching, have arranged for additional help for children with learning difficulties.

Increasingly, therefore, articles in the professional journals, particularly the journal *Remedial Education*, have reported on attempts to provide extra help to mixed ability classes. For example, Geddes and Crone (1978) have described a programme for literacy; Bailey (1979) has reported a system for arithmetic; while Senior (1979) gives examples of teaching science in a mixed ability setting.

Such initiatives demand new skills of remedial teachers. They must become involved in curriculum planning with other subject specialists, and develop curriculum materials for children with learning difficulties. This collaborative working is new to many remedial teachers and some feel unhappy about it, seeing themselves as becoming technicians, merely providing materials for other teachers to use.

A recent study by Ferguson and Adams (1982) highlights this problem. This sample of 36 remedial teachers spent between 9 and 39 per cent of their time team-teaching with subject specialists, but they were largely dissatisfied. Only five of these teachers prepared and taught lessons jointly with their subject colleagues; others adopted the role of teacher's aide and were seen as such — 'the classroom's faithful retainers'. Such a pessimistic view, however, need not be justified. This role can, indeed, be seen as of high status, advising fellow teachers — providing, of course, that the remedial teacher is indeed a specialist with particular knowledge.

As a result of moving out from a separate, closed environment into the main body of the school, the remedial teacher will become more aware of the issues affecting the school. As a result, there will be an increased need to become involved in the policy-making of the institution. Decisions on grouping of pupils and organisation of the timetable become very pertinent. Remedial teachers should have important views to offer in such discussions. The senior management of the school will need to consider how such involvement can be engendered, and how the best use can be made of this expertise in policy formulation.

This is not to deny the need for specialist teaching *per se*. Much can be improved by organisational change, but some of the children, for example those with profound, intractable reading difficulties, do require specific teaching.

In view of these concerns, a pattern for the organisation of help for pupils with learning difficulties will be suggested. It is loosely based upon the suggestion of Brennan (1979) that three groups of such pupils can be identified.

Remedial Help Across the Curriculum

First there is a need for the curriculum in class lessons to be appropriate, both in content and presentation. This is particularly necessary in a mixed ability setting, but it is still pertinent in the most carefully streamed school. Reading materials (books, workcards, writing on the board) must be pitched at an appropriate level. This is not easy: consider that a mixed ability class of 11-year-olds might usually have a span of reading ability of at least four years (9–13 years), and in some schools it might easily go down as low as 6–7 years, and up beyond 13 years.

Readability analyses of textbooks have revealed that many texts of, for example, mathematics, require a level of reading ability *above* the level of mathematical ability being developed (see Harrison, 1980). Harrison also provides a useful review of methods of analysing the readability of books and materials. It is not possible to carry out a complete survey of all materials but some schools have collaborated on such ventures and, with the advent of microcomputer technology, results can easily be stored, and transferred.

In order to carry out such a programme, the skills of the subject specialist and the remedial teacher should be harnessed. English specialists will also be of great importance for such a task with other subjects. Collaboration between departments is not always very easy as many schools have a history of self-contained departments with resultant loyalties — a factor determined, in part, by the issue of allocation of capitation. Also, as was stated above, remedial teachers have often been low-status teachers in the past. But for a truly effective programme to be instituted across the curriculum, such collaboration is essential. Its negotiation and implementation will be sensitive issues, requiring careful handling by the senior management. Remedial teachers must not feel they are 'hacks' providing materials for others; subject specialists must feel their interests are also being served.

Outside specialists, particularly remedial advisers and educational psychologists, also have much to offer here. For example, what scientific concepts and skills is it possible for children of different general cognitive abilities to learn at each stage? What are the implications for teaching? A history teacher once raised with myself the problem of a lower set fourth form who were undertaking a CSE History syllabus, devised by the school. While some aspects of the topics were easily understood, others appeared to be too abstract. Assessment grades therefore varied considerably, as did morale, interest and behaviour. Investigation of this and many other issues could be a collaborative affair with subject and remedial specialists, together with outside professionals.

Withdrawal

A report by Geddes and Crone (1978) describes how one school allocated first year pupils of varying abilities to different timetables. Those with a reading age greater than 9.5 years received a normal timetable. Those whose reading age was between 8.5 and

9.5 years received six extra periods of special English in place of five French and one library periods. The third group, with reading ages less than 8.5 years, received the same six periods of English in a mixed ability setting, plus five extra periods in lieu of French, RE and or music, and library. In place of French they also received individual help from sixth form students.

In this case, a school has instituted a withdrawal system in addition to mixed ability teaching. This has the benefit that the pupils maintain contact with the normal curriculum, while still providing special help in small groups. Of course, a major issue if this is followed is which subjects are missed? It appears perverse to remove children with learning difficulties from English lessons, but there is a danger of a restricted curriculum if other subjects are missed instead. The argument for missing a foreign language is that it is better to help the pupil's own language first. However, some teachers would argue that many pupils who fail in English language-related subjects derive great enjoyment from a foreign language, at least in the first year or so. Apart from any intrinsic interest in the subject, all pupils start from the same level.

Ultimately such a decision will be based upon the school's philosophy, the nature of teaching in each subject specialism, and the constraints of the timetable. It is, of course, to be hoped that the former factors are the main determinants, but the opposite is, unfortunately, often the case.

The number of pupils to be withdrawn is also an important point. This will vary from school to school, if absolute levels of ability are used.

In addition to the teaching provided by the remedial teacher, the use of other staff and older pupils can be investigated. Visitors to school, particularly parents, are another resource for some pupils, although the use of parents in secondary schools is rare at present.

Total Withdrawal?

Some children, even with the degree of extra help specified above, still find it very difficult to cope in an ordinary school. The time spent in the withdrawal group is not enough; the work in the ordinary class, although amended, is still too difficult. Some of these pupils may require a transfer to a special school, but some can be catered for in an ordinary school system, if it is sufficiently flexible. Jean, the girl discussed at the start of the chapter, attended a remedial department for about half her timetable, while still taking part in craft, art, home economics and other activities with a full range of peers. Some children with emotional difficulties (see Chapter 5) can also be helped by temporary placement in a remedial department, and gradually reintegrated into the mainstream.

Short-term Withdrawal

Some pupils can be identified as having specific problems which may respond to short-term intensive help. A child of generally normal abilities might have a very poor handwriting style. Assessment of this might suggest that a short-term intensive course in handwriting, with practice at home, should remedy this. Arrangements could be made for, say, four periods a week for half a term.

For such pupils, long-term placement in a withdrawal group would be inappropriate — they are, in fact, truly 'remedial' in that their problems can be remedied, usually quite quickly. Unfortunately many have been placed in bottom streams or special classes because an aspect of their work which is considered very important is poor. Such children miss out on a curriculum with which they are otherwise quite able to cope, and may become increasingly frustrated.

Matthew was placed in a low band on entry to secondary school on the basis of primary school advice. His written work was indeed shoddy, yet he was found, on assessment, to have an IQ of over 140 (well above the 99th percentile). Behavioural problems were arising due to the mismatch between his level of intelligence and the curriculum.

Of course, such difficulties should preferably be identified long before the secondary stage (see Chapter 2). Indeed, according to one headteacher it was this group of children who most concerned some primary teachers in the West Riding in the 1960s, resulting in the setting up of remedial centres for primary pupils (Tinsdeall, personal communication). However, such children are still entering the secondary school which must in turn make provision for them. In this context, an experiment in some schools in Sheffield is of interest. Here, pupils in years 1–3 with learning problems regarded as being likely to rapid amelioration (in this instance, 1–1½ terms) have been attending a unit attached to a school for moderate learning difficulties. An evaluation of this facility is being conducted, but initial evidence is favourable. Here good use of available facilites and expertise is occurring, although it could well

Table 4.1: Learning Difficulties and Curricular Needs

Type of learning difficulty	Curriculum
1. General and pervasive	Adaptive-developmental
2. Specific gaps in experience, knowledge or skill	Corrective or compensatory
3. Specific learning difficulties or disabilities	Remedial

Source: Brennan, 1979.

be argued that these pupils should be suitably catered for in their ordinary secondary school. Such a venture is reported by Galletley (1976) who reports that 20 different courses of different lengths had been staged, and that 300 pupils had been catered for.

Children with Special Learning Needs

In addition to the general decisions on allocation and organisation of resources, there are important specific curriculum decisions to be made in order to meet the special needs of these children. In some cases the main focus is on curriculum materials, in others it is on teaching method, but inevitably these two aspects interact. It is beyond the scope of this book to consider these issues in detail, but general principles can be proposed.

The terminology adopted here is derived from Brennan (1979). This is useful in that, although it has the disadvantage of bringing in new jargon, its emphasis is on pupils' *needs* rather than their difficulties. As such it emphasises the interaction between the pupils' own abilities and disabilities, and the provision necessary to meet the needs revealed, as shown in Table 4.1.

Pupils Requiring an Adaptive-developmental Curriculum

This will be required for pupils with generalised learning problems who require 'a special adaptation of the normal school curriculum from the beginning and all through formal education' (Brennan, 1979, p. 150). Modification of teaching methods may also be necessary. The criticism of the traditional curriculum for such pupils is that it is no more than a watered down version of that available to mainstream youngsters. Within maths, for example, pupils may have seemingly endless exercises focused on four rules and other elementary processes on the assumption that they are unable to understand more complex concepts and processes.

However, recent surveys by HMI have severely criticised this diet. Also, some maths specialists argue that seemingly more complex aspects can be successfully taught to, and enjoyed by, these pupils, particularly when these are inherently interesting and, hence, motivating. This view reflects the increasing belief that these pupils, and similar pupils in schools for children with moderate learning difficulties, have been underestimated in their abilities — a view argued in the Warnock Report (DES, 1978).

The work of Brennan (1979) has also shown that curriculum for these pupils is often ill-defined and lacking clear aims and objectives. When these are more clearly defined they are often limited to basic attainments and work preparation. Tomlinson (1982) has argued that such pupils are being prepared for 'good worker' roles in low-status employment, and are denied access to a large amount of knowledge thought worthwhile and useful for other pupils. Decisions on curriculum content are, of course, far from easy, and this applies to all levels of education. However, Brennan's suggestion is a useful one, namely to move the initial emphasis of debate away from *content* to *objectives*. He proposes a model of involvement of individuals (including teachers, LEA and parents) in these decisions — although, interestingly, pupils themselves are not included in this debate.

Across the country individual schools and LEAs have set up curriculum study groups to consider some of these issues, though emphasis does seem to have usually been on content. A project in Sheffield, funded by the EEC, has produced ideas for a curriculum for these pupils in their final years of school.

In the area of basic attainments there have been recent changes in approaches. During the 1970s there was an increasing vogue for the teaching of phonics and other reading sub-skills which were considered to be necessary prerequisites for the mastery of reading itself. Subsequent research questioned these assumptions, and there has been increasing interest in the methods of Direct Instruction (e.g. Becker *et al.*, 1981) and Precision Teaching (e.g. Haring *et al.*, 1978). A study of the former by Gregory *et al.* (1982), using the DISTAR programmes, demonstrated gains by the experimental group of 1.8 years in reading, compared with 0.2 years by the control group, over the five months the programme operated.

The adaptive-developmental curriculum, therefore, is far from obvious. In a time of increasing unemployment the pupils considered here are hardest hit, so raising fundamental questions about curriculum content. Critiques of teaching methods and of the content of the formal and hidden curriculum must also be answered. Although these youngsters have a general difficulty in academic learning it does not follow that they must have what Tomlinson (1982) calls a curriculum of 'non-knowledge', i.e. one that is the result of stripping the normal curriculum of aspects considered too difficult.

Pupils Requiring a Corrective or Compensatory Curriculum

A second group of youngsters are those whose learning experiences have been impoverished or restricted. In most cases the inadequacies do not operate over the whole of the pupils' learning. For example, although progress in academic subjects may be poor, practical skills might be well developed.

Two types of intervention may be defined. The first, corrective, is aimed at making right inaccurate or inappropriate learning. Poor handwriting styles, inappropriate and inefficient use of mathematical techniques, are simple examples. Compensatory education is necessary when there have been gaps in previous knowledge, skills or experiences which must be made good. Most of the work encompassed by these methods will be more applicable to young children, but some straightforward special needs at secondary level can be identified. However, it is important to recognise the danger of oversimplification. For example, does a youngster from an ethnic minority require compensatory or corrective education? At one level there are easy answers, e.g. correcting faulty grammar, improving knowledge of the new culture. But it can be argued that such an approach, based upon an assumption of a deficit in these youngsters, implicitly undervalues their own culture. A similar problem arises at the level of social class. Hargreaves (1982) argues that working-class children have their dignity destroyed by schools. Once more, therefore, it is necessary to consider the special needs of these youngsters within a wider context of the aims of education as a whole.

Pupils Requiring a Remedial Curriculum

The group of pupils under consideration here comprises those with specific learning difficulties. Although of normal general cognitive ability and with no adverse emotional, social or organic disabilities, they fail to learn satisfactorily, particularly written language (i.e. reading, spelling and handwriting). The earlier discussion of causation of learning difficulties indicated that our understanding of the reasons for these problems is far from complete (see Tansley and Panckhurst, 1981; Pavlidis and Miles, 1981). However, there is no doubt that they exist in our schools; that they often are undiscovered, at least until later in the pupils' school lives; and that these pupils do have special needs. An assessment of the incidence of these problems is not possible, as different studies have used different criteria, but the suggestion of Tansley and Panckhurst (1981) of about 2−5 per cent of pupils seems reasonable — even though this figure will vary from school to school.

Reading Difficulties. Helen was a girl of above average intelligence when tested at the age of 11 years, but her reading and spelling were more like those of a 7-year-old. Her mother, a successful professional woman, reported having had similar problems with written language which she had largely overcome, although she still felt unhappy about writing reports or papers. On transfer to secondary school Helen received extra help in a withdrawal class, supplemented by weekly visits to a special class run at her local dyslexia institute. By the end of her fourth year Helen had made very good progress. When seen by myself at that stage she was informed that it might be in her interest to have a reassessment in order that the examination boards could be advised of her history. She was very reluctant, preferring to put her problems behind her, and not to seek a dispensation. However, her mother and I were not sure this was wise, and she was indeed reassessed in the March of her fifth year. Advice was then provided to the examination boards.

Helen is one of a small but significant group of children who are intellectually capable of good examination results, but whose poor reading impedes their progress. Unfortunately, the problem of such children has been all but submerged under a debate on the 'existence' of dyslexia. Although there are many important issues here, including academic, political and educational ones, the fact remains that such *children* exist, whether a clearly defined *condition* exists or not. Increasingly the emphasis is changing to analysing the needs of children rather than categorising them as 'dyslexic' or 'not dyslexic' , a development which must be welcomed.

There is evidence that children with specific reading difficulties fall further behind their peers than do other backward readers, if not provided with the help they need (Yule, 1973). However, Hornsby and Miles (1980) provide evidence which is encouraging.

They review the work of three dyslexia centres and report significant gains in attainment. Although some criticisms can be made of this study, as of earlier reports of remedial teaching, namely that the gains are only short-term, an important difference is that all these children had previously been receiving remedial help in school. This suggests that it is something about the type of teaching or ethos of the centres that was effective.

Identification of such children is greatly facilitated by the school having a good process of screening and assessment (see Chapter 2). Any child considered to have such problems should be checked for visual and hearing difficulties, and assessed by an educational pyschologist. If such problems are still evident as the youngster is coming up to external examination, a referral to an educational psychologist should again be made in order that the examination board can be advised. This often used to be done via a GP, with the strange result that advice on educational problems was being given by medical practitioners. However, in the British Medical Association *News Review* of January 1980, doctors were advised that dyslexia 'was not basically a medical problem' and the 'certification of the disability . . . should be the responsibility of the educational psychologist'. This view was endorsed by the Schools Council who advised all chief education officers accordingly. Unfortunately, examination boards vary considerably in allowances they make for such children. This is a matter which is being pursued by the British Psychological Society's Division of Educational and Child Psychology. It is to be hoped that, very shortly, a common system of allowances can be agreed.

Spelling Difficulties. The case of Martin was presented at the start of this chapter. This boy was severely disabled at school by his inability to spell despite very high general cognitive ability, and this was not realised until late into his school life. In general it is not common for spelling to be systematically assessed in order to identify problems, so the extent of the problem is not known. Our understanding of the spelling process is also poorly understood, and this affects methods of teaching. There is an increasing emphasis now on a structured approach to teaching, and several spelling schemes and workshops on these lines are available. But, as with reading, there is also a need to go beyond a consideration of spelling as an almost mechanical process involving the learning of components (e.g. *ex-; -tion*). Just as reading is also about meaning, so also is spelling. The work of Merritt, through the Open University Reading Diploma, and Frank Smith (1978) emphasises the general intellectual processes of language knowledge, including *prediction*, which is true of both reading and spelling. For example, spelling errors are often called 'bizarre', particularly in the literature on so-called dyslexics. Yet these spellings are often, in fact, very sensible if the perspective of the *writer* not the *reader* is assumed.

Handwriting. Problems with producing written English can be of two types — spelling or the process of writing *per se*, i.e. manipulating a pen or pencil appropriately. The first stage, therefore, is to try to assess which of these processes is faulty. Often youngsters with spelling problems will have untidy writing as a result of frustration or crossing out errors. If spelling is not a problem the two likely areas of difficulty are in fine motor control and speed of information processing.

Some children, although generally sound in their body movements, have specific difficulties. Where this affects their writing hand, it can either render writing a slow and painful process, or else cause untidiness. In part the result depends on the nature of the disability; in part it depends on the youngster's reaction to it. Some will try to rush work, others to be neat. The former are disadvantaged when tidiness is a major criterion; the latter when speed is important. In some cases several problems can interact to produce a more complex problem.

Problems with handwriting often become more apparent as the need for note-taking increases. David, for example, was referred to me because of poor work. He was a third year and his rate of progress was said to have decelerated. Investigations revealed that he had great difficulty in writing quickly. This was partly due to a spelling problem, and partly because of poor fine motor skills. In a quiet one-to-one session, I was able to reduce stress, and this resulted in his accuracy, though not his speed, increasing. However, in class he had never had the time I gave him (as an experiment) so he was under constant stress. Not only did this further increase spelling errors and untidiness, it also led to frustration. In addition, as he often didn't correctly write down homework assignments, or notes, his homework was usually incomplete or incorrect. David was greatly helped by his teachers being advised always to give him time to write down notes, and to check that this had been done; by a support teacher giving extra handwriting lessons; and by David completing extra spelling exercises at home.

Learning Difficulties — Conclusion

The main focus of attention here has been the group of youngsters in the secondary school said to have learning difficulties which are in the mild or moderate range. The exact number of such youngsters is difficult to determine. Not only will it vary from school to school, but definitions are difficult. At the heart of this, and of the argument presented here, is that these youngsters have learning difficulties in relation to a curriculum. While some have problems within themselves causing problems with learning, many have difficulties for reasons more to do with the curriculum than themselves. The problem of identification, therefore, is one of determining the relative emphasis of these two causative components, which will in turn guide thinking on appropriate action.

5

EMOTIONAL AND BEHAVIOURAL PROBLEMS

Geoff Lindsay

Adolescence — a Time of Turmoil?

> Although the period of adolescence has provided a constant source of fascination to adults, psychiatric and psychological writings on the topic are characterised more by confident assertion than by the presence of well based knowledge. (Rutter *et al.*, 1976, p. 35)

So begins Michael Rutter's Chairman's address to the Association for Child Psychology and Psychiatry in 1974. Is adolescence really an age of upheaval and turmoil, or simply a period of development which has been characterised as such? Are the behavioural and emotional difficulties characteristic of pupils in secondary schools different from those in earlier childhood or adult life, and if so are the differences of quality or quantity?

In order to answer these questions it is necessary to study several different aspects of development. First, the different populations must be examined for their characteristics. Second, differences between these characteristics must be explored. Third, comparisons must be made with behaviours which appear to be similar in younger or older people. Finally, in order to be useful, these data must lead to some practical outcomes.

The first issue requires epidemiological studies where whole populations are investigated. This method avoids the misleading conclusions which can be drawn from other types of research. For example, much work in this field has been based on clinic samples, that is young people who have visited psychiatric or child guidance clinics. The obvious problem is that of knowing how justified one is in generalising to other populations. Unfortunately, there have been very few epidemiological studies, and that by Rutter *et al.* (1976) provides the most useful information.

Their study follows up the development of the children reported upon at 9 and 10 years in the Isle of Wight (Rutter *et al.*, 1970). Parents and teachers completed questionnaires on the total population of 2,303 adolescents age 14 to 15 years. Two sub-samples were then chosen for individual study. The first comprised 200 children randomly selected from the general population. The second consisted of 304 children with high (deviant) scores on the questionnaires. The children in both these groups were individually interviewed by psychiatrists (who did not know which sub-sample the child was in). Also, standardised interviews were held with the parents and teachers of these youngsters. In addition all the children designated as having a psychiatric disorder at age 10 years were followed up. Thus information could be provided on several issues: the current degree of disorder, a comparison with a normal population, and an analysis of the development over 4 to 5 years of a group of children with disorder at 10 years.

The conclusions of this study can be summarised as follows. First, parent-child alienation was not a problem for the general population at this age (14–15 years). Second, although there were increasing peer group influences these do not replace parental influences, except in a minority of youngsters. Those with a psychiatric disorder did tend to have more problems with parents. Third, feelings of misery, self-depreciation and beliefs that people were looking at them or talking about them were quite common. For example, 41.7 per cent of boys and 47.7 per cent of girls reported feeling so miserable at times that they were tearful or wanted to get away from it all. However, very few had thoughts of suicide (7.3 per cent boys, 7.9 per cent girls).

Fourth, there was *no* evidence for the view that psychiatric disorder is very much commoner during the mid-teens — it appeared to have a rate of just over 10 per cent among the 10-year-olds, 14-year-olds and adults (the parents of the children in the sample). However, the pattern of disorder did show variation with increased prevalence of both depression and school refusal.

Fifth, many adolescent psychiatric problems arise in early childhood. In fact just under half the youngsters who had psychiatric problems at 14, had been so diagnosed at 10 years. Sixth, there was evidence that parent-child alienation was associated with disorder, though it is probably not often a cause.

Seventh, conditions which arise for the first time during adolescence differ in certain important respects from those which persist from early childhood. They are more often found in girls and are unassociated with educational difficulties. Finally, there was no evidence that disorders arising in adolescence have any different prognosis from those which arise in younger children.

This study provides evidence that 'adolescent turmoil is a fact, not fiction' (Rutter *et al.*, 1976, p. 55) but that its importance has probably been overestimated in the past. However, it is unwise, they argue, to assume that adolescents will 'grow out' of their problems to a greater extent than do younger children. The study suggests at least 10 per cent have what they term a psychiatric disorder, although when others in the sample are included, who were not so diagnosed but who themselves report marked suffering associated with psychiatric symptomology not recognised by teachers or parents, the rate rises to about 21 per cent (Graham and Rutter, 1977). Also, it must be remembered that the Isle of Wight is not totally typical of the whole of the country. When comparisons have been made with an inner London sample, a rate of incidence double that of the Isle of Wight was discovered.

Classifying Problems

The preceding section was concerned with the general incidence of 'psychiatric disorder'. It is now necessary to consider the different types of problem exhibited by adolescents, particularly those most frequently encountered by teachers. The general distinction to be made here will be between emotional and behavioural problems. The former, often called neurotic problems or disorders, are characterised by an abnormality of emotions, but no loss of sense of reality. Anxiety states, phobias and depression are examples. Behavioural problems, often called conduct or antisocial disorders, are usually contrasted with emotional problems in the effect they have on other people, giving rise to disapproval and distress in others. Examples include bullying, disruptive behaviour, stealing and truancy.

Although there is evidence for the usefulness of distinguishing between these two groups of problems, there is also an overlap between them. Rutter *et al.* (1970) argue that in such cases the over-all pattern was closer to children with conduct (behavioural) problems. However, these are only crude groupings anyway and what is of greater importance is an analysis of particular types of problems. But this also is not easy. The classification of behaviour into categories (for diagnoses) is fraught with difficulty. All methods of classification are to varying degrees arbitrary, and this is even more evident in the area of psychoeducational difficulties.

Rutter (1977) proposes a coherent and well-argued 'multi-axial framework' which would comprise five axes. For example, in addition to a 'clinical psychiatric syndrome' (e.g. emotional disorder), the diagnosis would consider specific delays in development (e.g. specific reading retardation), intellectual level, medical condition (e.g. asthma) and abnormal social situation (e.g. family discord). Clearly such a scheme, even if it is useful in psychiatry, is of limited practical use to teachers. This is not to decry attempts to analyse and even explain problem behaviour.

A basic problem with attempts at classification is the type of explanation preferred. Should one aim at describing the behaviour, or at providing hypothesised causations? This is a similar dilemma to that posed by children with learning difficulties (see Chapter 4).

For present purposes the problems chosen will be those which are commonly used as reasons for referring children for advice. As such they cut across the more structured classification systems, but have the benefit of using constructs readily understood by teachers.

Types of Emotional Problems

In a short chapter like this it is not possible to cover adequately all types of problem (for a comprehensive review see Rutter and Hersov, 1977), so the emphasis will be on those emotional difficulties which are commonly presented by adolescents. For this reason relatively little will be said about psychotic disorders which are very rare (about 1 per 1,000 according to Rutter *et al.*, 1976). However, rare problems will be considered when their characteristics are such that they have a significant impact on teachers, e.g. by causing them acute anxiety, as in suicide attempts.

Anxiety and Worry

Many of the referrals made by schools of youngsters with apparent emotional problems are rather hazy and diffuse. Commonly teachers will report that the pupil seems worried, anxious or fearful, but that there is no obvious cause. Such cases require sensitive investigation to determine the exact nature of the fears and anxiety, and possibly the cause. The word 'possibly' is put in here as there are some cases where no cause is found after a thorough investigation, and to continue looking in the hope that one will be discovered might do more harm than good (see School Phobia, p. 94).

Throughout an investigation it is important to remember that the aim is action, namely to reduce the fear or anxiety and return the youngster to a more settled pattern of living. There is, of course, a danger that a less than thorough analysis of the problem will lead to the wrong action being taken. In this case we might solve one problem, only for another to appear in its place. This problem has been considered in some detail over the past 20 years with the increase in the number of behavioural approaches to psychological problems and the relative decline of psychodynamic methods which are characterised by a search for a full awareness of causation.

Fears and anxiety can be related to many different things and can derive from identifiable life events, such a being mocked by one's peers, to diffuse worries about something which can never quite be explained. In all cases, however, the main characteristic is a withdrawal from or avoidance of some aspect in the youngster's life. There are three components to this: the cognitive, the behavioural and the physiological. The pupil will have some ideas about what is causing anxiety, which may or may not be clearly formulated. A cognitive component can also be deduced by someone analysing the person's behaviour. Second, there is the behaviour itself — what does the person do? This may include not entering a classroom, avoiding a group of peers, and staying inside school when other pupils leave. Thus the behaviour can be active or passive, but the result is the same: avoidance.

Third, there are physiological reactions. Some of these are readily noticed, others require investigation. Jumpiness, muscle tremors, 'freezing' and flushing can all be observed while changes in heart and respiratory rate are not always evident. The pupil may also tell of subjective changes such as feelings of apprehension and worry. There is evidence for considerable individual differences in the way these three components correlate with each other. For example, some individuals during treatment have reported a subjective improvement before changes in heart rate were recorded, while others showed the contrary sequence.

If the problem continues it becomes complicated by secondary effects. For example, youngsters who constantly withdraw from social interactions reduce their opportunities to improve the social skills necessary to make such events a success. In many ways such pupils are caught in the classic Catch-22 situation.

One of the major causes of anxiety is in the area of relationships. During adolescence the changes of puberty render peer relationships more complex. These are still formed on the basis of common interests, sympathy and affections, but to these are added sexual attraction and the conflicts which arise therefrom. Teachers are well aware that some friendships blossom and end, only to be reformed again with great, not to say monotonous, regularity. For most this is a normal pattern of development. However, some find either the forming of relationships problematic, or the breaking of friendships very upsetting.

The optimal form of treatment for youngsters with such problems is a mixture of counselling and a direct change of behaviour. The former allows a trusting relationship to develop which facilitates the revelation of fears and worries. This is a common task for pastoral care staff in schools. Evidence suggests that the main attributes of a counsellor which are help this process are genuineness, positive regard and non-possessive warmth (see Truax and Carkhuff, 1967). Much counselling is derived from the work of Carl Rogers (e.g. Rogers, 1951), which emphasises a non-directive style. This can be very difficult for some teachers to follow as it may, for them, conflict with their normal style of interaction in school, which is more didactic and directive. However, since school counselling as a profession has never developed in this country, most of the work must be carried out by teachers with posts of pastoral responsibility, not all of whom are suitable for this work. This dilemma has often been discussed (e.g. see Marland, 1974; Best *et al.*, 1980). Increasingly it is being recognised that experiential as well as academic courses or reading about the subject are essential to develop the skills required.

The second component of the approach is that of direct behavioural change. Counselling can often help a great deal but may not be enough. Youngsters may be helped to explore their feelings, and reduce their anxiety, but they might still have the problem of what to *do* when next in that situation. There is now a good body of research on behavioural methods, including social skill training, which supports this approach (e.g. see Yule, 1977).

Jackie. Jackie was a girl who became very anxious at school. She had transferred to her secondary school later than her peers, moving into the area as a 'comer'. Her teachers noticed that she began to complain of headaches, stomach aches and other physical ailments requiring attention in the medical room, yet when spoken to in that setting she rapidly recovered and interacted quite well with adults.

On investigation it became quite clear that Jackie's lack of friends in school was becoming a serious problem. She had reached the stage of being in the classic Catch-22 approach — avoidance conflict: she desperately wanted to be friends with the others in her class, but was very anxious about being repulsed. The more she tried to approach others, the more anxious she felt and the greater the likelihood of disappointment became, leading to greater avoidance. In Jackie's case there were also problems within the family which were causing her great concern. Some she would confide in me, but with nobody else. I had, therefore, to respect this confidentiality but to devise a treatment plan which did not break it. Jackie was helped by regular counselling over a three-month period, which enabled her to explore her concerns about her peers, and family, while at the same time her teachers put into operation a plan whereby her contacts with peers were gradually increased in a systematic manner. Initially meetings of only one or two girls in a controlled setting were engineered. This was gradually extended to larger groups.

Jackie overcame her problems to the extent that she was happy at school, and had some peer relationships. But on follow-up she reported that there were still family problems and she did not have any close friends. On leaving school she took a job which was rather solitary but very fulfilling.

In this case an analysis of the reasons for Jackie's anxiety was necessary. Treatment was of two different types — one behavioural, one based on exploring relationships. But the dimension of her own personality should also be recognised. She was a rather introverted girl who, with help, reached the level of social integration with which she was happy.

Phobias

The distinction between fears and a phobia is not easy to make. Definitions usually make reference to the fear being 'irrational', or out of proportion to the situation or object causing the fear. Also, it tends to persist over an extended period of time, is beyond the voluntary control of the individual, cannot be explained or reasoned away, and is not age specific (cf. infants' fear of strangers). However, in reality these are all not discrete categories but continuous variables, and some psychologists would not wish to try to make rigid dividing lines.

The number of phobias described in the literature is very large, ranging from the common (e.g. agoraphobia) to the highly idiosyncratic. Usually phobias have been labelled with respect to the object or situation causing the fear reaction, usually by taking the Greek name for the phobic stimulus and attaching it to the word 'phobia'. At its most absurd use now we have phobophobia (fear of phobias). There have been attempts, therefore, to classify the phobias. One such scheme by Miller *et al.* (1974) comprises three main classes (physical injury, natural events and social anxiety) plus a miscellaneous category. Social anxiety, for example, is then subdivided into, among others: school, separation and performance (e.g. examinations).

Adolescence is a time of transition as far as phobias are concerned. Among younger children, fear of specific situations was found to be most common by Rutter *et al.* (1970). Specific animal phobias were only half as common and they occurred only in girls in this study. There was no case of a markedly handicapping social anxiety, nor of agoraphobia. Comparison of this with other studies suggests that insect and animal phobias almost always start by the age of 5 years, and rarely begin in adult life. Agoraphobias, however, start at any time from late childhood to middle life, with peaks of onset at late adolescence and around 30 years. In adults, agoraphobias are by far the most common with a ratio against specific animal phobias of 84:18 in a study by Marks and Gelder (1966).

Thus for adolescents some phobias will be manifestations of long-standing problems, which have perhaps differed in severity. Those which start to appear are either specific to the situation or more like the adult pattern. For example, now that few children suffer the stress of examinations at primary level, the first time this can specifically be shown is in adolescence.

The preferred treatment of most phobias is by behavioural methods, usually based upon classical conditioning. Monosymptomatic phobias (e.g. of spiders) show particularly good success rates. With more complex problems, particularly those of social settings, a more comprehensive treatment involving several approaches may be required. An example is given below under 'School Phobia'. Miller *et al.* (1974) suggest that the wide range of techniques used over the years can be reduced to four basic essentials: establishing a helping relationship, stimulus clarification, desensitisation to the stimuli, and confrontation of the stimulus.

The importance of the therapist's relationships with the child and parents is critical to the first of these. There must be a belief that success is possible. If parents and youngsters have such a trust it facilitates the exploration of the problem. This analysis is important to determine whether the phobia is simple or complex. Rutter *et al.* (1970), for example, found that most phobias in their sample were associated with other problems. In some cases, the phobia may be a symptom of a more serious problem. Once the phobia itself has been determined it is then necessary to build up a picture of events: the setting in which it occurs; the precipitating events; the effects of other people; the stimuli that evoke the anxiety; the reactions of others; situations or actions which reduce the fear. These and other factors will be investigated to gain a clear idea of the operation of the phobia.

Treatment involves a desensitisation of the person to the fear produced by the stimulus. The basic aim is to introduce a reaction which competes with the fear reactions; this is often relaxation. The method might involve a sequence of steps whereby the youngster is gradually introduced to increasingly anxiety-provoking stimuli, or 'flooding' where there is immediate confrontation with the stimulus in a controlled setting. In both cases the person's trust in the therapist is important.

In many, if not most, cases of phobias the purpose of the school is largely limited to identifying that there is a problem, arranging for expert help, and then handling the pupil sympathetically. In some cases, however, teachers can be very helpful either in carrying out a treatment programme, or counselling a pupil.

This is pariularly the case with 'school phobia'. An example of a specific phobia, which also demonstrates how treatment must be carefully monitored, concerns Robert.

Robert. During his second year at secondary school Robert's teachers suddenly became very alarmed when he twice collapsed at school. Investigation of the settings revealed that in one instance a film of a war had been shown in the school assembly; in the second, Robert's class were being instructed on the system of blood flow in the body with graphic demonstrations. It was readily apparent that Robert had what could be called a 'blood phobia'. A programme of desensitisation was therefore worked out, initially using an ideational method (where the person imagines the events rather than faces actual stimuli). Here a hierarchy of increasingly anxiety-provoking stimuli was evoked from Robert. Robert was taught to relax and over three weeks (one session per week) he was taken through most of the hierarchy. Each time he was asked to relax and then to think about the first stimulus. When he could do this with no anxiety, he moved on to the next.

Progress was quite good, but the method was not completely successful. Several factors could be identified. First, life in school had to go on and, while most of his teachers were made aware of his problem, one who didn't receive, or register, this information made a joking reference to the class which was sufficiently graphic to cause Robert to relapse. Second, a continued monitoring by teachers revealed that Robert was also showing anxiety in other ways, particularly when in large crowds, and especially during the assembly. In discussion Robert reported that he now became anxious that a teacher might make a reference which he would find upsetting, and he could not 'escape' from the middle of a hall full of pupils. He had now developed a form of claustrophobia.

Third, discussion with the parents revealed a family pattern of phobias. Although sensible and caring, by their circumstances they were now causing Robert more anxiety as they tried to sympathise with him by describing their own difficulties. Fourth, Robert was a very able boy, but was becoming increasingly concerned that he was dropping behind his class, because of his occasional absences, and the increasing 'free-floating' anxiety.

It was decided, therefore, that it was necessary to try to at least reduce the blood phobia to a manageable level as quickly as possible. A clinical psychologist, able to see Robert three times a week, was therefore contacted. This proved successful, although Robert continued to show some general anxiety in school.

'School Phobia' or School Refusal

School phobia will be considered as a separate issue as it is probably for teachers the most common type of problem called a phobia. The paper by Miller *et al.* (1974) referred to earlier claims that the ratio of school phobia publications to published papers related to other types of child phobias is approximately 25:1. This interest of the professionals is matched by interest in the press and magazines. However, its actual incidence is very low. Depending on how it is defined, different rates have been specified, but in general a figure of less than 1 per cent of the population (Yule *et al.*, 1980) seems reasonable.

There are some significant problems with 'school phobia' as a label, and many authors prefer to use the term 'school refusal'. Several different issues are relevant. First is that of consistency of categorisation. Phobias are normally named in accord with the stimulus which arouses fear and anxiety. In school phobia, however, it is not always straightforward. Many children do not seem to have a phobia about school *per se*, but rather have an anxiety associated with leaving home. This reveals itself as a 'school phobia' mainly because the youngster is supposed to attend and refusal to do so causes confrontation and more anxiety, in both parents and their child.

Second is the issue of treatment. Pupils who do not attend school have traditionally been divided into two types: truants, considered to be making a rational decision not to attend, and school phobics, whose non-attendance is due to a psychological disturbance. The former have been dealt with by ignoring them, or punitive measures (e.g. see Berg, 1980). School phobics, on the other hand, were often off school until their disturbance could be overcome, often using psychotherapy. It was not unknown for some pupils to be 'signed off' for several years while this treatment took place. One apocryphal story describes how one 12-year-old in a block of flats in an inner city area was so diagnosed, leading to an 'outbreak' of this disorder among his friends who were equally reluctant to attend school!

More recent studies have tended to the view that reasons for non-attendance are more complex than a simple dichotomy ('bad or mad'). The effects of the school itself, the family's health and financial circumstances and the peer group have all been shown to be important (e.g. see Berg, 1980; Galloway, 1980; Rutter *et al.*, 1979). Reports of treatment have also stressed the need for a more thorough appraisal of the circumstances as well as nature of the refusal, as was described under the general discussion of phobias. Yule *et al.* (1980), for example, identify four main sub-types of school refusal. The first occurs at entry to first school. The second occurs shortly after a major change of schooling, perhaps from a small primary to a large secondary school. This is substantiated by earlier studies of clinic samples, where 11 years was a peak time for referral (Chazan, 1962), but not by the epidemiological study in the Isle of Wight. Third, when school refusal first occurs in later adolescence it may be associated with the onset of a depressive illness or even early onset of schizophrenia. Fourth are those cases brought on by any of the large number of possible stress-provoking events that can occur in the youngster's life.

Judith. Judith was a very attractive, personable young lady of 15 years who had stopped attending school, despite the efforts of an education welfare officer. Although not keen on school, she was not thought to have major academic problems, or to be unhappy while at school. Neither was she a truant. Investigation revealed that Judith's home circumstances were very difficult. Her mother had poor health and had undergone several major operations. The father was a long-distance lorry driver and often away. The family lived in an area being cleared of houses, and so had few neighbours. One day Judith had returned from school to find her mother lying at the bottom of the steep staircase, where she had been for several hours. Her problem of non-attendance became particularly marked after an illness and school holiday resulted in her enforced absence for well over a month.

In this case, Judith's fear of going to school was a result of a reluctance to leave mother, but not in the unhealthy way described in the literature on separation anxiety, where mother and child have developed a symbiotic relationship. Her worries had a sound basis. Treatment involved a short series of counselling sessions together with a careful reintroduction to school, where she had free access to the payphone to call her mother.

Angela. Enforced absence through illness, especially when it follows on from or precedes a holiday, is often associated with school refusal. The anxiety related to other events becomes multiplied by having to return to school, and Angela's problem was of this type. An interview with the mother revealed that Angela had a history of minor illnesses, particularly respiratory tract problems, and the onset of her menarche had added to these. Also, her reluctance to go to school had started at the junior school where the mother helped in the kitchens. There was evidence, from the investigation, of a well-developed, if unintended, collusion between mother and daughter. Minor ailments were treated very seriously and with great sympathy, resulting in much time off school. Yet the mother recognised the harm being done to her daughter who was very able and well on top of her work, though now in danger of falling behind.

In this case, treatment consisted of a sympathetic teacher

collecting Angela from home and taking her to school. This teacher had herself gone through similar problems as an adolescent, but was now a vivacious and popular member of staff. This sympathetic 'self-disclosure' by the teacher, together with the lifts, quickly improved matters. The next stage was to let Angela go by bus with a friend. The problem was resolved within a couple of weeks.

These two cases exemplify some of the different aspects of 'school phobia', or as it is better described 'school refusal'. Further case studies are to be found in Yule *et al.* (1980). As with other problems described here, a careful investigation is very important. The intervention is usually a mixture of counselling and behavioural methods, the exact proportion and nature of which varies from case to case.

Unhappiness

Unhappiness in adolescence is a common event, as the study by Rutter *et al.* (1976) reported above shows. Some adolescents, however, develop a state of unhappiness in school which is more prolonged or ingrained and they are often called 'depressed'. The severity of interference with school and home life, in terms of both relationships and work, is usually taken as an indicator of whether the unhappiness can be considered a symptom of depression or, if severe, part of a depressive disorder. The dividing line is, however, very difficult to determine; and whether it is necessary to make a distinction is challenged by some psychologists and psychiatrists. The lack of a clear definition also makes it difficult to specify rates of incidence, but in the Isle of Wight study (Rutter *et al.*, 1976) only 9 out of 2,303 adolescents were described as having a depressive disorder, while another 26 were considered to have a disorder involving both anxiety and depression. These figures (about 1 per cent of the population) must be contrasted with the fifth of adolescents at 14 years who had feelings of misery and unhappiness.

For teachers the important point is to recognise unhappiness which does not go away within a matter of days. Even short periods of depression may, in fact, be suitable for some form of intervention, but in general the normal supportive interactions of peers, family and teachers are sufficient. With unhappiness continuing into several weeks action is required.

The causes of unhappiness are many and varied. One of the major groups of problems which precipitates events can be described as 'loss'. This includes loss of friendships, particularly when a best friend, or boy- or girl-friend is involved, and the loss of loved ones through death or marital separation.

Bereavement

Children and young people are less likely to encounter death of a loved one now than in earlier times, which renders any loss which does happen more of a problem. Not only is the youngster faced with a traumatic experience, but others often find it difficult to cope with their own feelings as they may not have experienced bereavement either. Problems of bereavement are of two kinds. There is the immediate emotional reaction to the trauma, but this may be followed by difficulties which are the result of the new family circumstances, particularly if the child is taken into long-term care, or if only one parent dies and the other brings the child or children up alone. These problems can also occur in adolescence, but by definition will be of much shorter duration. The financial plight of one-parent families was well illustrated by the Finer Report (DHSS, 1974) and this can cause conflict at home when fashionable clothes or expensive activities are desired. In some cases the loss of a parent can trigger off a range of other problems which were simmering under the surface. In one case, for example, the death of a father coincided with a difficult period of development for one girl who was working out her sexual and non-sexual relationships. Her need for a father figure became confused with the exploratory sexual encounters, resulting in her causing great distress to male teachers. She would seek sympathy, and receive it, as 'daughter to father', but then would start to interact in a flirtatious manner. Her teachers were confused and distressed as they were sympathetic to her loss, but sensibly aware of the danger of such interactions. Non-teaching male staff were not exempt, and one kindly man became the main focus of her attention.

The death of other loved ones can also cause difficulties, but these are generally limited to direct emotional problems. The death of a sibling can lead to disturbance if the youngster is convinced he or she was at fault. This can happen if siblings are playing together in dangerous circumstances, particularly if an older sibling is charged with taking care of a younger brother or sister. The reaction of parents and other family members can also continue a youngster's difficulties. Some families do not resolve their own grief, and this can be particularly worrying if the child is idolised.

Jason. Jason was a 13-year-old whose brother had been killed in a road accident, when in his company. Several years later the family still grieved, particularly at the anniversary of the death. The home was full of pictures of the dead boy, but not of Jason. His brother was proclaimed to have been wonderful at everything — little was said about Jason. At the time of an anniversary of the death Jason developed a range of problems. He was very unhappy, complained of various pains and truanted. At that time the extended family were meeting every night in his home, which had taken on the ethos of a shrine.

Divorce

The number of divorces has risen dramatically from 25,400 in 1961 to 148,000 in 1980. The steady annual increase in the number of divorces in the 1960s accelerated when the 1969 Divorce Reform Act became effective law. In 1980, 88,000 of the divorces made absolute involved children and young people under the age of 16 years. Those figures give some idea of the magnitude of this phenomenon. However, the majority of divorces occur in the first ten years of marriage, so there will be proportionately fewer occurring when a child is at secondary school. For most pupils the problems will be a result of long-term difficulties from an earlier divorce. There is little direct evidence on the effects of divorce on children, although a number of studies have indicated the greater likelihood of a number of difficulties following early loss. Loss of a parent through divorce, it is argued, is similar to that caused by bereavement. For example, younger children may think they caused the loss by their actions or wishing and so become distressed. Boys are usually found to be more vulnerable to the stresses involved.

However, it must be remembered that divorce will follow a period of marital conflict, which may be severe. It is more important, therefore, to consider the effects of this conflict rather than the divorce *per se*. Divorce, in this context, may be either a final straw or a release for the youngster. But in either case, there may be longer-term problems. Legal wrangling over custody and maintenance can prolong the ethos of conflict, even if the parents are divorced. Custody issues, however, are generally more of a problem with younger children.

In adolescence there may be concern about divided loyalties. Where violence is a factor, a boy might become involved as a protector of his mother against the father's anger and attacks. In addition to the trauma of the violence itself, a boy who still cares for his father will be torn in two directions, but feel powerless to resolve the problem. Such boys often reveal their problems in school by being involved in various misdemeanours caused by their frustrations.

Other problems can be caused during adolescence when the parents either over- or under-involve their son or daughter in the process of separation. In the former case, too much unburdening can confuse a youngster who is not ready to cope with the conflicting messages. But mature adolescents also feel they have a right to know what is going on. One boy, showing disturbance and unhappiness at school, had parents with marital problems of which he was aware. But despite being a mature and intelligent 15-year-old, he was not asked who he wanted to stay with, or indeed anything about *his* wishes. He felt powerless to control this, yet believed he should be asked to contribute to such discussions of his future.

For youngsters in secondary schools, divorce *per se* will probably be much less a problem than the various other factors which accompany it. Marital and family disharmony is often relevant when youngsters start to show acute or chronic unhappiness, or behaviour problems.

Suicide Attempts

Successful suicide is very rare among adolescents at school, but when it does occur it achieves national attention. Its importance to teachers is out of proportion to its incidence, both in terms of its finality and the effect on school staffs if they are accused of either failing to spot the problems, or doing anything about them. One or two famous cases, for example, received extensive news coverage when youngsters committed suicide claiming they had been bullied at school.

Shaffer (1974) reports that during the period of his 7-year study only 1 child out of every 800,000 alive in England and Wales aged between 10 and 14 years killed themselves each year; all were over 12 years. Suicide accounted for only 0.6 per cent of all deaths in this age group. Suicide among children under 15 years accounts for only 0.08 per cent of all suicides. However, the rate of suicide among the 15–19 age range increased by half between 1975 and 1979. Shaffer reports that boys are more likely to commit suicide (ratio 2.3:1) and that more were youngsters of above average intelligence than would be expected (12 out of 28 on whom test data was available). Attempts to use the information collected to predict potential suicides, however, were unsuccessful. While broken homes, antisocial behaviour and depression were often found, these were not very different to the rates found in other populations of disturbed youngsters. A common precipitating event was the reporting to parents of some type of antisocial behaviour or loss of face that had taken place away from home, but not fights or arguments with a member of the family. Only 2 from the 14 who left suicide notes mentioned fear of a peer.

Thus it is very unlikely that a teacher will encounter a successful suicide and, from evidence available, even if this should happen it is unlikely that a clear indiction will be evident. What is more likely is that he or she will have a pupil who *attempts* suicide, although this is probably an inaccurate description. Of all the people who make what can be described as a suicide attempt, or parasuicide, most are probably not intending to be successful: they are usually making a 'cry for help'. As a leaflet from the Samaritans states: 'Many of these people who attempt suicide don't want to die. They just don't want to go on living as things are.'

The number of parasuicides among the 15–19 age group increased in frequency during the later 1960s to early 1970s, despite a fall among older people. Unlike suicide, which is an adult phenomenon, parasuicide is very much a feature of late adolescence. The rate for girls doubled between the late 1960s and mid-1970s, and was about twice that of boys. In all about 750 per 100,000 15–19 year olds committed parasuicide per year by the mid-1970s. However, parasuicides were very rare among pre-pubescent youngsters. The reasons for the increase in the rate of parasuicides over time is not clear, and attempts at discovering predictor variables have also been unsuccessful. High rates of disturbance in the youngster's life are again indicated, but there is no straightforward pattern. For some, parasuicide follows a period of increasing stress which finally becomes intolerable. However, most youngsters under similar stress do not attempt suicide. For others, the gesture is almost a 'spur of the moment' affair, and out of all proportion to previous stress. In some cases the cause is a kind of game or pact which goes wrong. In others it is a deliberate challenge — 'If you don't let me do this I'll take these pills'. These examples are more likely not to be true attempts, but can of course go wrong. The more worrying type is the youngster (usually a girl) who feels that problems are mounting up and there is no solution. Such pupils may find the dividing line between a gesture and genuine attempt difficult to determine, having lost some sense of reality. Most attempts follow major disruption of a personal relationship, typically with parents or with boy- or girl-friend (Hawton, 1982).

Because of the nature of the result, all suicide attempts or gestures should be treated seriously. Even if it is clear that the likely cause is attention-seeking, it is necessary to take positive action. The simplistic interpretation of behavioural psychology, that responding will simply reinforce the behaviour, is both naive and dangerous. Even if the attention is itself reinforcing, this need not prevent a more appropriate treatment plan, based on reinforcement of appropriate behaviour, being instituted after the immediate crisis. In some areas all youngsters with drug overdoses are given a psychiatric interview after recovery, which may result in follow-up treatment. In other cases, support in school by teachers and educational psychologists will be provided. The short-term prognosis is good in the majority of cases of parasuicide, but at least one in ten makes a further attempt within a year. It is not clear what preventative and supportive measures are most effective, but the support of sympathetic teachers can often be of great benefit.

Anorexia Nervosa

This is another problem which, though uncommon, is discussed a good deal in the literature and press. Its characteristics are a wilful and successful refusal to eat associated with a preoccupation with food and weight loss. Adolescent girls form the main group affected with the peak in late adolescence. Crisp *et al.* (1976) reported an incidence of 1.3 cases for 1,000 girl-years for those aged 15 years and under and 3.9 cases per 1,000 for those 16 years and over in a survey of independent schools. However, the rate among girls at comprehensive schools was much lower. There is some evidence that the incidence was rising from the 1960s to 1970s. The reasons for this disorder are disputed. Some argue that there is a primary hormonal imbalance leading to a distaste of food. However, the main debate is between those favouring a psychological interpretation, and those who prefer a pragmatic explanation (e.g. see *British Medical Journal*, 7 January 1978).

Psychological interpretations focus on the person as a scapegoat in the family or the girl being in conflict with a mother where sexual attractiveness is an issue. The refusal of food has also been interpreted as a fantasy about impregnation through oral sexual relations. Such views have been extended to see the youngster as trying to deny a developing sexuality — this succeeds in as much as the menarche may be delayed, or periods may be halted; a related explanation concerns the feminist view that girls feel the need to fit into a shape which is determined by a male-dominated society. A more pragmatic view is that the problem starts as normal dieting which is mainly designed to increase sexual attractiveness, but for some reason the dieting gets out of control. In some cases it is a combination of factors.

Palmer (1980) has proposed a wide-ranging attempt at an explanation which he terms the *psychological regression of hypothesis*. In this, with its nine propositions, he attempts to include all the known relevant aspects of the disorder, and attempts to combine both psychological and biological causations. Thus he relates anorexia nervosa to slimming behaviour, often started for cosmetic reasons, but argues that it is also related to the stress experienced at adolescence. An interaction of these two sets of factors may result in a continuing downward spiral of weight loss, which brings with it biological regression — e.g. periods normally cease. He suggests that at this time the youngster is 'switched off', and in this state much of the pressure of life events is removed. Adding weight may therefore be seen as non-rewarding as this will bring the adolescent back into stress, so leading to a phobic avoidance of normal weight. This thesis is the most satisfactory at present. It seems to account for most if not all youngsters who do suffer from the disorder, being based upon both psychological and biological causative elements, while not resorting to the more extreme psychodynamic explanations which appear, in most cases, to be rather fanciful.

Ann. Ann was a small very attractive lady who was a successful doctor. She considered herself anorexic and reported that she ate very little and her weight had been stable at about 6 stones since adolescence. There was evidence of a long-standing conflict with a very attractive mother, despite Ann being sufficiently alluring to have had pin-up photographs in a national newspaper. In addition Ann's body perception was disturbed. Although very slim, she still regarded herself as too fat. Finally she now found the actual eating of more than a few mouthfuls of food physically discomforting. In this case, causation appeared complex, with different factors having varying degrees of influence at several stages in her life.

At the present time there is still a good deal of debate over both cause and treatment of anorexia nervosa (e.g. counselling or forced feeding). As with most human behaviour, the explanations are not likely to be simple, and it is probably best to assume that the dieting that goes wrong, repressing of developing sexuality and intra-family stress are all likely, partial or full explanations for different groups of girls.

Behaviour Problems

The problems of classifying problems have already been attended to. This difficulty is increased in the area of behaviour problems as a central aspect of the definition involves some concept of the behaviour being antisocial and causing harm to others. Violent behaviour and delinquency in general clearly fit this pattern, but what of truancy, or drug abuse? Furthermore, writers such as Rutter, and Herbert (1978), prefer the term 'conduct disorder' which can be viewed as placing the problem very much within the youngster. While for some this may be appropriate, it is clearly most inappropriate for many others. For example, one young person may take delight in hurting others, while another may live in an area where to be prepared to fight is necessary to 'survive'. There is, therefore, an even greater problem in conceptualising behaviour problems in terms of whether the person is 'mad or bad' — does this youngster need help or punishment? While this can apply to emotional problems, the general assumption is that it is help that is required.

A related problem is that of referral. With emotional problems many people seek help. Adults may consult a family doctor or take other steps to find assistance. With antisocial behaviour, however, it is usually another who decides what should be sought. Thus a court might determine that a person should receive psychiatric help rather than a custodial sentence. This problem is even more acute among adolescents. Most youngsters with emotional problems who are seen by psychologists and psychiatrists are not self-referrals. Teachers, parents or others have usually perceived a problem and suggested this action. However, commonly the pupil appreciates that help is being provided and is grateful. With behaviour problems a very different situation pertains. Often a referral is made after a crisis, and in some cases there is an explicit threat that either the pupil sees a psychiatrist or psychologist, or else a punishment of some kind will be given. But even if the referrer shows greater sensitivity than this, there is still a problem. A pupil who is about to be excluded from school is usually dubious about the good-natured help being offered, coming as it does at that time. Also such youngsters may not consider they have a problem; rather they may believe their action to be either justified or at least not an indicator of a need for 'help'. Such a pupil might challenge the referral either by not attending an interview, or denying a problem if they do. And they might well be justified.

In considering behaviour problems, therefore, it is important to be very clear about who has the problem, and to what degree. In some cases it is very clear that a youngster has a problem by its manifestations. Les, for example, was a boy of average ability who had a long record of under-achievement at school. When young he had been overactive and found settling to work very difficult. This problem, as is common, reduced during adolescence, but he was not motivated to make up lost ground. There were family difficulties, and he was not very popular with his peers. His school was concerned to identify youngsters with problems and the teachers regarded Les as a boy who was likely to be excluded if he continued in his present manner; he was therefore referred to me. At interview he readily accepted his difficulties and showed much insight, despite his not being very articulate. With regular counselling, and the support of key teachers, particularly his year tutor with whom he had a good relationship, he managed to avoid exclusion, although he continued to have low motivation to improve his work and take the examinations of which he was capable.

Other youngsters, however, regard themselves as perfectly normal and can't understand the fuss. If school is boring, why should I attend? Everybody 'pinches' so why shouldn't I? Indeed, in such circumstances does the youngster need 'help'? One mother became very concerned about her son when she discovered he had truanted for a week, and referrred him to me herself. Before interviewing him I inspected the class's register, and discovered he had the best attendance in the form! It transpired he had been goaded by his peers to be like them (i.e. 'normal') and had finally succumbed.

The preceding argument is not a justification for antisocial behaviour, nor an argument that youngsters who engage in it should not be helped or punished as appropriate. However, it is important for teachers and others to be very clear on whose behalf they are speaking. In some cases it is reasonable to talk explicitly about the 'good of the others', but this should be recognised. There are many ethical issues raised when one intervenes in someone's life, particularly if it is at the request of others.

The nature of behaviour problems during adolescence shows differences when compared with both childhood and adult life, but there is evidence for a persistence of problems over time for a minority of youngsters. A study by Farrington (1978) found that boys considered most aggressive at 8–10 years were more likely to be so considered at 12–14 years and again at 14–16 years. For example, 59 per cent of the most aggressive boys at 8–10 years were so rated at 12 to 14 years, compared with 29 per cent of the remaining boys. The boys who were severely aggressive were especially likely to become violent delinquents (14 per cent vs 4.5 per cent). Other studies have provided evidence for a continuity of problems, and for an antisocial personality (e.g. Robins, 1978). The longitudinal study of West and Farrington on a group of London boys, for example, suggests differences between delinquent and non-delinquent boys on a wide range of behaviours, which are not accounted for by factors which could be described as environmental.

However, there are also studies which reveal how some antisocial behaviours are related to environmental influences. Studies of schools, including Hargreaves (1967), Hargreaves *et al.* (1975) and Woods (1979), have done much to illuminate aspects of schools which contribute to problem behaviour by large numbers of youngsters. The different results derived from these two sets of studies are probably related to the severity and persistence of problems. The studies which have shown the persistence of problems have tended to reveal this in a small number of youngsters with severe difficulties. The work of Schacher *et al.* (1979), for example, on the prognostic importance of pervasive overactivity on disturbed behaviour at 14 to 15 years, is concerned with only 9 youngsters identified by their teachers from 1536. Within schools these youngsters with severe problems might represent only a handful of the population (although in some schools they could represent a sizeable minority). This confusion had recently led to misunderstandings when, for example, teachers who have been advised of the contribution of the school to the production of behaviour problems (by, say, 20–30 per cent of pupils), interpret this in terms of the 1 to 2 per cent of pupils with severe problems. Such a misunderstanding has led some teachers to reject the significance of work which shows school effects, and so reinforce the belief that the main contributing factors are the pupil and home background. A reasonable summary, therefore, is that some youngsters who exhibit severe behaviour problems, of various kinds, often have longstanding problems, which might require identification and treatment in the pre-secondary years. However, most of the behaviour problems exhibited in schools cannot simply be explained away by reference to home background. The relative influence, therefore, of a youngster's own personality, his present and past home circumstances, and the school's treatment and expectations, will vary from person to person.

This analysis has an importance also in the area of intervention. Youngsters exhibiting severe behaviour problems, particularly if they cause hurt and damage to themselves or others, will probably require individually organised intervention plans. Behavioural approaches appear to have the most to offer here (e.g. Herbert, 1978). In some cases the problems are such that the youngster may need to be segregated from society and placed in a community home, perhaps even one with secure accommodation. (Again, reasons for so acting are often confused: it is often argued that it is in order that the youngsters can receive 'help', yet it may in reality be a punitive measure.) A study of such youngsters reveals that they tend to have had a longstanding series of problems in their lives (Hoghughi, 1978), and are usually boys. Intervention with such youngsters may include attempts to reduce specific actions (e.g. violence) and increase other actions or skills (e.g. social skills). Such methods are in some ways easier in restricted environments (such as community homes and special schools) as contingencies can be controlled. However, there is then the problem of generalising any new behaviour to the normal school or home setting. These factors weigh on opposite sides of the equation of course, when modification of behaviour is tried in the normal setting. However, the literature on approaches in normal settings is increasing and this must surely be the main focus of work (e.g. Upton and Gobell, 1980).

One area of concern with respect to pupils with behavioural problems is the growth of unit provision. Looked at in one way this development has good features. It represents schools' attempts to deal with problems themselves rather than exclude or transfer the pupil to special school. In terms of levels of integration these units would seem to be preferable to such segregation. The declared aim of many units to reintegrate their pupils adds weight to this argument. Unfortunately the reality is different. These units have a variety of names, and a variety of functions, but in general they cater for those pupils who are disturbing to the ordinary school system. It is readily apparent that most have the task of solving a problem of the system (by removing the youngster) rather than specifically helping the pupil. A survey by the Advisory Centre for Education (1980) reveals a worrying picture of units not having governing bodies, and those that did having no parent representation. The curriculum is usually restricted (DES, 1978b; Dawson, 1980) and the goal of reintegration is rarely achieved (see Topping, 1983, for a review; Galloway *et al.*, 1982). As examples of integrated settings, 'least restrictive environments', and organisational modifications to meet the needs of pupils with special educational needs, these units fall a long way short of perfection. Also, as Galloway *et al.* (1982) report, they appear to fail to meet the needs of the schools — those which had introduced units failed to show a decrease in suspensions or referral to special school.

There is still much to be discovered about the provision which is most suitable for these youngsters. Some are both disturbed and disturbing, but in many cases the cause is the mismatch between pupil and task in mainstream classes. The provision of units can alleviate the school's problem, but it does not solve that of the pupil. In these instances a more radical examination of the educational process is required.

Conclusions and Implications

Adolescence is a time of change, and it is normal for adolescents to have problems. Many of these are the result of the differences in expectation of others and themselves as they change from child to adult; others derive from the stress of life events. But beyond these normal difficulties, some youngsters suffer problems which differ in severity and duration. Teachers, therefore, must be in a position to judge what are problems which require action, and what are best left alone. The latter form of action is important as adolescents are well known for their objection to what they call 'interference'. Individuality and self-determination must be respected, but in a context of a developing person who will still need help and guidance.

The evidence presented for the common forms of emotional problems of adolescence has re-emphasised the point made earlier that there is no simple way of predicting who will be unhappy, make a suicide gesture or whatever. Whenever these problems have been investigated, certain patterns have been identified, yet these are common, and most youngsters who fit the pattern do not then suffer the problem.

A similar result is found when the literature on antisocial behavioural problems is examined. With many youngsters who exhibit severe problems, a continuity can be traced back to early childhood. Often severe social stress is implicated, but there is also evidence that personality characteristics are important. But these youngsters are the minority, severe though the problems they cause may be. Many other pupils exhibit behaviour problems whose origins are in adolescence itself. With most the difficulties are transitory, and indeed may not be considered abnormal. For example, studies of delinquency have revealed that practically all adolescents have committed theft (though normally of objects with low value).

Intervention is needed on several fronts. Some youngsters, particularly those with severe problems, require specific help or attention. But for many the help is best provided not at an individual level, but at the level of the organisation or setting. Recent work on school organisation and classroom management has shown how these factors can be modified to improve behaviour. The ecology of the school and community is also a ripe area for develpment. The implications for teachers, therefore, are that a comprehensive system of monitoring is required, matched by a pastoral care system which is both sensitive and responsive. Teachers can often identify children with problems, even if they cannot work out what the problems are. A well-respected tutor can also be an excellent person to help a troubled youngster. Books such as that by Nelson-Jones (1982) provide good reviews of counselling as a process, although there is a need also to develop counselling skills through experiential learning. But the range of problems and the varying implications of each, require a partnership of teaching staff and outside professionals. In some cases this is less a partnership than parallel services: a practice to be deplored. Collaboration in both assessment and intervention is always beneficial, and often essential, if the pupil's best interests are to be served.

6

PROBLEMS OF SOME ABNORMAL CONDUCT IN COMPREHENSIVE SCHOOLS AND WHAT CAN BE DONE ABOUT THEM

Mike Pomerantz

I suppose it is tempting, if the only tool you have is a hammer, to treat everything as if it were a nail. (Maslow, 1966, pp. 15–16)

This chapter is about socially unacceptable behaviour in school. We are talking about actions which cause discomfort for teachers and possibly call their competence into question. This may be due to a lack of effective tools to do the job. We are talking about pupils' behaviour which interferes with the curriculum and is, therefore, wasteful of time and resources. It disturbs the progress of the more conforming majority. This behaviour is unlikely to diminish without someone making a new move. This chapter is about a series of moves that are possible.

Let us suppose that the author and reader of this chapter have a joint interest in helping a comprehensive school teacher who shall be called Mr Jones. The task of the author will be to provide a framework for this assistance and to raise a few questions. The reader is asked to reflect upon the issues and then formulate a reasonable programme of activities designed to help Mr Jones.

To make this exercise feel realistic, we will have to come to know Mr Jones as a person. His first name is Bill. He is 32 years old and a native of Derbyshire. Ten years ago, he obtained his qualification and began his career as a science teacher. He is still at the same school where he started, but did take advantage of a two-year break from teaching in order to gain experience doing research for a pharmaceutical company. In this regard he is up-to-date as a scientist and has a greater appreciation for the employers' perspective when training older pupils in chemistry. Bill has always been attracted to science and technology since his own childhood. He did well at school and college; thus he has not seriously failed at anything. He is married and has two young children.

Since Bill is only an imaginary character, the reader is given liberty to paint in other attributes at will. Bill is a fellow staff member; his classroom is just down the corridor. Of late, Bill seems

111

to be having major difficulties with some of the pupils in his classes. At this stage our knowledge of Bill's problem is uncertain; we hear some of the noise through his door, we hear troubling comments from pupils and some concern has been raised in the staffroom when Bill is not present. As of today, Bill has not actually asked anyone for help in a direct way. Possibly he never will. He does, however, like to talk and he seems to need support and sympathy from a few of his colleagues. In this case, we will assume that the reader is one of these colleagues.

Once again, let us suppose that after weeks of passive reflection the reader decides to intervene in order to assist Bill. The previous hesitation may have been motivated by a desire to avoid facing the issue which is so threatening to Bill. His classes have been characterised by outbursts of pupil to pupil aggressiveness and a breakdown in Bill's authority. The reader now begins a conscientious pattern of active listening on the assumption that it would be pointless to offer advice prematurely. Immediately, there is the suspicion that Bill's problem will not be solved by a quick and simple remedy.

A period of time now passes. Much greater rapport is established with Bill. Given these conditions, Bill begins to feel that he can trust the reader and let down his defences. A mutual sense of empathy develops and Bill perceives for the first time that he really does have a problem managing the conduct of some of his adolescent pupils and that other staff have also had problems in this regard.

If the reader does no more than what is cited above, that intervention of active listening without offering advice might not be sufficient. This is a very effective and respectable method of helping people. It is based upon the positive assumption that persons have the potential to solve many of their own problems given appropriate understanding and emotional support. Professional counsellors may refer to this method as a 'client-centred' or 'non-directive' technique. One can obtain training with this method; probably the best introductory book on the subject is by Carl Rogers. It is called *On Becoming a Person*. Without doubt it is an excellent resource for beginners and, furthermore, it is also a comforting base to return to if one finds the other types of interventions disillusioning or unsatisfactory.

What else can be offered if the reader rejects the non-directive method for any of a variety of reasons? Possibly it is too time-consuming or it appears weak or too passive. Possibly the reader just does not like it or fears that it is inappropriate for Bill's immediate needs. Perhaps something more scientific seems indicated; after all Bill is a logical sort of fellow who appreciates a rigorous objective method. He himself has been wrestling with his own analysis of cause and effect relationships in science teaching. This is familiar territory for Bill and the reader might want to focus on an approach that Bill will find respectable and understandable.

This leads us to a brief discussion about the nature of scientific investigations and car maintenance. Suppose we deliberately foul the spark plugs of a motor car rendering it unusable in this condition and we have it towed into a garage. We describe the symptom that the car will not start properly and place the matter in the hands of the engineer. At this point we realise that a variety of options are possible. The engineer makes a few investigations. Some of these are relevant and some are not. The fouled spark plugs may be located immediately or after some delay or not at all. If found and cleaned or replaced, the car engine will start properly. We pay for a reasonable diagnosis of the problem and a solution. In this case, the solution depends upon the correct identification of the cause (i.e. the fouled spark plugs). Any other form of remedy, such as supplying a new battery or changing the oil, would have been costly in two regards. The first would be financial and the second would be the waste of time as the car still would not start properly. We all know from experience that it is possible to benefit from a thorough cause and effect analysis of one's disabled car at a garage. We also know of cases where the analysis was faulty. With defective spark plugs incapacitating an engine, we must find the cause before effective treatment is applied and finding that cause may come as a result of an orderly investigation or as the result of luck.

In the study of classroom conduct problems, it may be helpful to look for causes. In Bill's case, several possible causes can be hypothesised. The first that comes to mind is a genetic cause. It could be suggested that at least three of Bill's most disruptive pupils have inherited a temperamental predisposition toward violence and a lack of internal constraint over outbursts of temper. This may be compounded by the social influence of living in households characterised by violence. Unfortunately, this cause, while plausible, does not lend itself easily to a programme of intervention or treatment. On the contrary, it may actually be a recipe for pessimism and inactivity on Bill's part because he realises that no one can alter genetic endowment in the classroom. Furthermore, we note that these same three pupils are not constituting a major behavioural problem with all of the rest of the teachers. Some staff manage to cope well with these three individuals. Finding a simple cause for Bill's problem is not going to be as easy and simple as locating fouled spark plugs. A teacher is not going to examine chromosomes under a microscope. Even if it were possible to agree that an abnormality had been sighted, as does occur with Down's syndrome (Mongolism), it would not have immediate treatment implications that are analogous to cleaning or replacing spark plugs.

A second cause of disruptive or aggressive classroom behaviour in an individual might be an unresolved internal conflict of long-standing duration. Current behaviour may be caused by something which went wrong during the child's very early development: for example the pupil may have had a genuinely traumatic experience, such as a specific physical assault or a more general feeling of rejection or jealousy regarding affection. The current aggressive behaviour may well be a symbolic substitute for some other internal conflict which needs decoding via time-consuming analysis. This might, for example, involve the child's perception of his or her own inferiority. Using this approach, a therapist may assume an underlying emotional conflict which is not readily apparent in the child's consciousness. This method of coming to understand the cause of abnormal human behaviour has a long tradition within psychology. However, it is a controversial approach on several grounds. Some practitioners argue that it is not sufficiently scientific. A more relevant criticism is that it is very costly in terms of both time and money. While some colourful insights do come from this line of enquiry, we have come some distance from Bill Jones's classroom setting. We have identified a second independent cause which is different from genetic factors.

Some would argue that this underlying cause is very real and valid. Others would advise us to move on to more fruitful techniques which hopefully lead to quicker interventions. Followers of the above thinking believe that the major focus of intervention should be an attempt to get beneath the surface of the problem. Aggressive behaviour may be considered only a symptom of a much deeper personal conflict. Comparisons are often made with an iceberg where only the tip is visible to the observer. To get beneath the surface of the problem takes time, effort, imagination and therapeutic skill. A major obstacle may be the child's resistance, which can be well developed with highly effective defence strategies. For example, the child may flatly deny the existence of a deeper conflict. He or she may want to project blame and responsibility on to someone else, like a parent. Rationalisation is another defence whereby the child attempts to excuse anti-social behaviour on the basis of an apparently logical argument. Minimisation is a defence by which the child suggests that the adult is making a mountain out of a molehill. Denial, projection, rationalisation and minimisation are all predictable forms of resistance which the therapist must approach with great care in order to move beneath the surface of a problem.

The reader may well be wondering how this approach to understanding and changing human behaviour might be of help to Bill Jones in his classroom. An easy response would be to suggest that it can offer nothing to Bill on the grounds that it is too time-consuming, that it lacks scientific respectability and that neither Bill Jones nor the reader are likely to undergo years of self-analysis and training to become a therapist. However, a minority of professionals do become therapists working intimately with a small number of clients over long periods of time. Many hundreds of books have been published in this field and the method has had a profound effect in the Arts. Both serious literature and the theatre have been influenced by these traditions and the overall effect has been to boost our insights into understanding human behaviour. In this regard, we could also turn to Shakespeare as someone else who seems to be able to help us understand behaviour and the more we understand about behaviour the more powerful we may feel in doing something about the actions of another, especially if those actions are disturbing to us. Any activity which will help either the reader or Bill to comprehend unusual adolescent behaviour is worthy of consideration. We are clearly in a situation where we can leave no stone unturned. What works for one individual may not do so for another. Staff need options. People who actually feel they have more than one option probably behave more effectively than those who feel limited to one course of action.

Thus far, we have explored two possible causes for abnormal behaviour observed in three pupils who are in Bill Jones's class. The first was genetic and the second was an inner emotional conflict of longstanding duration. Both of these causes are internal to the child and do not seem to involve Bill directly. For the time being, we will continue to look for other causes which seem to reside within the pupils and postpone questions about other sources of causation outside the pupils until later. These will involve both Bill Jones's behaviour and attitudes as well as the interaction between teacher and pupil.

One dominant influence affecting the pupils' behaviour may well be their respective families. Some teenagers tend to model the behaviour of adults within the home. Others reject these models and possibly strive to present a public image which is quite opposite to that seen in the parents. In single-parent families, the absence of the missing parent can have a profound influence on the child. Could we persuade Bill to become more involved with these three different families? Initially, this might be done simply to provide more diagnostic information upon which to base his scientific hypotheses about causation of abnormal behaviour in his classroom. He might find parents who seem like carbon copies of their teenagers. In this case, one, or both, parents present with attitudes and values which support the child's antisocial behaviour. Some parents are remarkably anti-school and do not hide this feeling. Possibly their child has internalised this message and adopted a similar value system. In other cases the parents may be very conforming and supportive of the school and the adolescent is blatently rejecting their influence. In some cases parents are already well informed about the conduct of their child in the school setting, but this is not always true. Occasionally there is a profound breakdown in home to school communication and this can be due to a variety of reasons. The adolescent may actively contribute to this by 'losing' written messages sent home. Some parents find large comprehensive schools threatening and would not initiate contact themselves. Sometimes an unknown crisis at home relegates school-based problems to an inferior status which is misinterpreted by school staff as parental indifference or negligence.

Bill's investigations via home visits may prove to be of greater value than merely helping him to find causes for disordered conduct. He may well find potentially powerful allies in mounting a successful programme for intervention. We will return to this issue later in describing behavioural modification programmes. Of course, he could formulate the opinion that the parents would not choose to co-operate with him, but Bill would certainly be on safer ground knowing that he had at least explored this possibility. The reader would have helped Bill simply by advising him to get more involved with the parents of a few of his pupils, but resistance to this suggestion may surface. Will the timetable allow for this activity? Will it involve evening visits when both parents are at home? Would the school administration be supportive? Would the form tutor or year head feel threatened by this? And what about Bill's feelings? He may not have done this sort of work before. A helpful introduction might be for Bill to accompany another member of staff who does this home visiting regularly and finds the practice worthwhile. School staff who employ this approach are probably the best advocates and may be able to assist if resistance of any type is encountered.

Another child-centred cause for the disordered conduct may be that he or she has a handicap of being restricted in the range of their responses to classroom stress. School life is characterised by some degree of stress from a variety of sources. For example, academic expectations regarding work or examinations are potentially stressful. So are the demands of the peer group and the pressure to conform. Not all teenagers respond favourably and in this regard Bill's three pupils are thought to be at risk. If it were possible to videotape Bill's lessons unobtrusively, we might look for patterns to emerge in the way his three antagonists respond to varying types and degrees of stress. Alternatively, we could substitute a member of staff for the video camera as this could be easier to arrange. The observer, ideally, would be someone with a keen interest in drama and theatre. We are seeking someone who is quite familiar with acting, role-playing and observation. Let us imagine that after a few periods the observer noted evidence that one of the antagonists (who will be called Tommy) does show definite signs of having a limited repertoire of responses to certain provocations in the classroom. For example, Tommy got involved in a personal property dispute which led to a fight because he took someone else's property without permission. He could have asked for the pen, which he desperately needed, but he did not do so. Another child accidentally bumped into Tommy who reacted immediately with flying fists. Tommy could have asked for an apology or responded in a more considerate manner, but he did not do so. In Tommy's conflict with yet another pupil, he could have expressed his feelings, which could have been anger, resentment, jealousy, rejection or admiration. He could have done this either with or without words, but he did not do so. His non-verbal gestures, facial expressions and body language did nothing to facilitate real communication with either the other child or with his teacher, Bill Jones, who had to intervene and separate the boys.

Bill and his classroom observer now withdraw to consider the new evidence. Bill is impressed that we are back to considering the very real problems he faces in his science lessons. He may derive some comfort in concluding that he is not personally responsible for all of the disciplinary problems which are surfacing. It may be supportive to feel that someone else has actually seen some of the behaviour in question. If the cause of the abnormal behaviour is a restriction in certain pupils' behavioural repertoire of responses, then what can be done about it? One answer might be to try to teach Tommy some of the alternatives which are socially more acceptable. This could be done via individual counselling sessions, but it would be preferable to do it in a group setting as a drama exercise. Tommy could be an active participant or he could sit on the side and learn vicariously. Either may work, but the former is preferable. The lesson could be taught by Bill or by the drama specialist or by both working together. The drama specialist would hopefully be able to provide a more suitable environment than Bill's science room. This environment does not refer only to props, a stage, lighting, sound effects, etc. It also refers to social conditions, necessary to engage adolescents in a creative exercise. One essential requirement is safety. If the circumstances appear threatening, defences will arise rendering the lesson ineffective. The director of this exercise would have to engage the pupils by clarifying the activities and objectives to the satisfaction of the participants. This is no easy task, but if it is accomplished then the director is placed in a potentially powerful position to influence the student participants.

The following is an example of one type of intervention that could be employed. The director is the drama specialist and Bill has elected to participate with a group of pupils which includes Tommy. Bill could have passed the entire matter over to the drama specialist or he could have opted to sit in the background and passively watch. He was persuaded that he would gain more from the exercise by direct involvement and it might improve his relations with his pupils. The director set the scene by describing an hypothetical incident in which one pupil (John) accidentally knocks over a second pupil (Ken) during a lesson. Ken, the victim of this 'assault' immediately retaliates with his fists. Two students volunteered to mount the stage and re-enact the confrontation through role-playing. The acting looked realistic, the audience were engaged in a meaningful session. The director asked for contributions to be made to an emerging list of alternatives that could have been acted out instead of the physical retaliation. With a bit of prompting, the following list was constructed on the blackboard:

1. Ken counts to 10 or preferably to 100 before responding.
2. Ken utters the statement, 'You knocked me down!' to John.
3. Ken requests an apology from John.
4. Ken demands an apology from John.
5. Ken exaggerates injury in a theatrical way to attract attention.
6. Ken cries.
7. Ken appeals for help from his peers.
8. Ken appeals for help from an authority figure.
9. Ken ignores the incident and walks or runs away.
10. Ken writes a letter to John.
11. Ken writes a letter of complaint and posts it on the school noticeboard.
12. Ken initiates a programme of exercises to build his muscles and enhance his body image.

Both the director and Bill could have made further contributions to this list but chose not to do so in this instance. Obviously a list of possible alternatives is almost endless, but to be practical it is best for the pupil participants to create their own list.

Next the director asked for volunteers to act out each of the alternatives without much supervision. Pupils were encouraged to improvise and experiment at will. After each scene the audience was encouraged to comment favourably or otherwise as to the usefulness of each approach. Some actions predictably produced humour, but others were received seriously. Bill volunteered to play both John and Ken at times. This gave the audience a chance to compare the same behaviour when played by an adult or an adolescent. Tommy was one of Bill's original three classroom antagonists and he chose to take a relatively passive posture. He may have felt slightly threatened but steps were taken to suggest that many people have the potential to retaliate violently and that the exercise was not done to get at him. Only time will tell just how effective this intervention was. Hopefully, everyone learns something and this was done experientially through action rather than through a lecture or reading a book. Tommy may now have a greater understanding of what it feels like to be the victim of his aggressiveness. Bill may feel that he has examined the subject of aggressiveness more thoroughly.

The previous paragraphs were based upon the assumption that one cause of abnormal behaviour is a restriction in the number of options available for some pupils in the face of stress. Bill may also have felt that his options had been restricted in the past. The treatment is to provide a safe and suitable context in which to practice other options recommended by peers. Some would argue that it would be better to focus on attitudes and beliefs that underlie abnormal behaviour, rather than to focus on the behaviour itself. Perhaps the cause of the unwanted behaviour is a faulty way of thinking. Let us go back to Bill's classroom and concentrate on another of the three antagonists and this one we will call Mary. Once again, we need to do some careful observation in order to provide diagnostic information to support the view that Mary's thinking is wrong. It may be irrational or maladaptive. In the latter case, her thought processes are not helping her to cope with the stress and demands of life at school. Bill is the one member of staff with the greatest disciplinary problem involving Mary. Therefore, he should have the motivation to do the observation work himself rather than to ask for outside help. He will have to establish a pastoral relationship with Mary in order to gain her confidence and overcome resistance. If he is unable to do this, Bill may have to recruit additional help or refer Mary on to another professional. The latter may be time-consuming and would certainly not guarantee a successful outcome.

Let us assume that Bill is able to get to know Mary, who co-operates and likes to talk. Other staff tend to ignore Mary and she is not particularly attractive to her peers. During the course of a few pastoral counselling sessions Mary reveals some of the following types of unhelpful beliefs:

1. 'I have to assert myself physically in the face of stress.'
2. 'I must get even with him.'
3. 'I won't get caught.'
4. 'If I did get caught, it wouldn't really matter.'
5. 'She deserves to be bullied. She's weak.'
6. 'Bullying doesn't really matter. Everyone does it.'

7. 'I'm not personally responsible for my actions.'

Bill may now come to the conclusion that these beliefs are the cause of his problems with Mary's conduct. He could choose to hold up a mirror symbolically in order for Mary to see just how non-productive her beliefs actually are and what they are costing her. Using his skills as a teacher, he could try to persuade Mary to examine her thoughts and beliefs critically. If Mary states that she has to assert herself physically or that she has to get even with someone, this implies a degree of compulsion. It suggests some external attribution beyond her control. Mary might be receptive to the suggestion that she claim greater powers for herself as a sign of maturity. Mastery over some previous form of compulsive behaviour might bring other rewards. Bill could hint at these. If Mary states that she won't get caught, this is a denial mechanism which is counter-productive because she has been caught repeatedly by Bill Jones in class. Denial mechanisms which fail to convince others may damage Mary's self-image or confirm an already bad image of herself. In either case, Mary loses. Does she want to continue as a loser? If Mary states that it doesn't matter if she gets caught, what does this really mean to her? Is it another superficial denial of her feelings? Does the message actually work when Mary utters it? Does it effectively bring relief? Do her listeners respond favourably or not?

If Mary tries to justify her actions by claiming that the recipients are weak and therefore deserving of bullying, then how does she feel? Does this attitude help Mary? Do people believe her? Does she really believe it herself? If Mary says that her behaviour is acceptable because everyone is doing it, does this statement conform with reality? Could Mary get other adolescents to confirm her position? This might make for a good classroom debate. Finally, Mary might try the approach of denying responsibility for her actions. In counselling with her, Bill could expose the fallacy in this line of thinking. How would Mary feel if that excuse were used when she herself was the innocent victim of aggression?

Direct, educationally-based counselling can indeed change attitudes and beliefs, particularly if attention is focused to the very specific environment of the classroom. It does, however, require time and motivation. If either is insufficient, the outcome is likely to be limited. Because of this, we must continue to search for other options in order to help Bill Jones. We are still looking for possible causes of abnormal school behaviour. Thus far, we have examined genetic influence, deep-rooted emotional conflicts, the family, restriction in the range of roles to play and faulty thinking. Let us now turn to a behavioural analysis of the classroom environment and try to discover other causes. Behaviourists suggest that it is fruitful to look for causation in one of two places, either before the antisocial behaviour or after it. An event or a condition which precedes a given behaviour is called a stimulus and sometimes this stimulus actually controls the behaviour in question. The sight of a hostile object rapidly approaching one's face might produce an automatic evasive response of ducking. The object's approach is the stimulus and the ducking is the response. Using this type of thinking, the stimulus may be called the cause of the response. Others might argue that the cause of the response is actually an anticipation of the consequences of ducking or not ducking. In one's past, failure to take evasive action has been painful while quick evasive moves have brought relief knowing that one has escaped pain.

There are a wide variety of stimuli in Bill's science room which might account for the aggressive behaviour in Carl, who is the third of Bill's difficult pupils or antagonists. For example, Carl finds there is an optimum range of temperature which facilitates his impulse control and span of concentration during lessons. If the temperature rises substantially above or falls remarkably below this range, then we may see a change in Carl's behaviour. If Carl's behaviour is somehow under the partial control of the stimulus of temperature, then the person who controls the classroom temperature in effect gains a measure of control over Carl. The following is an unfinished list of stimuli which may contribute to aggressive or non-conforming behaviour in the classroom:

1. Atmospheric pressure.
2. Noise.
3. Crowding.
4. Poor ventilation.
5. Apparatus failure during a demonstration.
6. Sleep deprivation or fatigue.
7. Hunger.
8. Physical discomfort due to illness, fever, headache, etc.
9. Materials missing (no pen, etc).
10. Provocation by peers.

The above stimuli are cited first because they could be identified relatively easily by a group of observers who would probably all agree with each other's observations. However, other stimuli may be present which are difficult to assess. Examples would include, but would not be limited to, the following unfinished list:

1. Boredom and lack of stimulation.
2. Distraction.
3. Inappropriate curriculum or method of teaching.
4. Fear of failure.
5. Teacher's lack of preparation.
6. Short-span of concentration.
7. Inappropriate teacher's attitude.
8. Frustration.
9. Confusion.
10. Preoccupation with something unrelated to the task.

If Bill were to attempt a behavioural analysis of his own classroom, looking for possible stimuli which precede abnormal behaviour in Carl, he would definitely benefit from some assistance. This could come from the reader or from some other member of the staff who perhaps is more familiar with behavioural approaches. This familiarity may have come from attendance at workshops on this topic or from independent reading. Bill would benefit from the assistance of a supportive but objective observer who might be able to find the stimuli which seem to precipitate the aggressiveness. If this can be done, the next step would be somehow to alter that stimulus, possibly reducing it or possibly obliterating it. Obviously not all stimuli are within Bill's control, but he may find it encouraging to experiment with these options. Even if he fails with this type of environmental engineering, he may gain further insights, particularly with reference to cause and effect relationship.

Behaviourists would further advise us to make a thorough analysis via observation of the consequences of Carl's antisocial behaviour. They might assume that Carl exhibits poor impulse control because it meets his needs. Bill Jones's classroom observer could help by monitoring several incidents and searching for signs that Carl's behaviour is somehow being rewarded. The record might reveal that while Bill Jones chose to either ignore or punish Carl's outbursts, several of Carl's peers provided social reinforcement in the form of laughter. It would not be too speculative to suggest that rewards outweighed whatever Bill was doing. Before planning an intervention, Bill needs to know as precisely as possible what is rewarding Carl's behaviour. In some cases, Carl himself might provide the answer, but this will not always happen. If Carl and Bill can work together in developing a self-control programme for Carl, then the chances of success are far greater. Specifically, they could try to remove or devalue the rewards for loss of self-control over impulses whilst simultaneously boosting rewards for greater self-control. Sometimes a reward menu is helpful, but it is always preferable for Carl to nominate what he will work to obtain or to avoid. An oral or written contract between Carl and Bill Jones can be established. Finally, the parents may be able to provide more powerful incentives than Bill has at his disposal. If they are invited to participate in this programme, again the chances of some success are increased.

Let us return to examining cause and effect relationships. We have now moved away from confining the causes completely to the child. Clearly some abnormal behaviour may be caused by Bill's actions as the stimulus. Alternatively, Bill may actually be rewarding the behaviour in Carl which he would like to see disappear. Initially, he may have been reluctant to consider just how influential his own behaviours are in precipitating or reinforcing incidents. He may have felt helpless and caught in the counter-productive bind of falsely attributing causation exclusively to his pupils. Through some of the above exercises he may have shifted his position a little.

The author would like to stress the value of the role which the reader can play. The latter, as a colleague, may have far greater potential in helping Bill at an early stage. The mechanism is peer support. The competitive nature of schools and belief in survival of the fittest both work to inhibit a fellow teacher like Bill from seeking help which he needs. The most practical offer of help is to be available to listen carefully and provide a few options. This can be done on a one-to-one basis or in a small group. Bill might respond by changing the way he teaches. He might be given a bit of in-service training time to sit and observe in colleagues' classrooms to see how they handle difficult pupils. He might elect to spend his time working on a staff committee to revise the curriculum on the grounds that this alone may be the greatest single cause of problem classroom behaviour. Bill might decide to start ignoring or tolerating some abnormal behaviour as practical strategy. Perhaps he will become more accepting of his own weaknesses and those in his pupils. Possibly he will learn to resolve conflicts without someone having to be the winner and someone else having to be the loser. Finally, he may have to accept that in some cases the search for a cause is unproductive and he will have to work on the symptoms with whatever tools are available.

7 SEX, ADOLESCENTS AND SCHOOLS

Kathleen Cox

Each school must by law inform parents of the manner and context for their sex education. (Education Act, 1980)

Introduction

Schools are no longer only for children; half the pupils now in secondary schools are sexually mature. One of the main tasks of the secondary school is to facilitate the development of its pupils through their entire adolescence from childhood to adulthood. However, although sexual development is an important part of adolescence it is often not seen as an integral part of schooling. It may be on the school's curriculum as 'sex education', varying from a series of information giving sessions and exhortations, of the type summarised in Schofield's survey (1965): 'The vicar told us not to do it, the biology teacher how not to do it and the headteacher where not to do it', to a fully coherent programme of education for personal relationships including sexual aspects as an integral part. Or it may be avoided and ignored.

Adolescents have various needs with respect to sexual development. All have a need to receive help in understanding their own changes, of body and behaviour, and how to cope with these not only at the time but also how to integrate them into a mature personality in the future. A minority have special needs in this area. For example, some are unsure of their own sexual identity, some have physical problems impairing sexual development with which they must come to terms. Others encounter sexual problems from their experiences, e.g. girls who become pregnant while still at school, and youngsters who are sexually assaulted. In most cases there are not special *educational* needs, but are certainly special *personal* needs.

Sometimes the sexual behaviour of the pupils impinges on the school as a problem; the pupils who are petting in the school field, the youngster who is considered homosexual. Teachers worry on behalf of their pupils because of their presumed problems,

126

although in some cases the emotional energy expended by adults bears no relation to importance of the problems as perceived by the young person. Teachers also worry because they feel uncomfortable with the topic of sex and about the reputation a school may acquire if the pupils are perceived as indulging in sexual behaviour.

Sexual learning is gained in a variety of ways: personal experience, informal learning and formal teaching. We learn directly the gender roles expected of men and women in daily life at home with family and friends and indirectly from books and television. In our culture jokes and graffiti contain many sexual references. Then there are our own physical and social experiences and sensations through which we learn sexual responses. Perhaps the least significant contribution comes from formal teaching and we would delude ourselves if we thought that sexual behaviour and attitudes were learnt primarily in the classroom. Nevertheless there is a task for the school and that is to help children to make sense of their observations and experiences to ensure there are no significant gaps in their knowledge so that the learning acquired in all ways is eventually integrated into a coherent, consistent, mature perspective.

This chapter will consider the problem in its broader perspective, academic and vulgar, before considering an approach to helping all adolescents come to terms with their own sexual development. It will also consider the way problems are conceptualised, in addition to the particular needs of those youngsters who have special sex-related problems.

No single, simple solution is being offered but a background against which to consider issues so that schools may produce responses which suit their own particular situations.

The Problem

General Uncertainty

Much of the problem is quite simply because we think it is. Sexual relations are a private matter and we don't actually know much about other people's behaviour. Our limited experience makes for many areas of ignorance. Furthermore, many of our attitudes are chameleon-like in that they vary with the audience; at one end of the spectrum sex is perceived as beautiful, at the other it is described as rude. Unstable attitudes add to feelings of uncertainty. The society in which we live is changing rapidly and does not have a coherent, consistent view with regard to sexuality. It gives conflict-ing overt and covert messages, and adolescents are confused by what they see and hear.

Alison Gingell, writing in the *Times Educational Supplement* (24 April 1981) about school, home and the media, wrote:

> adult confusion and insecurity had led to teenagers being denied the information and support they need in many areas; perhaps nowhere is this more apparent than in the area of sexuality and birth control.

At one school some students knew contraception was on the syllabus in 'O' level Biology but that the teacher was forbidden to bring contraceptives to school to show them. On the TV they see sexual innuendos in 'sit-coms' and blatant use of sex in advertising chocolates, soap powders and sports cars, but the advertising of contraceptives is explicitly forbidden (Hayman, 1977). At home, if the middle-aged father tells his daughter to beware of men because they are lecherous and evil, and ogles the nude on page 3, what is she to think? Her father is a man, and therefore evil: or that he is the exception?

The Quakers suggested in 1963 that: 'the insincerity of the sexual moral code may well be a cause of the wide spread contempt of the younger generation for society's rules and prohibitions'. Martin Cole (1983) considers the confusion stems from playing it safe. Adults who no longer espouse Christian values themselves think they had better play it safe since they have not replaced these values by anything else and preach what they do not practise — just in case.

Problems of Language

One problem is linguistic. Spoken everyday English reflects our attitudes, but does not contain a vocabulary available for ordinary unemotive conversation on sexual matters. An agreed vocabulary is an essential to communication but our choices are extremely limited. For example, for the sex act itself the short simple Anglo-Saxon word 'fuck' is regarded as vulgar, obscene and not socially acceptable, whereas Latin-derived 'copulate' is scientific but pedantic and not in everyday speech. Similarly for parts of the anatomy our language lacks words which are simple and permitted in everyday speech. The Goldmans (1982) refer to over 100 words used by small children for the penis. Teachers of reception classes give examples of the numerous words used when young children wish to use the lavatory, to the extent that the euphemisms can be so misunderstood as to lead to puddles on the floor. This early experience of the embarrassment associated with the part of the anatomy connected with sex can last a lifetime.

Informal Education

By the time children enter secondary school at the age of 11 or 12 they have received a considerable amount of sex education. It may not have been on the curriculum of the school or given purposefully by their parents, but they will have acquired knowledge and attitudes in this area. They will have learned about gender roles by observing men and women doing certain jobs at home and at school (dinner ladies but no dinner men), and will have learned to which sex they belong and some of the behaviours expected by our culture of each sex. They will have learned which public toilet to use and that genitals are clothed in our society; that you don't talk about certain things in certain company and many other taboos. They have probably learned to laugh at a joke which is described as dirty even though they may not know why they are laughing and they will have seen obscene graffiti on walls. There is therefore no such thing as no sex education but there is undesirable and bad sex education coupled with ignorance and lack of understanding even in our so-called permissive society.

Parental Attitude

In most adult behaviours offspring model themselves on their parents but sexual behaviour is a notable exception among human beings. The parental bedroom door is firmly closed to children from an early age, demonstrating the privacy of the act. This demonstration, however, provides few positive guidelines to the young — presenting yet another problematic aspect of sexual behaviour to them.

Silence is the rule between generations. The example set by most parents is deliberately non-sexual; demonstrations of affection between mature adults are stricly limited and the only implicit references to parental sexuality the few occasions which result in pregnancy. When adolescent sexual prowess is developing most strongly the important adults in his/her life (parents and many teachers) are reaching middle age. The combination of the decline

of the one and the growth of the other with the secret worries of
each is an additional difficulty in bridging the gap between the
generations.

In this confused society there is a point of view which says that
sex education is the job of the parent and not the school. This
opinion has been voiced by both parents and teachers, but it is not a
question of 'either-or' and such a question presupposes a quick
solution, whereas sexual behaviours and attitudes evolve throughout the whole of life.

Most parents are only too pleased to hear that the school has a
sex education programme, being well aware of the difficulties and
embarrassment they experience themselves. One parent kept her
secondary school daughter at home to watch the Merry-Go-Round
programme for primary school children on TV. She sent a note to
the school giving the reason for absence and added the suggestion
that their school should be doing something. Another parent, a
mother of seven, told me that she never talked about 'that' with her
daughter, but with a resigned sigh said that the school did, adding
'they made it sound nice there'. Under these circumstances the
school was the place where her daughter was likely to acquire
positive attitudes and accurate facts. Many, however, find the
school's contribution is complementary to their own for school and
teachers have knowledge that many parents do not themselves
possess. It is perfectly possible for a couple to produce a child when
they have only hazy notions of male and female anatomy and
physiology.

What and When

One of the main anxieties is about what to tell children and when,
with a worry that information is given 'too soon', especially if this
is on a formal curriculum for an immature child. But these worries
belong to the adults rather than the children, who do what they do
with all lessons they find boring or irrelevant — ignore it and make
little sense of it. Clearly, however, any teaching must pay attention
to the phases of development of the child by attending to the
questions asked by the children. If answers are confined to those
questions many of the adult worries take care of themselves.
Developmental phases of children with regard to sexual questioning
have been summarised by Bernstein (1976) using the Piagetian
concepts. She describes them as (1) Geographers — Where did I
come from? (2) Manufacturers — How am I made? (3) Agricul-

turists — What do you need? (4) Reporters — What does each do? (5) Miniaturists — Why does the pre-formed baby grow in utero? (6) Realists — How does genetic material unite and change? in their successive attempts to make sense of what they hear.

A clear example of following the lead given by the child can be seen in the junior school. With regard to where do babies come from, young and pre-school children are intrigued to discover how they grew inside their mother. Many who have younger siblings can see the bump, feel the movements and are happy to share this with their mothers. This knowledge suffices for a considerable time, probably co-existing with the hazy notion that babies have their own fathers. Much later comes the question 'how does it get out?' A truthful answer may get a surprised response from a young child who associates that area of the anatomy with defecation and urination, but his world is full of wonder and surprise and this is just one more. Such an answer also paves the way for the next question which probably comes months later: 'How did the baby get there?' The route out is obviously the way in and the involvement of the father made much clearer. Adults worry about these questions in reverse order, creating problems for themselves which need not exist if they were in the habit of encouraging children to ask questions by confining their responses to the questions asked.

The Issues

Physical Development

'Am I normal?' This is the commonest problem of the young person. Many children still enter adolescence unprepared for the physical changes they will experience and which they find so worrying despite increased efforts by the schools to give sex education in some form to more children. The agony columnist, Clare Rayner, writes as a result of queries from her postbag: 'I wish someone would spare time to give simple facts to adolescents who are worried sick about perfectly natural developments'. At a conference on human sexuality at St Thomas's Hospital, London, in 1976 she wondered if every schoolboy was born with a tape measure in his pocket as she received so many letters from boys worried that their penises were not long enough.

For boys many of the concerns focus on the genital area. This is less problematic as the genitals are external to the body and there is not the same ignorance as to the structure and appearance of the penis as is experienced by many girls towards their own vagina. Boys' genitals are handled several times a day during urination and so do not have the unfamiliarity and 'must not touch or look' feeling that many girls have towards their genital area. In other ways, of course, it is a disadvantage in that the ease of inspection means that a boy is aware of the size of his penis, whether or not he is circumcised and whether or not he has two descended testicles. In addition to the normal range of anatomy, boys also need to understand their physiology. From birth they will have been experiencing erections but the adolescent boy's concern is linked to control — will he have an erection when he wants to, can he avoid having one when he doesn't want to? As his body matures he may have erections at embarrassing times and may also experience what are popularly known as 'wet dreams', when semen is released during sleep. Nocturnal emissions are a natural way of getting the body working in its adult form but can be embarrassing for a boy who wakes up and feels he has wet the bed if he doesn't know to expect it. Another phenomenon of male adolescence is the temporary development of breasts in boys. This is not common but where it does occur the embarrassment is lessened if the boy knows in advance that this is merely excessive hormone secretion at a time when the body is changing its functions from that of a child to an adult. A deepening voice may be another source of embarrassment if it is difficult to control emitting an occasional squeak.

Growth of body hair at puberty is usually included in talks for boys and girls but often not the enormous range of distribution from one person to another. Pubic hair, for example, can extend in a line up the lower abdomen in both boys and girls and well down the thighs, as well as the inverted triangle said to be the typical female distribution. While the boys are worrying that they are only half men because they have no hair on their chests, some girls are worrying that they are changing sex because of the hair they do have on their chests around their nipples. Recent trends towards pictures of nude and semi-nude females may have altered our attitudes away from excessive prudery but have set new norms, particularly of breast development, causing girls to regard themselves as deformed if they are not the same even shape as the model girls chosen for their small, big-nippled, upturned breasts. Clare Rayner asserts that bodies vary as much as faces and this piece of knowledge is one of the most vital lessons any sex educator can give.'

Menstruation

Some girls will start menstruating without any preparation with the attendant fears of bleeding to death, being ill or being punished for playing with themselves. Girls in this situation often have the additional problem of not having anyone to turn to for help because of the taboos placed by families on that part of the body. Preparation of this sort can be done by school or home but it is a personal job. A respondent amongst 6,000 replying to a survey conducted by the magazine *19* in 1982 said 'I feel a bit cheated by my mum, she told me nothing about sex, not even periods,' (Newman, 1982). This is not quite so simple as it sounds. A marriage guidance counsellor of my acquaintance felt she had prepared her daughter for the start of her monthly periods with both theory and practical advice over a considerable amount of time but was somewhat confused when reminding her of the possibility of this event by her daughter's question as to 'how would she know when it happened?'

Boys need to know about menstruation if only because they have an interest in the subject which if not assuaged leads to a prurient curiosity. Offensive graffiti in schools about Tampax is often a boy's aggressively gauche attempt to gain information he is aware he does not have but feels he ought to. Excluding boys from talks to girls is one way to promote this, although girls need specific help in learning to cope.

Both boys and girls need some knowledge of hormonal changes and their effects on behaviour, especially in women. Pre-menstrual tension (PMT) has featured in several well-publicised court cases. Dr Katarina Dalton (1979) has demonstrated some effects the menstrual cycle has on some girls and achievement in schools. Such knowledge can help girls to be aware of the unpredictability of mood changes at certain times and the advisability of controlling this with medication if it is severe and beyond personal control. Dorothy Dallas (1972) reports girls have been personally relieved that there is a biological basis for some of their moods and boys also relieved to understand their girlfriends' behaviours better. Behaviour related to hormone secretion also raises issues of control and is an example of the subject about which the teaching is information-giving initially but leads to open discussion and awareness of ethical issues. For example, can women be given responsible jobs if they are subject to such mood changes, should they expect exceptions to be made by others or should they take action themselves?

This awareness of PMT can also help relationships with teachers. One girl I knew complained bitterly that her German teacher was unpredictable and inconsistent, varying from helpful to quick tempered and sarcastic: 'You just got used to her being nice when she would be nasty again'. After discussing the probability of PMT the girl recorded the incidence of the contretemps and decided that was the teacher's problem. Whether it was or not is less important than that the girl was more tolerant and this was an advantage to both.

Masturbation

One of the great unmentionables is masturbation. Masturbation is for pleasure and it is sometimes called onanism. The old taboo is confused with Onan in Genesis 38, verse 9, in the Old Testament. Onan 'spilled his seed on the ground', but in fact he was practising coitus interruptus (withdrawal) with a woman he had been duty bound to marry and did not wish to impregnate. This was declared a sin because the ancient Hebrews wanted to increase the population and did not want birth control.

The *Oxford English Dictionary* definition of masturbation, 'to practice self-abuse', carries very strong moral overtones of badness. SPOD (Sexual Problems of the Disabled) leaflet No. 7 advises parents of the mentally handicapped that they 'must realise that masturbation is not wrong or wicked. Indeed it is part of growing up for almost every child and it can give relief from tension and stress'. Pamphlet No. 6 suggests 'It is usually possible to teach the mentally handicapped youngster that it should be done in private rather than where it will bother other people.' This is the advice for the primary caretakers of the mentally handicapped who wish to face up to issues with sympathy and understanding. It contrasts sharply with advice by White and Kidd (1976), who pronounce 'masturbation can be used in much the same way as casual sex, with some drug-like effect; but it conditions to associate sex only with self-gratification rather than with pleasing someone else.'

However, masturbation is common. Ninety-eight per cent of adult men are said to admit to masturbation at sometime — and the other 2 per cent to be liars. Fifty-five per cent of the 6,000 female respondents in the *19* survey said they masturbated.

In clinics for sexually dysfunctioning adults self-masturbation is a skill encouraged before progressing to mutual and sexual intercourse (Masters and Johnson, 1970). It is regarded as preparatory learning for successful sexual relationships in which self-awareness and communication are considered important and problems of embarrassment about touching or looking at oneself deliberately dispelled.

The function of the school is to inform in order to allay any lingering fears, not only of guilt but also of madness and blindness, still associated by some people with masturbation.

Homosexuality

Homosexuality is another one of the topics the children in the National Children's Bureau Survey (Fogelman, 1976) wanted to learn about in school. The word means a sexual association between members of the same sex and in females is known as Lesbianism. Lesbianism has never been against the law in England and Wales because Queen Victoria could not image homosexuality applying to women. Homosexual acts between consulting adult males (over the age of 21) have been legal since 1967.

Contemporary social psychology regards homosexual preference as a developmental phase which precedes and prepares for the heterosexual interest. This phase begins in late childhood as adolescence approaches and takes the form of preferring to be with members of one's own sex exclusively. This is particularly strong in boys who regard girls and girlish activities as 'cissy'. In this way sex and gender identity is learned from members of the same sex before beginning to relate socially, physically and eventually exclusively with one member of the opposite sex. It has been identified as a normal stage of development, although recent research by the Goldmans (1982) shows that in Scandinavia best friends at this age can belong to either sex.

From the developmental point of view homosexual behaviour in adult life is a phase of development from which individuals fail to progress. Practising homosexuals would reject this, claiming that their behaviour is as adult and mature as a heterosexual's and the Campaign for Homosexual Equality demands an equal place in society, including the option to take their same-sex partner to official functions.

The Catholic Church condemns homosexual relations unequivocally seeing as it does the sole purpose of sexual relations as procreation. The Quakers, however, were sufficiently troubled by their own inability to provide comfort and guidance for one of their members with this inclination to meet for several years in the late

1950s before producing a pamphlet *A Quaker View of Sex* (Heron, 1963).

Ian Kennedy began his Reith lectures in 1980 by stating 'in 1964 the American Psychiatric Association *voted* on whether or not homosexuality was a disease'. The vote went against, so since 1964 homosexuality has not been a disease in America, although it is so regarded by many other countries. Although now legal in Great Britain the topic is an easy joke in TV sit-coms and practising homosexuals are still possible blackmail victims, although behaving within the law.

There are some situations which promote homosexual behaviour — e.g. single-sex communities of war, prison and boarding schools — but most people revert to heterosexual behaviour when members of the opposite sex are available.

The ancient Greeks idealised this relationship as a higher form than a heterosexual one but our culture worries about homosexuality. In schools boys tease others by calling them 'puffs'. It is a powerful weapon to hurt someone, seldom 'true' but effective because it can be a secret fear of the boy himself in a homosexual phase of development. It usually indicates a more general lack of respect from one pupil to another perhaps from someone with similar fears. Some boys worry they might be 'queer' or 'gay' and seek to compensate for this by extreme 'macho' behaviour, boasting of sexual exploits, violence, vandalism, drinking, and even rape, in an attempt to convince themselves and others that they conform to what they see as masculine norms. Models of gentle masculinity can help to dispel these stereotypes. Furthermore, by raising the issues openly a student may be stopped from prematurely joining an homosexual organisation and prevented from making a commitment for what is a passing phase.

However, Dorothy Dallas warns 'teaching about homosexuality in schools is one of the surest ways of teachers to lose their jobs'. Teachers have lost their jobs when they are known to have homosexual preferences. This reflects a confusion by authority of different deviations in this instance with paedophilia (a preference for children). It is no more logical to dismiss a teacher in a mixed school who prefers sexual partners of the same sex than one who prefers the opposite. Homosexuality is a fact of life and school is one of the places where the facts are given.

Nudity

'None of us', says Paul Abelman in his *Anatomy of Nakedness*, 'can take the naked body for granted; we either idealise it or dismiss it as obscene'. We accept parts of our bodies and reject others and worry particularly about the bits most frequently covered. Quite young children in our society are taught to cover themselves modestly, i.e. cover their genital area, and by the time they start school 5-year-olds are well aware of these parts and have developed quite deep attitudes of shame towards their own bodies. The unwillingness to take showers after games in school is an extension of this modesty which cannot be shed as easily as the clothes. Young adolescents find nakedness embarrassing and are not attracted to nude public bathing, which is becoming more popular. The attitudes we have to our bodies are important. Nudity has certain values attached to it. The times to be naked progress along a scale from always when alone in the bath, often or sometimes in the bedroom, occasionally on the beach, but never in church.

Nakedness of the wrong parts in the wrong places occurs regularly. In the early 1970s there was a phase of 'mooning' when young men exposed their rears in public. The climate of the times was for the young to shock and this was one way of doing it. It seems as if the desire to shock is the prime motivation with men and boys who expose their penises to girls in public; the look of shock and horror on the face of the female is what the exposer seeks. For a woman to have the presence of mind to reach for a magnifying glass would be to reverse this power struggle.

Clothing

Being clothed is often infinitely more provocative then being naked. The fig leaf sported by Adam and Eve accentuates, not hides, their sexuality. Garments emphasising parts of the body, hinting at what is not seen, are more tantalising than the original birthday suit. The current fashion of tight clothes emphasises attributes of both males and females. Experiments in dress by girls in school can mean that their outfits are flamboyantly seductive. If a fashion calls for a slit skirt or blouse not completely buttoned then the length of the split and the number of buttons left undone may go beyond what is acceptable. However, this may merely be experimenting and the full impact of the style of dress not known to a girl who in aping her heroine presents an appearance unintentionally enticing.

On the other hand for both males and females learning to appear attractive is part of our culture. One of the difficulties encountered in mixed schools is by young male teachers embarrassed by the girls' clothing. Women teachers, too, can embarrass by their dress. Going without a bra may be a political statement for her but it can be a source of extreme embarrassment to colleagues and pupils.

Flirting

Flirting is an ancient, enjoyable pastime which seems to come naturally to some and is learned by others. It can occur in the initial stages of a new relationship or in order to maintain a long-estab-lished one. Basically it is using clothes, bodies and words to say 'I like you and want to spend more time with you, to become more intimate. How do you feel about me?' It can go wrong, however, if someone flirts for its own sake, trying to see how many conquests can be made or, unaware of the effect s/he has on others, gets into situations which were deeper than ever intended.

Relationships

An essential part of adolescence is learning to feel comfortable with one's own sexuality in the presence of the opposite sex to precede the development of a full sexual relationship.

Although in many cultures young people have been initiated into sexual life by older people, the ugly old man who deflowered the geisha and the matron who 'taught' in the boys schools, we now expect the older person to appreciate what is good, advise occasionally and contain the relationship at that level. There are romantic liaisons between members of staff and the pupils in school but such relationships are not only difficult for those concerned but for other staff and pupils in the school. Discouraging such relationships while both have different roles within the same organisation makes for the greatest comfort of all.

Problems about friendships, especially for girls, loom large in adolescence. 'She's taken my friend', is something often heard by teachers at this stage. Learning how to make friends, special friends and friends of the opposite sex is a concern of many teenagers who worry they won't achieve this, and may be left on the shelf. This is a particular problem in a school where it is the done thing to have a special friend of the opposite sex and also a problem in the age of shifting relationships.

Alvin Toffler (1970) considers that suburban man may meet in one day more people than the medieval villager met in his entire lifetime. The number of relationships, from superficial to intimate, is much greater for each person than it used to be, and the duration of each relationship in this world of rapid transport is likely to be shorter. This also applies to 'permanent' relationships such as marriage. Establishing, maintaining and ending personal relationships are skills required by today's children for the 21st century.

Courses on parenthood and family life must include an awareness of changes of types of families and relationships within new families. We do not know the proportion of children living with both their natural parents by the time they finish secondary school but some estimates put it at about 50 per cent in Britain today. One in 8 children is living with a one-parent family and a baby born in 1982 in England and Wales had a one in six chance of his parents being divorced. Some pupils have a series of 'uncles' in the house for differing periods of time when the mother is a single parent. Rather than avoid such topics for fear of embarrassment (whose?), it would help pupils to understand clearly what they are already vaguely aware of: that perfect TV families in cornflake advertisements are not the norm and to come to terms with this situation rather than hanker after an unobtainable ideal.

Not only in personal but also in working life the need to relate temporarily to strangers is increasing. A multidisciplinary approach to a task or a project means that individuals from different backgrounds must work together and relate to each other at least briefly for a job to be successful.

Sexual harrassment is an issue in the working situation but is also present in school and part of many pupils' own experience. In dealing with this adequately the school is preparing its pupils to cope with the same situation in the world of work.

Satisfactory sexual relationships depend upon efficient communication in which verbal bodily messages are transmitted and received. What a child wants to know is the answer to what one remedial boy felt able to ask his biology teacher: 'When you're in bed at night with your wife how do you tell her what you want?' A difficult question but one to which each must work out an answer that is acceptable to the other concerned, for sexual encounters can be gauche both within and outside marriage. The complaints received in school by girls who have been fondled and molested by boys, occur when the encounter has been unsatisfactory and not welcomed by the girl. If she is approached subtly, and signals agreement, a mutually acceptable level of intimacy takes place. If a boy recognises when his advances are not welcome and desists there is no cause for complaint.

Love

What about love in sex education? Making love and having sexual intercourse are expressions sometimes used interchangeably. They can be the same or they can be different. It is possible to have sex without love and love without sex, but ideally the bonding function of sex develops and strengthens a relationship between two people which is reciprocated and mutually exclusive.

Love is experienced and learned. New babies first love their mothers and other members of their family. After that they extend their circle and love friends, eventually hoping to fall in love with a man or girl of their dreams with whom to start a new family.

Martin Cole (1973) says:

> the average adolescent does not have too much difficulty in loving. Social pressures are on his side — loving had always been approved and the need for romantic association is normally quite strong in both sexes unless there has been severe emotional deprivation earlier in life. Indeed such romanticism is often too strong leading to the establishment of unstable and unreal pair bonds which if they persist for too long end in unsatisfactory marriages.

Adolescence is the time of the first love affair. Typically with an unattainable person — a pop star or maybe a teacher or older pupil at school. The crush may not be so common as formerly and often the loved one is in blissful ignorance of his new status. This phase can last several months while causing agony to the person in love. It has many delights because the loved one is never attainable and therefore entails no disappointment as the would-be lover is satisfied by the slightest word. This is well described in the poem 'First Love' by Gerald Bullett (Cooper, 1981):

> When I was in my fourteenth year . . .
> . . . Nothing I asked but to adore

All the world still loves a lover, which is a great relief to the publishers of the light romance of the Mills & Boon variety with its own vocabulary of smouldering, tempestuous relationships, heaving bosoms and cosmic kisses — the clinch that makes the earth move. One in 3 women in Britain read bodice-ripper romances at the rate of 1 per week (Emerson, 1982). Teenagers, especially girls, read a great deal of romance at this time. Whilst living vicariously through the heroine of the book there is also much learning and attitude forming taking place. Unfortunately the romantic being swept off her feet amongst many euphemisms is different from the real thing. Similes for below-the-belt biology of a consummated relationship necessary for the tone of the novel would be a PhD in its own right. The heroes do not have erections but 'bulging ardour'. A girl for whom education comes solely from novelettes may be no better prepared for the sight of an erect penis with which to make love than the brides of Victorian and Edwardian days.

Loving and liking are different. John Steinman of the rock group Meatloaf understands this when he sings 'Two out of three ain't bad, I want you, I need you, but there ain't no way I'm ever going to love you'. The all-consuming nature of love can be hard for a teenager to understand and pop music has explanations as a favourite theme. Much of the popularity is gained by putting into words what their listeners are experiencing but cannot say for themselves. Hearing others expressing their feelings is a source of comfort to a bemused person.

> She was a phantom of delight
> When first she gleamed upon my sight;
> A lovely apparition, sent
> To be a moment's ornament.

The school response again is twofold. Love and romance should be on the curriculum, classical poetry used to be there and has much to say on the subject. The more romantic and intelligent pupils can perhaps identify with Keats and other romantic poets but for most they are quite meaningless. Modern writers make a more effective bridge between the written word and the pupils' feelings. Developing easy relationships with members of both sexes and all ages should also be part of school life, expected and demonstrated as well as formally taught.

Virginity

Virginity, chastity, celibacy are issues of immediate interest to teenagers — the 'should I, shouldn't I?' dilemma. The system of no sex outside marriage was developed in a society when every act of intercourse might lead to the birth of a baby: babies needed a family to care for them properly so the simple strict taboo made sense, even though history records that it was not completely observed. These conditions no longer apply. Intercourse need not lead to a baby, and systems other than families in which children can be raised are being considered, for example, the kibbutz in Israel.

Christine Farrell (1978), in *My Mother Said*, discovered that 12 per cent of girls had had sexual intercourse before the age of 16 and the *19* survey (Newman, 1982) quoted a figure of 25 per cent. This means that in a fifth year class of 30 students, at least 3 or 4 will have had and probably are having sexual relations fairly regularly. To be effective, teaching must be within the situation which does obtain, not the chaste one we would pretend or prefer to have.

Of particular concern are issues relating to the age of consent. The age of 16 was introduced during Victorian times to protect young girls from child prostitution. Periodically it is argued that this age should be altered. As it is disregarded by so many young people it clearly makes no sense to raise the age of consent. To lower it could equally imply that 15 was an age when young people were sufficiently mature, which many are not. Those in favour of retaining some age limit often argue that this is protection for a girl. It is probably doubtful, but in any case this method denies a girl 'protection' the moment she becomes 16, when she may still be too immature for sex. Rather than seeking to give rules it should more helpfully consider some of the pressures currently experienced by today's teenagers, for example from the pop culture, from their peer group, their own desires and even from 'liberated' parents eager to put their daughter on the pill. A good discussion is included in *Will I Like It?* written for teenagers. Mayle (1978) says only have sex if you, in your total situation, want to; if you believe in chastity before marriage stick to that. Sexual behaviour should be responsible in that sexual partners are respected as people, not as objects, and children not conceived that cannot be provided for.

Contraception

Concepts of contracption can be introduced at a very early age.

Very young children understand the idea of being wanted and hoped for without understanding the mechanisms of family planning. To understand lessons on contraception it is necessary, however, to understand that sex is for recreation and health as well as procreation.

A child's thinking must clearly have advanced beyond the stage of sex for reproduction with some help perhaps, before he can understand the idea of contraception. Knowledge of a need for contraception, of various methods available, is an essential prerequisite for contraceptive practice. If 'hands on' experience is regarded as essential when learning about computers the same attitude could be adopted towards the contraptions of contraception.

Many women and girls, however, although technically knowledgeable fail to use contraceptives because their attitude, not their knowledge, is faulty. One young lady expressed it succinctly when she said 'Me I just forget all that school stuff when I'm making love'.

Current advertising promoted by the Health Education Council is concentrated on attitudes of acknowledging that many prefer to trust to luck or hold romantic views of love which has no consequences. The 'macho' man on a motor bike with a Durex teeshirt is challenging the idea that it is cissy to use birth control.

Schoolgirl Pregnancy

Question: What do you call a girl who doesn't believe in contraception? Answer: A mother.

Some girls do conceive while still below leaving age. Donald Reid (1982) puts this between 1 and 2 per year in a school of 1,000 pupils. This was the incidence we discovered in our work in Sheffield of an average of 1 girl per school per year who had a full-term pregnancy (Preston and Lindsay, 1976). One of the main problems in this situation is the emotional response of the adult to the subject. Other people's sexual behaviour and young people today separately tend to trigger strong responses and together they exert a powerful influence. Responses vary from outright 'It is the policy of this school to exclude on pregnancy' to excessive concern to be helpful. Common responses include questions such as 'Did it happen in school?' and 'Was it one of our boys?'

On Dame Margaret Miles' working party which published *Pregnant at School* (1979) we were concerned that no automatic practices should be recommended as the girls were not a homogeneous group. We found that they were alike only by reason of their youthful pregnancies (Lindsay and Cox, 1982) and agreed with Schaffer *et al.* (1978), after conducting our own survey and a review of the literature, that the girls did not form a pathological group and differed only from the normal population by virtue of their pregnancy. Donald Reid (1982), on the other hand, concludes from his survey of the literature that there was a tendency for British schoolgirls to exhibit some certain characteristics often regarded as indicators of deprivation. Significantly, however, there was little overlap of references between Reid and the Miles report.

The help that schools can give varies with different stages of the pregnancy. Sometimes school is aware of a schoolgirl pregnancy before the family. It may be other girls that know and persuade the girl to confide in a teacher, or a teacher may overhear girls chatting in a needlework lesson, for example, where working and talking take place side by side. Sometimes the teacher has suspicions that the girl will admit. Sometimes a girl tries to impose impossible conditions on a teacher — 'you mustn't tell my mother'. If a girl is pregnant her family should be told. Most girls are in fact surprised when prevailed upon to tell their families, with or without the help of an outsider, that the worst does not happen; they are not beaten within an inch of their lives and shown the door, despite their assertions 'you don't know my dad'.

Most girls do tell the parents themselves sooner or later that they are pregnant and this may be communicated from home to school. However, out of every 8 schoolgirl conceptions, 5 are aborted (Miles, 1979) and the majority of these are probably not known to schools. There is a good chance that an abortion can be performed during a school holiday. An absence note can merely give a vague reason for non-attendance. Abortion is a more middle-class solution; the middle-class parents are more ambitious for their daughter and have money if necessary as well as the knowledge of where to get help. Additionally they adopt a generally less fatalistic view of life and are accustomed to being in control rather than being controlled by events. Hopefully abortions are accompanied by pre- and post-abortion counselling in which the girl's decisions are owned by rather than imposed upon her.

Counselling, which allows a girl to explore her own attitudes, is essential on detection of pregnancy and perhaps this is where the help of an outside agency such as the educational psychologist would be of use. It is too easy for the adults in her life to take over and make decisions for her, as girls frequently regress to a dependent state at this time. Procreation, however, is an adult activity and these decisions can no longer be made on her behalf.

Parents who are highly involved in such dilemmas have needs of their own which often go unrecognised. One mother of a pregnant schoolgirl said to me 'everybody is asking her what she wants. What about me, I'm going to be left looking after this baby. I don't want any more babies, my husband had the operation to make sure we didn't but she just sits there saying she wants it'. Other parents may not voice their needs so clearly but being made grandparents prematurely is a shock. A sensitive ear at school from someone who is concerned but not so involved can be of great comfort.

It is preferable for a girl to continue in school for the majority of her pregnancy so that she can stay with her friends and interrupt her studies as little as possible, although in addition to the normal curriculum she will need antenatal care and, if she is to be the primary caretaker of the baby, education in parent craft. The effect of a girl staying in school during her pregnancy has never in my experience encouraged others to try to achieve the same — rather the reverse.

Parental Sex

If adolescents have difficulty in coping with their own sexuality they have even greater difficulty in coping with that of their parents. This silence is so strong that in a survey (Pocs *et al.*, 1977) of college students who regarded themselves as sexually liberated, most of those interviewed were unable to consider their parents as sexual beings. A quarter of the respondents believed their parents no longer had sexual intercourse, even though less than 50 years of age. They further believed that most of their parents were happily married and in love. Sometimes it can no longer be denied and in several situations children must accept their parents are sexual beings. It is not common in these days of small families for mothers of teenagers to have additional babies and a mother's pregnancy can be met with great resentment. With some this is normal jealousy but comments such as 'it's disgusting at their age', relate more to children having to reappraise their view of their parents and acknowledge their sexuality than sibling rivalry.

Curriculum teaching which informs that sexual activity and drive is normal into old age prepares the way for the idea in themselves and others that sex is not the prerogative of the young. Sympathetic counselling for youngsters in distress is necessary to help them to reassess their long-established views of their parents.

Incest

Sexual relations between blood relations is incest. Although brother-sister relations are incestuous and against the law it is the older man-young girl situation in the family which is of most concern when the relationship may not be voluntarily contracted and the girl is unable to refuse the sexual advances. In law, however, the consent of the woman is irrelevant, the law is broken by both parties if the relationship is known. The frequency of incest is quite unknown. The 312 cases recorded in the Criminal Statistics of England and Wales, 1980, represent the unhappy, unsuccessful tip of the iceberg. The National Children's Bureau (Highlight No. 50) is concerned that 'as marriage breakdowns and family reformations become more prevalent, the sexual abuse of girls by stepfathers and mothers' lovers is an increasing problem.'

For a girl in an incestuous relationship with her father the confusion of society is played out before her eyes. She learns often without so many words to say nothing of this aspect of family life and becomes guilty by association. The ambivalence and uncertainty of a girl towards her father whom she loves and with whom she must live, but about whom she feels uncomfortable, are often compounded by the girl's own mother. The scenario is as follows: nice, decent woman brought up to believe in marriage and family but that sex is dirty and unpleasant does her duty upon marriage and provides a child or two. The man, with a warm loving nature knows how his wife feels, gradually turns his attentions to his daughters whom he also loves. The childish caresses become more sexual and gradually full sexual relationship develops, greatly aided by the parental power in the relationship a man has over his daughter. Meanwhile mother is aware that less sexual demands are being made on her and chooses not to think too deeply about why this is so. The likelihood of this happening in an isolated community is greater than in towns where other outlets are available. The daughter's attempts, if any, to discuss this with her mother are unsuccessful and the situation is established.

Although for some girls incest may not be traumatic, these are probably the minority. For most youngsters a variety of problems follow. Some of these are associated with the incest itself, and the psychological trauma that may accompany it, while others result from the legal process which may follow. If a father is accused a girl might suffer the traumas of giving evidence, seeing her father imprisoned, and her family split with herself being taken into care. Whether punitive or therapeutic measures are more appropriate for those found guilty of incest is an issue presently being explored (see Renvoize, 1982).

Incest should be on the curriculum because it is a word pupils can read in the newspaper about which they require accurate information. Schools need to teach that incest is against the law in our country as a protection for minors from abuse by adults. Punishment for the offence is officially severe but there are also uncontrolled punishments from fellow inmates in prison and opprobrium from society. However it might also be worth referring to incest in other societies, notably ancient Egypt, where it was the only relationship allowed for the royal family and where it caused so many problems for contemporary genealogists working out the family tree for a king whose father was also his maternal grandfather.

When a girl or boy has been involved in an incestuous relationship counselling is necessary because of the ambiguity, secrecy and guilt involved and this should be referred to an educational psychologist or the school counsellor with the caveat that children's perceptions differ from those of adults and the child's reconstruction of events is the important one.

Rape

Rape is when any person is obliged to have sexual intercourse without consent by 'force, fear or fraud' and must involve penetration by the penis into the body. Indecent assault and sexual assaults are also offences with specific legal definitions. These words, however, are not taught in schools with a consequence that girls are unprepared for what to do if they are so unfortunate as to be rape victims. One girl described in the *19* survey had been held and entered by three boys in turn but didn't think she had been raped as they didn't take her clothes off, therefore she did not report this serious assault. There are, of course, other reasons why rape is often not reported; the desire to forget and the gruesome cross-questioning and examination which have left some victims feeling guilty rather than victimised are disincentives. The incidence of rape is unknown because it is seriously under-reported.

Conversely one anxious mother cried her daughter was raped at the age of 8 and demanded retribution without ascertaining the, facts. The girl's playmate pulled her knickers down in childhood exploratory play to discover if what he had heard was true that she didn't have what he did between his legs. Ignorance leading to scaremongering of this sort can be just as damaging to children concerned, not to mention unnecessarily fraught relationships between parents and children.

Unforunately some children are sexually assaulted or raped and the knowledge that this has occurred sweeps rapidly through a community like school. Such a situation is serious but is the perfect breeding ground for rumour if the people in the community find it difficult to discuss sexual matters.

An attitude which accepts normal sexuality and regards most people as good is helpful when difficulties do arise. Situations in which all strangers and newcomers are regarded with suspicion is not healthy, let alone appropriate with constant shifts in population.

Prostitution

Prostitution is when a person sells his or her body for sexual purposes. Usually this involves a woman selling to a man, but it can be a man to another man, or a man to a woman. It has been called the oldest profession and certainly has a long and colourful history. In a world where everyone had a deep satisfying relationship with another perhaps there would be no need for the selling and buying of sex. In some places, Hamburg in Germany for example, the prostitutes are accepted as a way of life and have regular medical check-ups to control the spread of disease. To some people this is condoning immorality and in England we do not license prostitutes, although since 1956 in England and Wales prostitution is no longer illegal. However, as with many activities on the fringe of the law, more seedy aspects can intrude, including coercion, exploitation and blackmail.

Occasionally schoolchildren do become involved in prostitution and the response of the school is that a pupil is being exploited by an adult. She may be in a situation of fear and bribery over which she has little control. Often these girls have a very low opinion of themselves and accept exploitation as all they deserve. In this case the school role would be of caring adult and perhaps a need to involve a social worker and parents. We must not, however, assume that all prostitutes are victims. Xavier Hollander in *The*

Happy Hooker gives a convincing account of the pride she takes in her work.

There have been instances of pupils in school performing or simulating sexual performances in public even for financial gain. Such behaviour is clearly a flagrant violation of our norms and perhaps seeks to shock. In many aspects, though, there is an element aping the special world of the adult movies.

Pornography

Pornography is disapproved of in education establishments but adolescents have easy access to sexual material. Popular newspapers regularly feature girls, and sometimes men, either as pin-ups or to add spice to a piece of text. What is acceptable in such a forum has gradually changed over the last ten to twenty years. Similarly some magazines, books and films have also become more sexually explicit. In addition to the soft porn easily available at the local newsagent or cinema, older youngsters could also visit some of the 'cinema clubs', watch videos and now cablevision brought directly into the home.

There is no consensus on what is pornographic. Art books, works of literature, medical texts have all at some time been suspect. Some materials, particularly those linking sex with gratuitous violence, are difficult to justify on any grounds other than complete lack of censorship; although there is a lack of evidence on their effects, there are good *a priori* grounds for controlling material of this nature. Adolescents, and younger children, are developing a concept of sexuality and it seems reasonable to promote certain caring behaviours as the norm. Degradation and sexual violence are not desirable, neither is the more invidious message that women are merely sex objects. In a few cases youngsters may be affected by extreme materials and require specialised help. There is a need to help youngsters develop an understanding of displays and uses of sexual materials, to help them distinguish between eroticism, sexuality and sexism. However, it is worth considering if there is censorship as to materials brought into schools, whether this extends to staffroom members looking at girly magazines — particularly if confiscated from pupils.

Sexually Transmitted Diseases

A lesson on VD is usually included in the curriculum of schools with even a cursory health education policy. Sexually transmitted diseases are on the increase, three times as many cases being treated in 1974 than in 1959 and the film on STD, *A Quarter of a Million Teenagers*, had to be retitled *Half a Million Teenagers*.

The term sexually transmitted diseases includes more than the traditional venereal diseases, in particular genital warts and genital herpes which are transmitted by direct sexual contact.

Although only a few pupils in school contract an STD, the Leverhulme Health Education Project based at Nottingham University suggests that 10 per cent will seek treatment within five years of leaving school. Before the statutory school leaving age is the last opportunity for society to ensure that its members are adequately educated to cope with this problem. A detailed approach is suggested under curriculum aims.

Final Comments

The topics mentioned are all facts of life. We may disapprove and wish it weren't so but refusing to teach about disagreeable things does not make them go away and leaving youngsters ignorant or ill-informed does not bring about the world we might prefer. Prostitution, rape and incest do not normally feature in programmes on health education and personal relationships but need to be included — if not emphasised. The approach can successfully be one of open discussion with such facts and opinions as are known and an avoidance of becoming too heated or opinions polarised. It is easy in adolescence to push youngsters to an extreme view from which they retreat with difficulty in later life. There should be no assumption that the situations mentioned don't refer to anyone in the class as some studies (NCB, 1982) suggests that one-quarter to one-third of children and adolescents have had a sexual experience with an adult.

The School Response

Curriculum Aims

It is possible to have negative aims and easier to evaluate the efficacy of such programmes than many with a more positive aim. If you have reduction or elimination of pregnancies, or sexually transmitted diseases, amongst school age pupils as an objective you can discover with relative ease whether this has happened and attribute it to your programme.

Positive aims are more difficult to specify and take lifetime to evaluate fully but curriculum objectives can be clearly specified as in all subjects. Is the education intended to be for now or future reference? Is it to inform so that the pupil may acquire knowledge, is it to promote understanding and to develop attitudes so that a child may be more tolerant and socialised, is it to alter behaviour or is it to develop skills? It used to be assumed that giving information to people affected their current behaviour. The girls who have become pregnant at school have often 'done contraception', usually in the context of when you are married and wish to delay starting a family. By failing to pay attention to current lifestyles and behaviours of pupils the teaching does not leave the classroom. Teaching aimed at the future can not be assumed to apply to the present.

Many of the confusions surrounding the area evaporate when the curriculum aims and objectives are defined, by attending separately to the areas of information, attitudes and skills. Some education has been discouraged by saying that to teach about sexual intercourse would encourage fornication in schoolchildren; such criticism is to confuse knowledge acquisition and skill development. An example of possible curriculum aims with regard to teaching about sexually transmitted diseases is as follows.

The knowledge aims would include the names, signs and symptoms of sexually transmitted diseases, the name and address of the nearest clinic; the fact that sexually transmitted diseases do not cure themselves, unlike many other diseases, and are highly contagious with hidden characteristics. The attitudes aims would include the idea that anyone who copulates with a person who has had a previous sexual partner is at risk, sexually transmitted diseases are no respecters of persons, that sexually transmitted diseases are treatable despite myths of penicillin-eating gonococcus, that treatment is not painful and that clinics are to treat not lecture. The skill aims would include how to minimise the risk of contracting sexually transmitted diseases, how to recognise the disease once you've caught it and finally how to get treatment if you think you need it. Teaching about tertiary syphillis makes very little contribution to the understanding of life to the average 16-year-old as the condition is now extremely rare, although the progression of the disease in a well-known character such as Henry VIII belongs to history. Sixteen-year-olds require skills for life, the minutiae of diseases are easily forgotten but 25 years after leaving school they may need to remember when they need treatment, how to find a clinic and that they have nothing to fear from the staff. These are appropriate educational aims for the future of young people.

The Organisation

> It is a waste of time to fuss about what we think the children should learn if we do not understand how to organise a system of pupil-teacher relationship which is productive of our intended learning. (Marland, 1974)

In no aspect of school life must this be more true than when it comes to sex education. Before any curriculum content is determined the mood, atmosphere and ethos of the school must be such that learning about intimate aspects of life is possible. The developing educational process mirrors the development of a sexual relationship. For it to succeed, the school must deliberately foster the same growth of trust, warmth and mutual concern to become intimate as is necessary for two people to develop a full sexual relationship. From the outset the mood created in school needs to be one that inspires the pupil to feel confident. This is the stage of soft lights, sweet music, pleasant and welcoming situations with people who seem interested and interesting. In this situation, the pupil feels secure enough to reveal a little of his personal self and move closer to a teacher as he feels more relaxed. The atmosphere is created for greater revelation and intimacy where personal concerns can be discussed.

Such an atmosphere must also exist outside the lessons of the timetable and the concern of the school for its pupils must pervade its entire life. Children cannot feel the concern of the school if forced into inhospitable, cold, wet school yards for breaks. The pupils' feelings must be considered before considering curriculum content in the area of personal relationships.

Many secondary schools now have the type of organisation which overwhelms the child on entry and contrasts sharply with the junior school that has just been left. Relationships are lived, not talked about, and if a child has a dozen or more teachers in the course of a week it is not so easy to develop anything other than a superficial relationship with each. To compensate for this many schools have now constructed elaborate pastoral care systems to try to ensure the children are cared for. An alternative, however, would be to return to a system wherein each child has no more than five or six teachers, when the teachers and the taught can get to know each other and where form teachers always teach their own classes as well as perform registration duties.

Sexism in the Organisation

The general deployment of staff within a school conveys many subtle messages as to the values of the organisation, in particular the relative role of the sexes in our society. What is women's work and what is men's work? In girls' schools not only was the head of a school a woman but also the heads of departments as well. Some girls' schools have recently boldly broken with tradition and appointed a man as head, which is theoretically all right but it would be more convincing to see a woman heading a boys' school. In our mixed comprehensive schools how many headteachers and heads of departments are women? What departments do they head beyond girls' PE, commercial and domestic studies?

If the female deputy headteacher is seen to spend much of her time tending to fainting pupils and handing out sanitary towels what does this say about her role in the life of the school? The latter problem could be dealt with by dispensers in toilets, as it is in other places of work. If the toilets have to be kept locked for fear of vandalism the atmosphere in the school can scarcely be one where teachers and pupils work together in mutual trust and respect towards a common goal.

Such organisational issues involve personnel at all levels. If parents and teachers believe and teach that menstruation is a normal function of a healthy woman the organisation must support it. One cleaner in a junior school never replaced the polythene bags for disposal in the girls' toilets saying these things should not be necessary there in her opinion. Such an attitude has an effect on girls' learning to cope with menstruation.

Some schools are now declaring the anti-sexist policies of their organisation in the booklets for staff and pupils. Effective policies seem to be increasing an awareness of the presence of sexist ideas by consciously and deliberately challenging instances of sexist behaviour. This awareness led to the pupils in one school to rewrite some worksheets on their own initiative. To ensure equal opportunities for boys and girls it may even involve returning to single-sex groupings in some subjects.

Curriculum Contributors

Without a curriculum policy over-enthusiastic teachers can see it as
their duty to 'tell all' to the children. This may be because of their
own embarrassing lack of education, or because the dearth of
formal policy in the school results in some glaringly obvious gaps.
But this overkill approach is perceived by the children as 'oh no,
not sex again' and becomes one more dull lesson which meets the
teacher's needs rather than those of the pupils.

Subject teachers, both as individuals and specialists, can make
separate contributions of direct relevance in areas of sexual growth
and development, and self-awareness in personal relationships. All
teachers contribute to the ethos of the school. Form teachers can
promote a type of atmosphere deliberately by having a programme
of the Active Tutorial Work type published by Lancashire LEA
(Baldwin and Wells, 1979). This scheme sees the formteacher as the
centre of the pastoral system and its principal aims are to facilitate
the child's progress in school through adolescence and prepare him
for adult life. All departments could contribute something to the
formal timetable within the school. In this complex area individual
interests and competences of the current staff are important. Traditionally it has been a subject in the science department. But each
department has a different perspective and these perspectives need
co-ordinating. The Schools Council Health Education Project
suggests an approach based on a list which itemises all the topics
considered to be important and shares them out between the people
who feel they can deal with them adequately. In schools retaining
separate departments the biologists could talk about anatomy and
physiology of adolescence and reproduction in a biological manner
but the chemistry of the body is of relevance here; the physicists
might make a contribution related to the use of sonar scanners in
antenatal clinics and mathematicians' knowledge related to probability and risk-taking in sexual activity. Population growth and its
control is important in geography while in history the relationships
between people — sexual or otherwise — has always had an important influence in the turn of events.

English specialists teach drama and self-expression as well as referring to great literature where relationships feature in both poetry
and prose. In modern languages the words children learn from each
other not quite accurately could be taught properly by the teachers.
Music is to do with the expression of feelings, as is well understood
by pupils, the prime consumers of pop songs. In art the nude form

is a feature of classical art and physical education is concerned with the development of the human body. If the traditional and old subject areas exist, the act of co-operating, and working together, is an excellent example for the pupils to observe when the subject boundaries are broken and each is respected for their own contribution: a practical demonstration of the groups of the future referred to above that come together to do a certain job.

Sexism in the Curriculum

In recent years we have been made aware of the sexist nature of our language (Spender, 1980). Feminists have objected to the use of 'he' referring to single people and in this chapter I have used the device of the plural 'they' to avoid the sexist implications of the singular 'he'.

Maraget Sutherland (1981) considers sexism in the schools in detail. The promotion of co-educational systems was intended to eliminate sex bias but has actually promoted 'girls' subjects 'boys' subjects. Girls now stand a better chance of choosing sciences in girls' schools and to a lesser extent boys of studying languages in boys' schools than under the co-educational system. The actual timetable may no longer forbid girls to do woodwork and metal-work under the Equal Opportunities Act, 1975, but it can continue in its sexist thinking to ensure the traditional divisions are maintained. One headteacher explaining the equal opportunities curriculum offered in his school qualified it by adding he couldn't resist a smile when a boy asked 'Please sir, where is my needlework lesson?' Needless to say not many boys chose needlework, although the opportunity existed on paper.

The content of textbooks used in the classroom is worth scrutinising to see what sexist attitudes are portrayed; the roles played by men and women in the stories used in the languages department tend to perpetuate stereotypes. Do 'men and their wives', or 'people', take initiatives and colonise the new world in the history books in use?

Teachers as Experts

Traditionally sexual matters have been taught by the outsider coming into the school specifically for the purpose. Originally this was the priest or the vicar warning about overindulgence in the guise of moral education. More recently it has been the doctor, the nurse or the health education officer invited into the school. If a celibate, or a person who is concerned with sickness and disease, is invited what attitude is conveyed in this way? Teachers as people leading normal healthy lives — including sexual behaviour — are the ones with the best skill to do any teaching. Sex is not only for those with medical qualifications: it is a normal part of adult life; teachers who are also parents have produced their children by sexual reproduction.

A series of speakers coming to school to 'do' menstruation, VD and birth of baby may salve the conscience of the school organisers in that they can point to our list of prestigious lectures, but often this has limited educational gains for the children.

Many medical and para-medical people want to go into schools to bridge the gap between the schools and the clinics. Health visitors in particular have a large educational component in their work. One solution is for teachers and their community health workers to collaborate on a joint venture to reproduce a syllabus using the experience and skills of both. The teacher knows the class and can follow up questions months after a visitor has gone, the doctor or nurse communicates a lack of embarrassment when speaking freely and has real examples to illustrate ideas. Such a joint approach helps visitors to the school in that the preparatory work enables it to be made clear just what schools expect the visitor to achieve and the visitor can say whether or not this is possible (Cox and Lavelle, 1982).

Where can teachers gain the guidance they feel they require if they wish to embark upon such a programme? There are many books written upon the subject by people who hold strong opinions and qualifications to support these opinions: 'medical practitioner, JP, C of E, and mother of three'. Who could quarrel with such claims to expertise, stemming as they do from medicine, law, church and motherhood? No one who always seeks for a higher authority. But rule-based education for living is inappropriate for the teenagers of today because no one knows what rules will work in the 21st century.

Teaching with regard to sexual behaviour must be genuine and sincere, coming from beliefs honestly held and personally formed (*A Quaker View of Sex*, Heron, 1963). Wilson (1970) says the more educated a person is the better he is able to make a responsible and informed choice between possible courses of behaviour. The more aware he is of these possibilities the more freedom he has in the way he conducts his life. Sexual behaviour involves being informed, knowing about how the decisions are made and the factors which influence them.

One way of helping teachers to determine their practices is described elsewhere (Cox, 1982), consisting of training where teachers acquired information, experienced their own reactions and decided their own policies on these bases. Each must decide his or her own views, philosophy and the boundaries of how much of themself they will reveal. Some revelation is necessary if it is to be a personal communication. Helping each teacher to determine their own personal style comes through sensitive in-service training.

Teaching Methods

Having decided the curriculum content it is apparent that different styles of teaching would be necessary to accomplish aims relating to behaviour change and attitude formation from those used in knowledge transmission. Surveys (e.g. *19* magazine) find that most young people's sexual information comes from friends, it is the minority that look to schools and parents when they want information or help. Sometimes the friends' advice or information is not the best but rather than deplore this the best way is to acknowledge and improve these informal tactics, particularly if the aim is to influence behaviour.

A system of training older teenagers to act as group leaders is one suggested to promote contraceptive behaviour based on success in smoking education by the Health Education Council. When girls do become pregnant at school their classmates do begin to believe it can happen to them and do not so easily reject the facts as those given by middle-class, middle-aged ladies. Although we formally teach that every act of sexual intercourse carries a risk of pregnancy many people reject this at some level of awareness because in their own experience they have had intercourse and not become pregnant.

To do this we must acknowledge the existence of human desires. Sex for pleasure is formally taught neither at home nor at school. Sexual intercourse is for reproduction but the majority of time it is for pleasure, a leisure activity between people for bonding as well as for relief of physical tension. Lessons on contraception make more sense in this context than following those which imply that the purpose of the act is to conceive. The girl who said 'Nobody told me I'd want to' defined the gap in her curriculum.

The teaching should be enjoyable and about what interests the pupils. They basically want to be sure they are normal and develop enough confidence to cope with the present and the future. They want to know about many of the things referred to above which some adults have decided should be of no concern to them. One health visitor did not seem to think that the questions like 'how long does sex last?' were genuine.

The climate and the opportunities to discuss issues of genuine concern are more important than expensive materials. Gillian Crampton-Smith's *Too Great a Risk* (1977) is an example of the comic format being adapted as classroom material. This format is both familiar and credible concerning characters with whom the pupils can identify. The stories told are stimulus materials for pupil discussions supported by the fact sheets for the teacher.

Teachers will have only limited participation from groups if they are felt to be actively promoting certain ways of behaving which are not conducive to the pupils.

School Resources

The school library should be well stocked with the type of book the pupils want to read as well as the more academic text. *Are you there God? It's me Margaret*, by Judy Blume about a girl worried about her periods which hadn't started, and *Will I like it?*, by Peter Mayle, are examples of this sort. In a subject where information and daily life are so intertwined it is essential that pupils have access when they want it rather than when others judge the time is right. The time will never be right for a whole class of individuals. Michael Schofield (1973) found that brighter children who were used to going to books for information were more knowledgeable in sexual matters, although the likelihood was that they had had less formal sex education at school. Being able to learn something when you need to is a valuable life skill.

Furthermore, by equipping one of the institutions of a school, the library, with books of sexual interest this creates an ethos which says 'we the authorities think that this is a normal aspect of life and the books are freely available and can be consulted openly'. Such an approach makes the subject less furtive and encourages healthy questioning. Obvious censorship of books, such as cutting out a single story from a collection of short stories, serves to draw attention and makes more attractive something which would otherwise have been overlooked.

In addition to a pupils' library the staff, too, need support resources, including films and videos as well as books, pamphlets and worksheets. More expensive materials, such as films, are owned centrally by some LEAs for use in different schools throughout the year and health education officers also are a valuable resource.

The Educational Psychologist

The educational psychologist can make a contribution to any school considering introducing such programmes. In the first place, as outsiders with a knowledge of the school they can act as sounding boards for teachers discussing ideas still in an introductory phase. This can be done informally or more formally via a specifically designed course in which ideas, methods and materials are introduced for the consideration of the teachers. The psychologist also will have a knowledge of normal behaviour and can put some behaviours into perspective when discussing sexual matters. Discussions between psychologists and teachers may, furthermore, help to make the teachers more comfortable with this aspect of their work.

Secondly, the educational psychologist can help teachers develop techniques required for this type of curriculum; techniques from social skills training, effective listening, awareness of group dynamics and influences of situations on behaviour.

Thirdly, the educational psychologist can be directly involved with a child. Often, however, children are referred to the psychologist because the teacher doesn't know what to do and the psychologist can talk with the teachers who then go on to deal with the child themselves. On other occasions the psychologist will see the child for a single interview or a series of sessions if the teacher does not feel comfortable dealing with the issues or the pupil prefers to discuss his difficulties with a stranger.

The fourth main contribution that a psychologist might make is in terms of evaluation. This would mean helping to establish clear curriculum goals at the outset in such a way that it is possible to assess how successfully they have been met (Ainscow and Tweddle, 1979). Psychologists' skills in the assessment of human behaviour may be of value in this area.

Conclusion

In writing this chapter I have indicated what I see as a practical philosophy to precede organisational and curriculum initiatives. I have tried to produce facts which describe the sexual lives of everyday people, the way they are and not the way they ought to be. People do masturbate and do have sex outside marriage with more than one partner despite the presumed Christian ethic. Distinguishing between the real world and the ideal world is one way of ordering some of the confusions outlined in the Introduction.

The views expressed are inevitably subjective, personal opinions based on the three strands of sexual learning: formal teaching from academic reference sources, informal learning, and my own limited direct and vicarious experiences. A personal statement is integral to an effective sexual communication but need be in no way embarrassing or excessively self-exposing — as I hope to have demonstrated.

I have aimed to produce a chapter wherein an essential part of the message is in the medium, both serious and humorous, believing these elements are present in successful sexual relationships. The combination of clear aims with light and serious notes is an effective mood for organisation: the firm and friendly manner traditionally recommended for those who deal with young people.

8 DRUGS, ADOLESCENTS AND ADULTS

Martin Desforges

Introduction

We live in a drug-oriented society, where the use of drugs is widely accepted as a solution to a variety of medical and social problems, as well as an important method of relaxation. Most people accept the widespread medical use of drugs; a large number are available over the counter in pharmacies and supermarkets. Many people would feel thwarted if a visit to the doctor's surgery did not result in a prescription for some form of drug to alleviate the symptoms of their complaint.

Drugs are commonly prescribed for a variety of physical and psychological conditions (see Table 8.1). They can be used to control pain, cure bacterial infections, alleviate psychological distress, as well as in many other ways. The use of painkillers for head or back aches, the popularity of sedatives and tranquillisers, is well known. A national survey of drug use in 1972 showed that 11 per cent of the sample had taken a sedative, sleeping tablet, tranquilliser, antidepressant or stimulant in the previous two weeks, 9 per cent had used one within the last 24 hours. A total 41 per cent of the sample had used analgesics within the previous two weeks, with 3 per cent using them daily. Close to 10 per cent of all prescriptions written by GPs are for tranquillisers, antidepressants or hypnotic drugs, accounting for 20 per cent of the National Health Service annual expenditure on drugs (Kennedy, 1981).

The success of the pharmaceutical industry in manufacturing products that ameliorate the effects of many diseases and painful illnesses is well known, and the use of drugs to relieve anxiety, tension and frustration has led to the expectation that anything short of complete psychological well-being should not be tolerated. Widespread advertising by the pharmaceutical industry and the working practices of the medical profession create a tendency to flight into drug support for life experiences that previously would have been accepted as mere vicissitudes. Young people observe this casual and frequent use of drugs by adults, and they are influenced by what they see.

161

Table 8.1: Medical Uses of Drugs

Physical pain	Psychological distress
a) Improve health	a) Aid to relaxation
b) Combat infection	b) Combat depression
c) Control pain	c) Reduce anxiety
d) Accelerate healing	d) Cope with phobias
e) Prevent illness	e) Change moods

The use of drugs for relaxation, social and recreational purposes is widespread, with different cultures emphasising different substances — alcohol, nicotine and pills from medical sources in the West; alcohol and opium in the East; cocaine in the Andes and marijuana in many regions of the world. As Aldous Huxley wrote, 'vegetable sedatives and narcotics, all the euphorics that ripen in berries or can be squeezed from roots have been used by Humans for chemical vacations'. The use of these drugs often develops into an experience to be enjoyed in its own right — the gourmet approach. The variety of alcoholic drinks and cigarettes available in European countries illustrates the point.

Problems with drug usage arise when the borderline is crossed between the legal, accepted drugs used in quantities and frequencies that are socially approved by most adults in a particular culture, and the use of unacceptable drugs or the misuse of acceptable drugs. Within any one culture there are obvious historical trends and short-term fashions in drug use. The opium dens of nineteenth-century London are no longer common, but the consumption of alcohol has risen steeply in the last 50 years. LSD which was used with increasing frequency in the 1960s, now seems to be on the decline. It is against this changing background of the acceptance and use of drugs for a variety of purposes by adults in the United Kingdom that the use of drugs by adolescents must be considered.

Drugs Commonly Used and Abused

A drug can be defined as any substance which can alter the structure or function of living organisms. Such a broad definition, which is concise rather than precise, would include many industrial and environmental pollutants, medically prescribed substances, socially accepted drugs such as alcohol and nicotine, as well as those drugs taken by abusers. Generally the term drug is applied to those psychotropic substances (those affecting mood or states of consciousness) used by individuals outside a medical context.

Drug dependence or addiction refers to a psychological and/or physical state which results from taking a drug, and is associated with a compulsion to go on taking the drug either because of the desired effects it produces, or because of the ill-effects if not taken. As Parish (1980) points out, by this definition most of us are psychologically dependent on substances not usually thought of as drugs — can you face the day without a cup of tea or coffee? Do you feel restless during a break from work without a cigarette to help you relax? What kind of alcohol do you need to help you unwind at the end of day?

Many drugs can cause dependence, but it is difficult to predict who will become dependent, and under what circumstances. Some drugs are more likely than others to cause dependence, and some individuals become dependent more easily than others. It appears that dependency is most likely to arise when three factors come together: a potential drug of dependence, a vulnerable personality, and some adverse aspect of environment. The importance of the context in which the drug is taken is demonstrated by the evidence that only a small minority of American soldiers who used narcotics while they were in South East Asia, and who considered themselves addicted, continued to use the drug when they returned home. Exposure to even the most addictive drugs is not a sufficient condition for addiction; other factors are also important (Stepney, 1981).

Drugs can be classified in many different ways: medical and non-medical, legal and illegal, by pharmacological action, clinical usage, etc. Drugs of abuse are usually classified according to their predominant effect, and are usually divided into three main groups: sedatives, stimulants and hallucinogens. Sometimes a further category is added: deliriants. Any system of classification will run into difficulties in that many drugs have diverse effects and may fit more than one category. It is also far from certain that the pharmacological action will follow a particular pattern. For example, although amphetamines generally stimulate, in a small proportion of people the effect is calming. Barbiturates are sedatives and depress the central nervous system, yet some individuals are initially excited by them. LSD is regarded as an hallucinogen, yet studies in an experimental setting suggest that its hallucinatory effect is by no means primary, or experienced by all users (Willis, 1973). Particular substances tend to acquire a magical reputation, and so little is known of their effects that people are free to speculate and build fantasies around them, which are then transmitted as facts. An attitude of caution and informed scepticism is needed when looking at information on the effects of abusing a particular drug.

What follows is a brief summary of the main types of drugs commonly abused in Britain. Further details on particular substances, methods of taking them, the main effects and dangers are available from many sources. The Teachers Advisory Council on Alcohol and Drug Education (TACADE — 2 Mount St, Manchester M2 5NG) and the Institute for the Study of Drug Dependence (Kingsbury House, 3 Blackburn Road, London NW6 1AX) have many publications if more detailed information is required.

Drugs Which are Predominantly Stimulants

These excite and stimulate the central nervous system, causing an increase in bodily and mental activity. Fatigue and tiredness seem to be reduced and users feel alert, restless, anxious or even panic-stricken. They are often used at discos or parties to increase excitement, ward off tiredness or to counteract the effects of sedative drugs. When the effects wear off the user may be left depressed and exhausted, with the temptation to take more stimulants to combat these effects. Tolerance develops quickly and large doses may be needed by experienced users.

Methedrine, dexedrine and cocaine are the main stimulants commonly abused. Caffeine found in tea, coffee, cocoa and cola drinks is a stimulant. The dose required to produce stimulation is between 100–300 mg, a level often reached by people taking these drinks, and a large number of people in Britain are probably psychologically dependent on caffeine (Parish, 1980).

Drugs which are Predominantly Sedatives

These are usually divided into the narcotic analgesics and the sedatives. Narcotic analgesics have a powerful pain-relieving action and produce alterations in consciousness. They act principally on the brain, and possess the most intensive dependency-producing potential. Confusion may be caused by the different meanings of narcotic — a drug which depresses central nervous system functioning, a drug derived from opium or morphine-like substances, or simply a drug which easily causes addiction. Here its use will be limited to substances derived from opium and morphine. Traditionally opiates were obtained from the opium poppy, morphine being the active component. However, there are now many synthetic narcotics: heroin, methadone and pethidine being the common ones. Dependence can develop fairly rapidly after repeated use of small amounts, and tolerance develops quickly.

There are many different terms used to describe drugs which depress central nervous system functioning. A hypnotic induces sleep, but a sedative calms without inducing sleep, and together drugs having these effects are called hypnosedatives. Barbiturates are the common drugs used. Tranquillisers calm without impairing consciousness, and are usually divided into two groups, major and minor tranquillisers. Major tranquillisers are often used to treat serious mental disorders, and can produce a state of emotional quietness or indifference known as neurolepsy. Minor tranquillisers are used to treat anxiety and are known as anxiolytics. The term anxiolytic sedative may be used to include sedatives and all minor tranquillisers.

Although a particular drug may be classed as an anxiolytic, tranquilliser, hypnotic or sedative because of clinical applications in medical practice, these terms do not represent discrete categories of different drugs. It is usually the amount used which determines the effect, and many drugs can act as an anxiolytic, sedative, hypnotic or anaesthetic depending on the amount used (see Figure 8.1). The point can be illustrated by alcohol, the most commonly used sedative. A glass of wine may act as a tranquilliser, a bottle of whisky as a hypnotic, two bottles as an anaesthetic. Death can result from drinking an excess of alcoholic spirits over a short period of time.

Sedatives reduce anxiety and stress as well as inducing confidence in the user. Feelings of relaxation, well-being and competence can be intense, creating an atmosphere of pleasure and adding to the enjoyment of other experiences. Sedatives affect both cognitive and motor activities, impairing judgement and slowing down the rate and accuracy of responses to emergencies when driving vehicles or monitoring machinery at work. Because thought processes are affected, users may make damaging decisions and get into dangerous situations as a consequence of using sedatives.

Fig. 8.1: A simplified Guide to the Effects of Increasing Doses of Drugs that Depress Central Nervous System Functioning

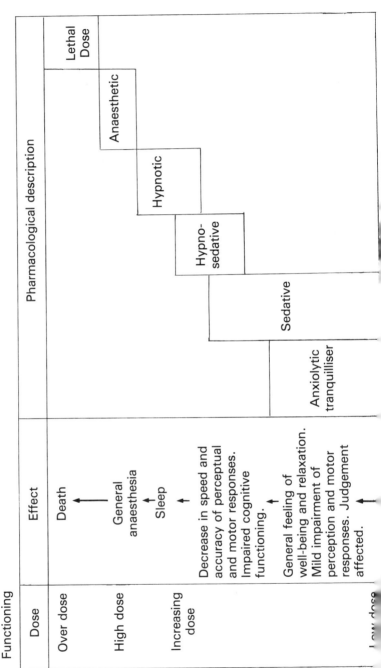

Dose	Effect	Pharmacological description
Over dose	Death	Lethal Dose
High dose	General anaesthesia	Anaesthetic
	Sleep	Hypnotic
Increasing dose	Decrease in speed and accuracy of perceptual and motor responses. Impaired cognitive functioning.	Hypno-sedative
		Sedative
	General feeling of well-being and relaxation. Mild impairment of perception and motor responses. Judgement affected.	Anxiolytic tranquilliser
Low dose		

Drugs which are Predominantly Hallucinogenic

These drugs induce marked changes in mood and may induce fundamental alterations in perceptions. LSD and cannabis are the best known, with a reputation for inducing mystical or religious experiences. There is good evidence that LSD experiences can go drastically wrong for some individuals, causing severe fear, anxiety and depression that may last weeks or months. Psychotic reactions lasting months sometimes occur, and there is no way of predicting who is prone to such reactions.

Cannabis is usually included as an hallucinogenic drug, but it also acts as a sedative, producing a complex effect on the central nervous system. It is obtained from the cannabis plant, and a variety of drugs are made from it. The crushed leaves, flowers and twigs are called marijuana (also known as grass, pot, weed and by many other slang terms). Hemp is made only from the flowering heads, whilst hashish (or hash) is made from a relatively pure resin of the plant and is much more potent than marijuana. There is a great deal of debate on the effects of cannabis and whether it should be legalised. Depending on the strength of the source and how it is taken, the various effects include mood elevation or anxiety, a dreamy state of happiness, distortions of time and space and feelings of insight into complex problems. Hallucinations tend to occur only with potent preparations, but effects also depend on personality, expectations, previous drug experiences and the social setting of use.

Deliriants

These are the volatile substances inhaled in a variety of ways from tissues, cloths, cellulose or plastic bags and aerosol sprays. The commonest are the impact adhesives, but may include dry cleaning fluids, petrol, paints, sprays and a wide variety of chemicals. The general effects are relaxation of social inhibitions followed by sedation and a feeling of relaxed well-being. Some users report hallucinatory experiences, although symptoms of drunkenness, confusion, nausea and vomiting are more frequent. Little is known of long-term effects, and with such a wide variety of substances used it would be difficult to generalise.

Table 8.2: Number of Notified Addicts of Narcotic Analgesics between 1970 and 1980

	1970	1971	1972	1973	1974	1975	1976	1977	1978	1979	1980
Age											
Under 16	1	0	0	0	0	0	0	0	0	0	0
16	1	2	3	2	1	0	0	0	0	0	1
17	18	13	12	9	7	4	3	1	5	2	0
18	30	34	24	24	15	10	3	7	9	12	7

Source: *Statistics of the Misuse of drugs in U.K.*, supplementary table, 1980, Home Office Statistics Dept.

Use of Drugs by Young People

It is difficult to piece together a national picture of the illicit use of drugs by adults in Britain, with even less known about abuse by young people. There is virtually no data on age at first use or recent use, with little on the personal characteristics of drug users. Although the domino theory of an inexorable progression from 'soft' to 'hard' drugs is held by many people, developmental aspects of drug use have rarely been studied, and there is little evidence to support or refute this theory. Most workers have equated the use of illegal drugs with a problem, but failed to investigate the extent of any social or medical problem associated with this use, begging the question of what sort of problem and for whom (see Stimson, 1981). There is a need to get beyond the anecdotes of the professionals and mass media, to look at acute and long-term effects of different drugs from medical, psychological and social perspectives, to find out how many drug users suffer from what complications. As yet there is no co-ordinated research on a large scale to study these issues (Ghodse, 1981). At present information on drug use comes from the following three main sources.

Home Office Statistics

In the United Kingdom there is no registration of addicts, and statistics cover two aspects of drug abuse. First the number of notified addicts receiving treatment (see Table 8.2). These figures apply only to those dependent on narcotic analgesics, with methadone as the most commonly supplied drug. The precise relationship between notified addicts and overall use of narcotics is

Table 8.3: Persons Found Guilty or Cautioned for Drug Offences from 1973 to 1980.

	1973	1974	1975	1976	1977	1978	1979	1980
Age								
Under 14	5	3	1	5	0	4	4	12
14 and under 17	609	322	193	164	180	138	209	267
17 and under 21	5,973	4,264	3,312	3,138	2,929	3,043	3,088	3,594

Source: *Statistics of the Misuse of Drugs in U.K.*, 1980, Home Office Statistical Bulletin 15/81.

impossible to determine, with many factors making it more or less likely that an addict will appear on the register (Edwards, 1981). However, it is reasonable to assume that the figures will reflect whether use of narcotics is increasing or decreasing. The trend since 1972 has been downwards in the adolescent age group, despite an overall increase of 2½ times in the numbers of notified adults between 1970 and 1980.

The other available figures are the numbers of individuals given official cautions or charged under drug offences Acts (see Table 8.3). These figures include all offences involving controlled drugs (many stimulants and sedatives as well as narcotic analgesics).

Again there are problems in relating these figures to overall use in that they reflect levels of police activity, and there may be variations in current practice between different police authorities, as well as many other variables. However, the figures show a downward trend in the period 1973–80, although there is some evidence of an increase in the last year. Under 17s account for less than 2 per cent of those cautioned or charged for drug acts offences. Over 80 per cent of all offences in the under 21 age group involve cannabis, and about 15 per cent amphetamines. Narcotics and all other drugs make up the remaining 5 per cent. Perhaps the most striking feature is the small numbers of individuals involved, and although alcohol may not be commonly regarded as a drug, it is of interest to note the numbers of young people convicted for drunkenness offences in the last 15 years (see Table 8.4).

Surveys on Use and Knowledge of Drugs

These surveys have looked at a number of aspects of drug abuse,

Table 8.4: Numbers per 100,000 in the 14—17 Age Group
Convicted of Drunkenness Offences

	1965	1967	1969	1971	1973	1975	1977
Numbers per 100,000	103	150	160	200	300	290	300

Source: Central Statistics Office, *Social Trends 12*, 1982, HMSO.

including knowledge of drugs, personal use of drugs and knowledge of use by personal friends. The data for Britain was critically
examined and summarised by Stimson (1981). He noted that most
surveys dealt only with illicit or recreational use of drugs, with little
attention paid to the misuse of prescribed or over-the-counter
drugs. Information on age and extent or frequency of use was rare,
and there were often shortcomings in terms of sampling methods
and information on response rates. In summary, between 1 per cent
and 23 per cent of 11—19-year-olds had ever used illicit drugs, with
cannabis and amphetamines the main ones mentioned. In most
surveys of secondary schools between 5 and 10 per cent of pupils
admit to have misused drugs (Dorn and Thompson, 1976). The
surveys of Wright and Pearl (1981) suggested an increase in drug
use (mainly cannabis) by school age children from 1969 to 1974,
but no further increase from 1974 to 1979. During this time the use
of amphetamines appears to have declined and cannabis now seems
to be the main drug used. The latest fashion in drug abuse by
schoolchildren, solvent abuse, was mentioned by respondents for
the first time in 1979 by 1 per cent of the sample. Solvent abuse
awaits an epidemiological study and remains shrouded in a mist of
anecdote, prejudice and myth as to the extent of its use or its long-
term effects.

Anecdotal and Unsystematic Reports

These come largely from field workers in the helping professions,
education and law (social workers, youth workers, GPs, teachers
and the police), from the mass media, as well as 'the autocratic
utterances by "name" and "fame" persons of scientific repute in
an area somewhat tangential to the field of drug abuse' (Harms,
1965). Half truths, misinterpretations, generalisations from a few
sensational incidents flourish in the publicity given by press, television and radio. Such reports may cause anxiety in parents and

set young people wondering if they are the only ones not involved in drug abuse. An unhealthy interest is generated, focusing on the dangerous and the unusual, rather than looking at the central issues of an informed choice on the use of drugs and medicine with reference to health and disease, as well as their social and recreational use.

Clearly individual clinical case studies and limited information on referral trends from particular areas or agencies are of interest, and add to our understanding of drug abuse, but it is dangerous to generalise from this selected sample to the population at large.

Factors Influencing Use of Drugs by Adolescents

Knowledge

This comes from a variety of sources, and may add up to a fragmented and contradictory collection of facts and opinions. The oral folklore of the peer group may be an important source of information on effects of drugs, where they can be obtained and how to use them. Sensational accounts of drug abuse in the press and media may be important in spreading knowledge of current fashions in drug abuse. By creating the impression that most teenagers are using a particular drug, perceptions may be altered, causing an increase in experimentation — what am I missing if so many others are using it? Information may come from adults in authority — parents, teachers, youth leaders. The context in which the information is given may have implications for future use of drugs. Are the facts and opinions provided by the adults congruent with their own use of drugs as seen by the adolescents? Are drugs discussed in the context of health education, including the variety of reasons why we use drugs, or is it just an alarmist presentation of drug abuse, likely to cause anxiety and possibly increase the chances that drugs will be used?

Motivation

Adolescence is the transition stage from childhood to adulthood, the end result being integration and acceptance into adult society. Particular problems arising out of the major themes of rebellion against adult care-givers, hostility to adult conventions and a rejection of their values are often over-emphasised. There are many exceptions to this picture, and the majority make the transition without serious turmoil or trouble (see Rutter, 1979). However, there are a number of characteristics of adolescence pertinent to any interpretation of drug abuse in young people.

Emergent sexuality and changes in hormone production have implications for assertiveness, sex drive and emotional development. Marked mood swings become more common, and possibly associated with fluctuations between childish and adult behaviour. Impulsive changes in attitudes and behaviour may also occur. Although most are still generally happy, moodiness and periods of misery are more frequent than in early childhood. Learning to cope with these bouts of misery may lead to experiments with drugs as a possible escape by altering moods or blotting out reality for a time.

In psychological terms Erikson (1965) suggests that the major task of adolescence is to establish a personal identity. In our society adolescence is an ill-defined period between childhood freedom and adult responsibilities. Development is from dependency to independency, from accepting the views of adults to establishing a personal point of view. It is a period of trying on roles, probing the possible alternatives. What sorts of person can I be? What sort of person do I want to be?

This search for an identity distinct from the family group can cause feelings of anxiety and insecurity that the use of drugs may help to reduce. Peer group relationships, values and activities can be a source of support outside the family during the search for an independent self-identity. The peer group will depend on shared activities to bolster unity, and self-esteem may be dependent to some degree on group acceptance. Conformity to group values is the price to pay for group acceptance, even if it means the use of drugs which an individual disapproves of and may not wish to take.

Although peer group influences increase during adolescence, especially as guides to current situational dilemmas, there is still a tendency to turn to parents for guidance on basic principles and major issues (Rutter, 1979). Peer group influence is at its strongest in areas of fashion and leisure activities. As leisure activities with peers increase, shared activities with parents decrease, with increasing opportunity for peer group pressure to influence behaviour. The authoritarian style of the hero leader in teenage groups may mean that one individual determines group conventions, and if he introduces drugs to the group, it is likely that members will use them.

Efforts to establish self-identity and independence may involve challenging not just parents, but teachers and other adults in their standards — tastes in hair style, clothes, politics may be used to bolster feelings of separateness. The parameters on which these challenges occur will depend on the importance invested in them by society. Personal appearance, music, the role of personal transport and the use of drugs are all major themes in our society. These will be reinterpreted by adolescents, and fashioned in a way to emphasise their separateness from adult values before the process of reintegration into mainstream adult life begins. Drug use is just one set of behaviours in this differentiation of adolescent and adult activities. Glue sniffing seems to be a good example of a drug used almost exclusively by adolescents, and amongst its attractions are the facts that adults neither indulge in the practice nor do they know as much about it as the teenage practitioners.

Finally, these physiological and psychological developments may lead to a probing of personal strengths and weaknesses in a variety of ways — a testing out of self, and comparing self with others in the peer group. This testing out of personal limits may be accentuated by dares and the excitement generated by risk-taking activities. The risk-taking aspect of drugs use may be heightened by sensational treatments in the press and by adult over-reaction to the practice. Skiing, hang-gliding, rock climbing, motor cycle racing, sport generally and the use of permitted drugs such as alcohol, are all socially accepted ways of satisfying these needs. Stealing and joy riding in cars, playing chicken on roads or railways, gang fights, muggings and the illicit use of drugs are all anti-social ways of meeting these needs. Which set of activities is chosen seems to depend on money, skills, access to resources and a wish to identify with a particular sub-group.

The attraction of the new and the role of crazes in teenage life are well known. In the context of drug use it would be expected that there would be fairly rapid changes over time in substances used. Amphetamines were commonly used in the 1960s and the use of narcotics and LSD seemed to increase in the late 1960s before falling back in the early 1970s. The use of solvents seems to have increased in recent years, and doubtless there will be a move to other substances in the next few years.

Access to Resources

Substances must be reasonably cheap and widely available if they are to be abused by young people. There may be legal restrictions to their sale — a complete ban or sold only on licensed premises at certain times with age restrictions in force. Can these restrictions be easily avoided? Can the substance be obtained by theft, shoplifting or from within the homes of the teenagers? What are the distribution networks? Parties, discos, youth clubs, regular meeting places of truants such as amusement arcades or large indoor shopping precincts are all likely places where drugs can be obtained and distributed.

Opportunity for Use

The most important factor is lack of supervision with little chance of disturbance or interference by parents, teachers or other adults. Access to unsupervised buildings or areas offering privacy and reasonable comfort are an added bonus. Parents on holiday, warm weather and light nights offer greater opportunities than the cold dark winter nights when it is more likely that both adults and teenagers will stay at home. For the practice to continue for a prolonged time without detection by parents or other caring adults, a low level of care and disorganised social structure is necessary. It is possible that boredom, caused by few alternative activities to fill available time, might be a factor. School holidays and an increase in unemployment with little money for leisure activities might cause an increase in drug use.

Cultural Context

We have seen how common is the use of drugs in Britain, and any consideration of drug use by adolescents will only make sense when looked at against this wider context. Attitudes of parents and teachers to the use of drugs, and even more important, the actual use they make of drugs, is another factor in determining use. There is a clear link between parents using medically prescribed stimulants or tranquillisers, and their offspring using illegal drugs. Children of mothers taking tranquillisers daily are three times more likely to use illegal drugs than children whose parents are nonusers. Watson (1979) found a link between solvent use by teenagers and parental drunkenness. Similar findings for use of tobacco and alcohol have been reported.

Adult Reactions to Drug Abuse by Adolescents

The role of a parent, and to a lesser extent that of a teacher, is to provide a secure, emotional base for the developing child, and to create a protective environment in which opportunities for independence and exploration can occur within the context of socialisation. There is uncertainty in the minds of adults about the capabilities of children, a desire to see them as independent people, but also a fear of the physical and psychological harm that may result from autonomy.

There is ambivalence, too, on the part of the adolescent, who may question parental decisions and values, struggle to exercise autonomy, but often fall back on the old dependency relationship in times of stress, so reinforcing adult doubts about the capabilities of the young person. Parents themselves will vary in their attitudes to independence, with differences between overt and covert actions. They may dislike the clash between family and peer group values, and undermine the uncertain independence of the adolescent. Similar disputes will occur in school between teachers and teenagers. Mutual expressions of puzzlement and bewilderment may be felt by adult and adolescent at the actions, attitudes and values of the other. Each may find it increasingly difficult and trying to understand the other, with an increase in tension between them.

Adult reactions to drugs will depend on many factors, but whether or not they use the drug themselves will influence how they deal with the young person. Parental or teacher reaction to a child drunk with alcohol is likely to be very different from that of a child delirious from glue-sniffing. The range of reactions may include some of the following:

(1) Ridicule and amusement, leaving the adolescent feeling immature, childish and silly. This may work in the short term, but if used frequently may cause deep resentment. The results are likely to be a retreat to the safety of the peer group, thus spending less time with parents, and a gaining in support and reinforcement from the peer group for the values being ridiculed by the adults.

(2) Shock-horror sensationalism, highlighting the dangers and risks involved, assuming that experimentation will inevitably and inexorably lead to the use of 'hard' drugs and long-term addiction. By emphasising the dangers, the attractiveness of drug use as a risk-taking experience may grow, increasing the chances of further use.

(3) A major explosion of wrath and hysteria, using threats of punishments that cannot be carried out. This may well cause resentment and anger, making it less likely that parents can offer

positive help that will be accepted by the teenager.

(4) Silence, ignoring the problem, hoping that it will just go away. This may be interpreted as covert collusion in approving the practice, or as disinterestedness, both making it more likely that drug use will continue.

(5) Talking with, not at, the child in a calm way. Listening to what he has to say rather than interrogating. When you have a clear picture of what is going on, let the child know your views, but make it clear you want to help improve the situation and that you are prepared to consult and co-operate with outside agencies if necessary. In this way it is likely that many of the child's worries and concerns will be surfaced. If parents or teachers can't provide sufficient information and support, they can make use of other agencies. In this atmosphere of co-operation the chances of achieving a satisfactory outcome are high.

Prerequisites to a Solution

Throughout this discussion it has been stressed that any behaviour has a multifactorial causation (see Figure 8.2). We each have our own hypotheses as to why people indulge in certain activities, and these hypotheses are often simplistic, imply unitary causation, and are held either without or despite evidence. Until we can put aside our prejudices it is unlikely that we will be able to analyse the important factors causing and maintaining drug use in an indiviual or group. Without this analysis any attempts to reduce drug abuse are unlikely to succeed.

The anger and anxiety of parents and teachers dealing with the drug users needs to be acknowledged. The ambivalence in how they think about and treat adolescents needs to be accepted. We must separate the activities that parents and teachers indulge in to reduce their own anxiety from activities that offer positive help for the drug user. There is a need to keep a sense of proportion. Most cases will be the 'one-off' or short-term experimental use, and as Harms (1965) wrote, 'In most cases we are likely to be dealing with a contempory "Rite de Passage", and should be careful not to fixate it by clumsy handling of the situation'.

Before deciding on an intervention strategy, establish the facts. Find out who is using what and by what method. How long has the drug been used? How often and with whom is it being used? This

Figure 8.2: Causative Influences on Behaviour — an Interactive, Multifactorial Approach

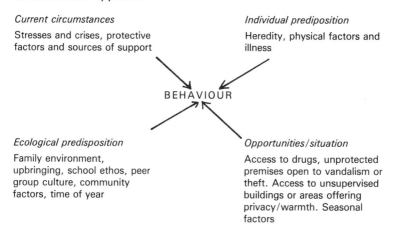

Current circumstances

Stresses and crises, protective factors and sources of support

Individual prediposition

Heredity, physical factors and illness

BEHAVIOUR

Ecological predisposition

Family environment, upbringing, school ethos, peer group culture, community factors, time of year

Opportunities/situation

Access to drugs, unprotected premises open to vandalism or theft. Access to unsupervised buildings or areas offering privacy/warmth. Seasonal factors

is the difficult stage that often leads to confrontations between adults and adolescents. Parents and many teachers come into contact with drug abuse only rarely, and may feel ignorant about the drugs used, their effects and dangers. There are numerous books available written for such people (Rice, 1980; Willis, 1973) and Figure 8.3 shows an information sheet prepared for teachers to help them establish the facts in cases of solvent abuse.

Having established the facts it is important to decide who has the problem: the drug-using child, the involved adult, or both. Adults, especially parents and teachers, must accept that they are important behavioural models for the child. Are they using medicines and drugs in a sensible way? If not are they prepared to join with the child in an attempt to change drug use patterns?

Possible Interventions

For a young abuser with good family support who is using drugs in an experimental way, disapproval and mild punishment in a caring atmosphere will probably be sufficient to control the problem — treat the child as naughty. If use is occurring within a group, co-operation between parents will increase the chances of getting over the problem, and can be a useful source of support. Similarly, if a school has an outbreak of drug abuse, consultation with

Figure 8.3: Dealing with Sniffers — Establishing the Facts

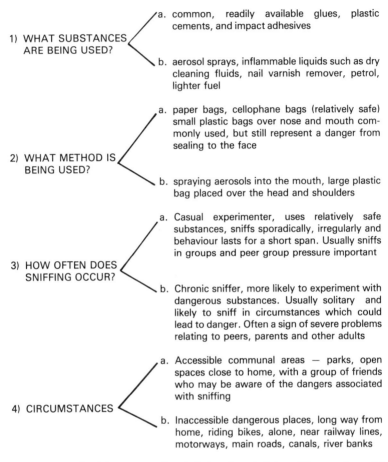

1) WHAT SUBSTANCES ARE BEING USED?

a. common, readily available glues, plastic cements, and impact adhesives

b. aerosol sprays, inflammable liquids such as dry cleaning fluids, nail varnish remover, petrol, lighter fuel

2) WHAT METHOD IS BEING USED?

a. paper bags, cellophane bags (relatively safe) small plastic bags over nose and mouth commonly used, but still represent a danger from sealing to the face

b. spraying aerosols into the mouth, large plastic bag placed over the head and shoulders

3) HOW OFTEN DOES SNIFFING OCCUR?

a. Casual experimenter, uses relatively safe substances, sniffs sporadically, irregularly and behaviour lasts for a short span. Usually sniffs in groups and peer group pressure important

b. Chronic sniffer, more likely to experiment with dangerous substances. Usually solitary and likely to sniff in circumstances which could lead to danger. Often a sign of severe problems relating to peers, parents and other adults

4) CIRCUMSTANCES

a. Accessible communal areas — parks, open spaces close to home, with a group of friends who may be aware of the dangers associated with sniffing

b. Inaccessible dangerous places, long way from home, riding bikes, alone, near railway lines, motorways, main roads, canals, river banks

NOTE: Alternative 'a' represents the relatively safe end of the sniffing spectrum, 'b' represents the more dangerous end. It is important to note that these alternatives do represent extremes of a continuum, not a tight, exclusive taxonomy of sniffing. The more 'b' alternative is used, the more dangerous the behaviour.

parents to ensure school and home work together will make for a satisfactory outcome. Realistic aims should be set for the child or group. If a break from a circle of acquaintances is needed, careful structuring and support to gain entry to other clubs, activities and to establish new friendships may be needed. Changes of this nature are not easily imposed, and the teenager needs to be convinced of the necessity for such action, and to accept the proposals.

The decision whether or not to involve a professional agency is important, and will depend on the skills and knowledge of the parents and teachers involved, as well as the extent of use and type of drug being used by the teenager. Trained workers skilled in discussing personal matters and with experience of dealing with drug abuse are in a good position to assess the situation and suggest possible courses of action. Professionals can offer help, but adequate motivation for change on the part of both parent and child is necessary.

Preventative measures rather than crisis intervention are widely discussed with reference to drug abuse, but their effectiveness is rarely evaluated. The concept of different aims for different target groups is a useful starting point in considering prevention of drug abuse (see Figure 8.4). In non-users the aim may be to prevent the

Figure 8.4: Aims of Preventative Health Education on Drug Abuse

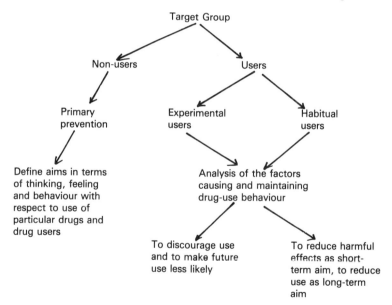

occurrence of drug abuse. For experimental users the aim may be to discourage use, to help them through the stage with least damage and to make future use less likely. For hardened users secondary prevention aimed at reducing the dangers involved may be the short-term aim. Such a programme is often misinterpreted as representing a pro-drug stance. However, this aim of reducing harm is only the first stage, and the long-term aim would be to reduce drug use, and finally to stop it completely.

Education on drug use is full of difficulties, and the effects of teaching about drugs are likely to be mixed rather than either preventative or counterpreventative. Attitudes to drugs may change one way, whilst attitudes to drug users may change the other way. A lesson on cannabis may lead to an urge to experiment with this exciting substance, yet also confirm opinions that other cannabis users are lazy, foolish and should be prosecuted for taking the drug. Attitudes are only one factor that influence behaviour, and a change in attitude does not necessarily lead to a change in behaviour. Learning that alcohol impairs perceptions, motor control and judgement may lead to an attitude that it is wrong to drink and drive, yet the individual may continue to drive after drinking alcohol. The effects of drug education may be specific to a particular drug: it is possible to change an individual's intention to take LSD, making him unlikely to accept the drug if it is offered, without changing his response to accept cannabis if it is offered (Dorn and Thompson, 1976; Dorn, 1981).

It appears from the small amount of research evidence available that it is relatively easy to increase pupils' knowledge about drugs, and possible to make attitudes more anti-drug. But neither knowledge nor attitudes necessarily hold implications for whether drugs will be used or refused in particular situations. Behaviour is a response to a specific situation, with many other factors involved, and not just an application of a general rule or attitude about one aspect of the situation. It is easy to be anti-drug in the health education lesson, rather more difficult to resist social pressure to use a drug at a party.

One approach sponsored by TACADE (1981) is to look at ways of increasing personal autonomy in relation to drug use. A skilful decision-maker will have more personal autonomy and greater control over life's events. Learning decision-making skills may increase the possibility of an individual achieving what they value as important, and make it less likely that they will be diverted by other pressures. The teaching pack consists of pupil material and teacher notes, and is aimed at secondary school pupils.

Conclusion

In many societies drugs are widely used by adults for a variety of purposes. Adolescent use of drugs is affected by this environment as well as by particular characteristics of adolescence. Concern over drug use by young people is just one aspect of adult anxiety that young people will fail to make the transition from childhood dependence to the status of an independent individual integrated into adult society. There are few facts on the extent and frequency of illicit drug use by adolescents. What is known does not suggest a rising epidemic of drug abuse, and the majority are not involved in the illicit use of drugs. For those who do become involved it is likely to be a passing phase best dealt with by the parents, teachers or other adults who know the child well. Most short-term drug experimentation is not a symptom of personal pathology, and will only rarely lead to major problems. Short-term counselling may be needed in some instances. Habitual drug abusers and experimental users of narcotics and LSD should be taken more seriously and are likely to require professional intervention to help both parent and adolescent.

By reacting in the wrong way adults can increase the chances of drug abuse continuing, and cause problems for the adolescent. Spreading negative stereotypes of drug-users — addicts, criminals, social incompetents — may be self-fulfilling prophecies, confirming adult prejudice and making it more likely that the young person will continue to use drugs.

9 WORKING WITH PUPILS WHO REFUSE TO ATTEND SCHOOL

Phil Budgell

The irregular pupil has generally a weakly mother who requires a great deal of help. She has a number of delicate brothers and sisters who require a wonderful amount of nursing. She is very liable to catch cold and is a martyr to sore heads. Washing day occurs twice a week and half the family is kept to assist. The irregular pupil is blessed with many relations near and far off and if a father's second cousin happens to visit them the whole family is kept at home in consequence. John is absent today because he has to go with his father's dinner and Mary will be absent tomorrow if she has to go to the shop — for two red herrings perhaps. These are not exaggerations. (George Leith, Greenock School Board, 1877)

Introduction

That there are children who habitually stay away from school is a fact that has attracted considerable attention in both the mass media and the more serious academic literature. Many of these accounts give the impression that non-attendance can be satisfactorily 'explained' in simplistic terms and that strategies for dealing with the problem follow logically from such 'explanations'. Unfortunately these common-sense explanations rarely constitute an explanation in any real sense — they are frequently little more than partial descriptions of some detail of a small population of children who don't go to school. This chapter is based upon work carried out at the Sheaf Centre — an action research project established in Sheffield LEA, the aim of which was to contribute to the Authority's understanding of non-attendance. But first this work must be put into the general context of non-attendance.

Non-attendance — the Problem

The vast majority of pupils of secondary school age, up to 16 years, are expected to attend. Exceptions include those whose parents have arranged alternative education for them, which appears to be a small, but increasing population. Such parents (and their young-sters) are often disenchanted with the school system and arrange provision either as individuals, or collectively, which they believe provides a better education than that otherwise available. Other exceptions include the chronically ill (although they would be expected to receive schooling either in hospitals, or from teachers visiting the home).

However, a significant minority of pupils who are supposed to be attending school do not do so. Some might stop attending alto-gether, others attend on certain days, or for certain subjects, while others have the odd days off. Over recent years a number of studies have been carried out which have investigated aspects of incidence of non-attendance, relationship with school and home factors and methods of treatment, (see Hersov and Berg, 1980; Galloway, 1982; Reid and Kendall, 1982). These general findings will be considered and then the results of a study of a centre for non-attenders will be presented to amplify meaning.

Definition

The first problem with this topic is that of definition. There has been a general division between pupils who 'won't' and 'can't' attend school. The former group is considered to be making a rational decision (albeit unlawful). They might be generally bored, or perhaps 'wag it' to watch a football match. The second group comprises those pupils who are considered to have a problem. This issue has been discussed in Chapter 5 when school refusal and school phobia were considered. In brief, such pupils are thought to basically want to go to school but anxiety at leaving home, or induced by school itself, or even the journey there is causing an aversion, and so non-attendance.

Such a dichotomy, however, does not stand up to scrutiny. Some pupils may want to attend school, but are kept off because, for example, they have no shoes (something which still happens), or to help with younger siblings. Debates on the issue of non-attendance have often been confused, especially when held in the press, because of these definitional problems. Currently it is common to divide the group of pupils who 'won't' attend into two sub-groups: those who do not attend but whose parents do not know this (truants), and those whose parents either condone absence or are powerless to enforce attendance.

Incidence

Given these problems of definition, rates of incidence reported in the literature must be examined with some care. Galloway (1976) in a study of Sheffield schools reports that about 1,000 pupils (of all ages) were absent for at least 50 per cent of possible absences per year (about one per cent of the school population). However incidence varied with age. Only 0.5 per cent of primary school pupils had such a rate of absenteeism, while four per cent of pupils in their final year of compulsory education were included. When Galloway considered the categories of the absentees he found that, for secondary schools, only six per cent were in the school phobia, psychosomatic illness category, eleven per cent were truants, while the majority were absent with their parents' consent or knowledge, or the parents couldn't enforce attendance.

Reid and Kendall (1982) in their review of several studies report similar findings. They report that the results of a national study of absenteeism on one day, revealed that about 9.9 per cent of pupils were away from school. Most had genuine reasons, but 2.2 per cent of pupils had no legitimate reason for absence.

Family and Ecological Factors

Galloway (1982) presents compelling evidence for the majority of *persistent* absentees coming from the most disadvantaged sector of the population. He compared three sub-groups of persistent non-attenders, and a control group of regular attenders. He reports that the regular attenders lived in the same areas but in significantly less disadvantaged conditions. Further support for this finding is reviewed by Reid and Kendall (1982). They compare the findings of the National Child Development Study when the children were at different ages, and show there is a consistent relationship between rates of attendance and social class. At 16 years, for example, the proportion of non-attenders was two to three times higher among pupils whose fathers were manual workers.

Many family factors contribute to the definition of 'disadvantage', in addition to those which are related to poverty (e.g. low income, poor housing). For example, the persistent absentees in Galloway's study were significantly more likely to be concerned about the mother's health. In fact a very high 74 per cent were concerned, as compared with only 24 per cent of the regular attenders.

The School

Schools are also known to be an important factor in absenteeism. Rutter *et al.* (1979) investigated fifth form pupils in London secondary schools and found that the rates of poor attendance varied between the schools studies from six to 26 per cent. A study in South Wales by Reynolds *et al.* (1980) also presented evidence for rates of absenteeism being related to processes within the pupils' schools. Both studies suffer from the problem of deciding whether the school factors are the *cause* or the *result* of rates of attendance, but it seems reasonable to conclude that, while both are likely, it is the former to which we must attend.

Action

If non-attendance is seen as a problem originating within the child or family, it seems reasonable to treat the child or family. If, however, it appears that the school is a contributor to the problem, there should also be a focus on what is happening within the school. The evidence reviewed here suggests that both views are correct but not sufficient. There is a strong relationship between social disadvantage and absenteeism, but also between school process variables and absenteeism.

However, the work of Berg (1980b) has shown that, whatever the cause of the non-attendance, those pupils who were brought to court and received a legal sanction (adjournment of the case and reappearance in court), attended better subsequently than those who received support from supervision by the social services department.

Non-attendance — an overview

The studies reviewed here have revealed that non-attendance is by no means a rare event. Whether it is seen as a problem depends on the school; or the parent or child. For example, one mother asked for her fifth year son to be seen by an educational psychologist because she had discovered a week's truancy. An inspection of the class register revealed that he was by far the best attender. At interview, the boy made it clear that he was 'got at' by his friends because his attendance was a sign of deviance!

However, while many youngsters miss some school, persistent

absenteeism is a characteristic related to severe and multiple disadvantage. Some remedies are beyond the education system for such pupils. However, there have been initiatives both within mainstream secondary schools, and special centres, which have addressed the needs of these youngsters positively. The main section in this chapter describes one such initiative, and the lessons that can be learned.

Sheaf Centre

As an action-research project the very existence of the Sheaf Centre acknowledged the lack of understanding of the problems of children who refused to attend school. This lack of understanding was specifically reflected in the quite deliberate decision by the LEA not to provide artificial guidelines which might constrain or deflect the work of the Centre. Thus, in an unspecified way the overt aims of the Centre were to contribute to the body of knowledge and understanding of the problems of non-attendance and to 'help' a small number of children to reintegrate into a mainstream comprehensive school.

Despite an administrative setting which placed few constraints upon the functioning of the Centre, certain decisions had to be taken in order that the Centre could commence work. It had to be decided, for example, whether the Centre was to be a neighbourhood resource or a resource for the whole city. Preliminary discussions with the Education Social Work Service revealed that within the neighbourhood of the Centre there was a considerable number of pupils presenting attendance problems. On the assumptions, therefore, that it would

(a) be easy for both parents and children to get to the Centre and,

(b) that it would also be easy for the staff to visit the children's homes when necessary,

it was decided, somewhat arbitrarily, to restrict the Centre to a neighbourhood resource offering help to pupils who lived within a mile of the Centre. On further investigation this *ad hoc* catchment area for the Centre was found to lie almost totally within the joint catchment area of five of the city's comprehensive schools. The boundary to the catchment area of the Sheaf Centre was modified, therefore, to coincide with the catchment areas of those five schools. This modification made particular sense in the light of the major objective of reintegrating pupils back into mainstream schooling — that is to say it facilitated reintegration because it restricted the number of schools with which it was necessary to establish and maintain close working relationships.

The reintegration of pupils back into mainstream schools also determined one of the referral criteria for pupils: in order that there should at least be the prospect of reintegration it was decided that only pupils in their first three years of secondary education should be considered, and that pupils should be reintegrated, at the latest, by the beginning of their fourth year.

By this stage, the administrative criteria (i.e. age and address) for establishing the client population had been set. Determining the educational/psychological criteria initially proved to be much more difficult but in the end proved remarkably easy — there weren't any. Discussions with social workers, psychologists, education welfare officers and teachers clearly showed the lack of knowledge and understanding in the field of non-attendance. There were often extensive case files on individual children and families but there were no obvious educational or psychological factors which could parameterise a homogeneous client population. It was decided, therefore, to substitute yet another administrative criterion — the children had to have attended school for less than 50 per cent of the time for at least one term in order to be considered for the Centre.

Essentially, therefore, an action-research project which was established in order to contribute to the understanding of the educational and psychological needs of children presenting major attendance problems at school defined its client group in purely administrative terms. The decision not to invoke educational/psychological criteria, however, had a face validity in that it would be difficult to comment on the educational/psychological needs of the population of children presenting attendance problems if that population were already restricted on educational/psychological criteria. It did, however, pose difficulties in both the ongoing work with pupils once they were attending the Centre and in the later attempts to reintegrate pupils.

The Pupils

In the discussions which took place prior to the Centre actually opening, the objective, as far as the staff were concerned, was to establish the criteria which might isolate the client group. For the other professionals (i.e. the social workers, the psychologists, the EWOs and the teachers) the discussions necessarily focused not so much on issues relating to the nature of the client group, but on individual children whose behaviour and attendance had proved unchanged despite their considerable efforts. Thus by the time the Centre was ready to open, the key professionals in the area had a hard and clear view of which pupils made up the initial group of children. This is in no way to suggest that it was an inappropriate group of chidren — they were clearly manifesting intractable problems for the professionals involved. It is more to suggest that the initial client group was almost self-evident to the key workers outside the Centre, the very visibility of this group of children being a result of the severity of their problems.

This presented an immediate dilemma for the staff of the Centre. As a new experimental project it might have been advantageous to start with less intractable problems. And yet the credibility of the Centre and its staff in the eyes of the key workers would depend on the Centre accepting their clearly defined group. Needless to say this group had to become the first group of pupils.

In retrospect the first group of pupils and the regime established by the Centre established a 'conventional wisdom' amongst the key workers of which pupils it would be appropriate to bring forward for consideration. It must be said, however, that like many a conventional wisdom or 'common-sense understanding' it was partial, incoherent and inconsistent; and more particularly it changed over time or more accurately with the nature of the problems being faced by the key workers.

The pupils referred to the Centre did present at one level a fairly consistent picture of education and social dysfunction. In terms of their formal intelligence (as assessed using the Wechsler Intelligence Scale for Children) the mean IQ for the pupils was in the low average range — although there were two pupils of very high intelligence. More interestingly, however, there was an average of at least 15 points difference between the verbal and the performance scores, the performance scores being consistently higher, even for the most able pupils. For one pupil there was 50 points difference between the performance and verbal scores — with particular scale scores (e.g. information and vocabulary) in the ESN(S) range.

These difficulties in the formal intelligence area were also reflected in the pupils' literacy and numeracy. All but the most able pupils demonstrated problems in reading — a small number of pupils at the Centre being fundamentally illiterate.

The pupils demonstrated a marked inability to form and maintain stable social relationships — although it must be accepted that the regime established and the physical setting of the Centre meant that the pupils' social problems were visible to the staff in a way which is not true for pupils in a large comprehensive. That is to say, a regime which set out to allow the pupils to be individuals in their own right and allowed for more close personal interactions between adults and pupils inevitably led to the pupils' problems as individuals being particularly manifest.

Similarly, the family dynamics of the Sheaf Centre families were visible to the staff in a way which pupils' families are not normally visible to teachers (Budgell, 1982). It is also true to say that many of these families indicated the most severe level of social dysfunction.

As the population of pupils at the Centre began to increase the most evident feature was the level of social disadvantage suffered by the children and their families. Of the children who came to the Centre:

in 75 per cent of families the head of the household was unemployed;
65 per cent were single parent families;
60 per cent of the homes were damp;
in 55 per cent of the families the head of the household was sick;
40 per cent of the households had no indoor sanitation;
the families averaged five children per family indicating overcrowding in the houses in which they lived.

Furthermore, a report produced by the Department of Planning and Design of Sheffield MDC delineated the area around the Sheaf Centre as a priority area within the inner city. Similarly the Corporate Management Unit of Sheffield MDC in their 'Sheffield Household Survey' showed that the Sheaf Centre was situated in the largest area of severe multiple deprivation in Sheffield.

Case Studies on Individual Children

It had already been suggested that the referral and selection criteria

Figure 9.1: Barbara — A Summary of Her Circumstances

		GRAVE RISK	CONSIDERABLE DISTRESS	SOME DISCOMFORT	LIMITED STRENGTHS	SUBSTANTIAL ASSETS
INDIVIDUALS	PARENTS AND ADULTS		▲				Father is a very heavy drinker, Mother pretending her home situation doesn't exist.
	CHILDREN	▲					No control exercised on her out of school and is progressively opting out of the family.
FAMILY	QUALITY OF CARE AND RELATIONSHIP	▲					Only the bare physical needs are being met within the family.
	HOME AND FINANCIAL CIRCUMSTANCES				▲		The financial resources of the family are certainly adequate to meet their needs.
COMMUNITY	SOCIAL NETWORK				▲		Older daughter provides refuge for mother and sister.
	GENERAL ENVIRONMENTAL CONDITIONS	▲					The house is currently unfit to live in. It is damp, filthy and lets in water badly when it rains.
SCHOOL	ACADEMIC ABILITY AND ATTAINMENTS			▲			Barbara has average ability but even so rarely achieves her potential.
	BEHAVIOUR AND ADJUSTMENT	▲					Her behaviour is such that she risks being suspended if she returns to comprehensive.

for pupils who were considered for the Sheaf Centre were, in terms of the pupils' educational needs, fairly arbitrary. That is to say, non-attendance at school does not isolate a group of children with similar educational needs. The range of those educational needs can best be illustrated by considering in some detail the case histories of two of the pupils: 'Barbara' and 'John'.

Barbara

In the unsystematic discussion which preceded the opening of the Centre, Barbara was one of the first pupils who we were asked to consider for admission — she also remained at the Centre long after the other children who comprised that first group had returned to comprehensive school. Hopefully, the reasons why Barbara remained at the Centre and never returned to comprehensive school will be made apparent in this case study (see Figure 9.1).

From the moment of her arrival at the Centre Barbara was almost continually the cause of considerable concern for the staff at the Centre. When the first group of children arrived at the Centre Barbara and Gwen, the other girl in the group (John's older sister — see next case history) formed an immediate friendship. They talked to and about each other as if their friendship was the only relationship that either had ever had. After two weeks another girl (who should have started at the same time as Barbara and Gwen, but with whose family it had been extremely difficult to establish contact) started at the Centre. This girl was totally rejected by Barbara who behaved as if to ensure that the newcomer could in no way threaten her 'one and only' friendship. Unfortunately Barbara's behaviour led directly to there being considerable difficulties in integrating the newcomer into the daily routines of the Centre — difficulties which were never really overcome.

The next intake of girls however, was far more robust than the previous 'newcomer' and they established themselves without any real assistance from the staff. One of the girls in this group totally severed the relationship between Barbara and Gwen without any real reaction from Barbara. This led the staff to interpret Barbara's earlier behaviour as being a function of the smallness of the initial group and the fact that the 'newcomer' was the first new person to come to the group. Subsequent events, however, demanded a reappraisal of this explanation — every new girl was subjected to Barbara's hostility and rejection, and her attempts to encourage rejection by the other girls. Only the most secure newcomers were able to weather Barbara's rejection and 'testing out' without considerable help from the staff.

As has already been indicated Barbara was only rarely not the focus of concern for the staff. Her effect on the daily routines of the Centre were such that when she gave no immediate cause for concern this itself became a point for discussion. Barbara's difficulties within the Centre are particularly illustrated by her relationships with the male members of staff. She, at different times, directed her aggression, abuse and total rejection at each one. The focus of her disdain at any particular time would be sworn at, openly abused in front of and to other pupils and other members of staff and goaded into overt rejection of herself. On the other hand, she could totally ignore that person; for example, she would be charming and friendly to all the other staff, ask if she could make coffee for the staff and then deliberately make one less cup of coffee than was necessary.

The other members of Barbara's family also gave considerable cause for concern in their own right — not merely in terms of their relationships with Barbara. Her father had, in her mother's words, 'a drink problem'. There was no evidence to suggest that he was an alcoholic, but his daily intake of alcohol was such that he was incapable of playing an effective role within the family — a problem that led to Barbara's mother leaving the household for short periods and threatening on a number of occasions to leave her husband altogether. Barbara's older brother frequently joined her father in drinking bouts and there was some evidence that Barbara and her mother were physically abused when both men were drunk. The effects of the assaults were never physically serious but they were of course symptomatic of the deeper problems in the family. The behaviour of the adult males in the family could have been a partial explanation of Barbara's attitude and behaviour towards male members of staff.

Barbara also had an older sister about whom little was known but who was a significant member of the family in that she frequently provided a refuge for both Barbara and her mother when their home situation became totally impossible. When the relationship between Barbara's mother and father was very bad then her mother, at one stage, used the Centre as a 'drop-in centre' in order to talk about the family situation. It became evident, however, that Barbara's mother was progressively seeking more of her personal satisfaction away from home. What also became apparent, and this was very difficult to make clear, was the extent to which she began to talk about the difficulties at home and with her children in the 'third person' — it was almost as if they were nothing to do with her and she was a professional describing someone else's home situation. At this time Barbara's mother also secured full-time employment and began to take a real pride in her own appearance — she would arrive at the Centre very well dressed and with frequent changes in outfit. The state of dress of her children meanwhile suggested that she regarded her new income as being for her own personal use — all the children in the household were inadequately dressed with poor-quality clothing which was usually filthy.

There were two other brothers in the family. One, ten months younger than Barbara, appeared in court and was found guilty of setting fire to a motor bike. As a result of this court appearance he was made the subject of a supervision order. His mother's attitude towards this encounter with the court was that 'he was mad anyway' and that the involvement of the social worker allocated to the case was limited to her son who had to be punished.

Barbara's youngest brother was offered an emergency place (see below) at the local nursery school and was found to be totally untoilet trained — a task which the nursery accomplished within a few weeks. Barbara's mother limited her involvement to the very basic physical needs of her youngest child — but he was treated as a much younger baby and was fed, watered and clothed.

All this reinforced the impression that Barbara's mother 'bracketed-off' her domestic situation as if to deny its existence and that she 'lived' for her job and her social life outside the home — situations in which there was reason to believe that she was more successful.

The Family Situation. The situation in which Barbara lived was so complex and so potentially damaging that the extent of her problems at home only gradually became apparent — although it is of course possible that they deteriorated while Barbara was at the Centre. Her circumstances are probably best appreciated, therefore, if they are presented as they became apparent to the staff at the Centre.

At the beginning of her second term Barbara was absent for about two weeks. Her father informed the staff that Barbara's mother had left home and had taken Barbara and the baby with her. Her father, who was considerably drunk at the time, would not (or could not) say where his wife and children were. After a number of home visits it was eventually established that they had gone to live at the elder daughter's home at the other end of the city. Despite frequent attempts being made it was not possible to contact Barbara or her mother. At the beginning of the third week, however, Barbara returned to the Centre and explained that her mother had decided to return home.

After the midsummer break Barbara was again absent for a week but her mother, without having to be contacted first, informed the Centre that Barbara was on holiday with her elder sister. There was, however, some evidence to suggest that Barbara was being left to babysit for her mother and sister while they went out together. For the rest of that summer term Barbara had few isolated absences and visits to the home were received in a friendly, affable manner by her mother — provided, that is, that her plausible excuses for Barbara's occasional absences were accepted without question. It was over this period that the house, which was already in a poor condition, began to deteriorate even further.

With the reopening of the Centre following the long summer holidays Barbara again did not return and on visiting the home it was discovered that she had been left to look after her baby brother who at that time was less than three years old. Her mother had gone away 'on holiday' and her father and older brother were at work. The basic material provision of the household had, by this time, almost totally disintegrated. There were doors and windows missing and the interior of the house was squalid, filthy and damp. Furthermore there was little adequate food or clothing for the younger children in the family. When it was suggested to Barbara that she could bring her baby brother back to the Centre she was immediately frightened of what her father's reaction would be if he returned home while she wasn't there. Despite her apprehension she returned to the Centre and appeared relieved to have someone else to talk to and to help with the baby. The head of the local nursery school was contacted and despite the fact that the baby was too young she helped immediately by offering to take the baby and Barbara (if she wished to accompany him). The local health visitor was also contacted because of the concern about the condition of the baby: she immediately contacted the duty officer at the NSPCC.

By coincidence Barbara's mother returned home at this point

and Barbara returned to the Centre and attended regularly for the rest of the term. It was during this period that Barbara's mother frequently used the Centre as a 'drop-in centre'. She talked about the deteriorating state of the house (even more windows were missing and the roof now leaked badly) and her relationship with her husband (who was drinking even more heavily).

As a result of the contact with the nursery school Barbara's baby brother was offered a part-time place as a priority admission. Within two days of him starting at the nursery, however, his mother requested a full-time place for him because she had a full-time job. To a large extent it was felt that the nursery were being coerced into offering a full-time place to a child who would normally be considered to be too young. The mother's attitude led to the belief that if full-time provision were not made available then she would make *ad hoc* arrangements and that these would be far less satisfactory than full-time placement in the nursery. It was at this stage that it was becoming more and more apparent that Barbara's mother was opting out of any responsibility for her family.

Further evidence of her mother's attitude was provided when Barbara arrived one Friday and said that the previous evening her mother had gone out to the club and that her father and brother had come home drunk and started to 'bash her about'. Barbara ran away from the house late that night and ended up at the house of another pupil where she had spent the night. Barbara went to her sister's house that night and spent the weekend with her sister. The following Monday she arrived at the Centre and asked if she could contact her mother. It turned out that despite her not having been home since the previous Thursday evening her mother had made no attempt to discover her whereabouts. The following week the same thing had happened but this time Barbara ran straight to her sister's house and refused to go home; a decision in which her mother appeared to take no interest.

It was at this time that Barbara's 12-year-old brother appeared in court, was placed on a supervision order and a social worker was allocated to the family. After the allocation of the social worker there had to be frequent co-operation and consultation. It was as a result of this close co-operation and consultation that any understanding of the problems of this family was reached and any joint decisions were made.

When she returned after the Christmas break it became apparent that Barbara, like her mother, was progressively opting out of the family situation. She slept wherever she was welcome, either at the home of a friend at the Centre or at her sister's home. There was no evidence that she was in immediate moral danger but there was no doubt that the home situation put her 'at risk'. Barbara's mother took no interest in where she slept and made no attempts to ascertain her whereabouts.

It is possible to see Barbara's change in attitude towards the family situation reflected in her attendance at the Centre. In her first four terms at the Centre her termly attendances were 85 per cent, 62 per cent, 68 per cent and 89 per cent. The low attendance figures in the middle terms were a result of demands made upon her by her mother and her sister. This interpretation is given more credence if one makes allowance for the times when her non-attendance was a result of pressure from her family, in which case Barbara attended 87 per cent of the time. This also suggests that despite the difficulties Barbara created, especially for the male members of staff, an adolescent who attended for 87 per cent of the time was saying something very significant about her attitude to the work of the Centre.

Education and Reintegration into a Comprehensive School. As a result of the involvement of a social worker it became possible to hold full discussions of Barbara's needs and not to have to discuss either the provision for her education or her care in isolation. This co-operation was vital because the two are inextricably linked and needed to be discussed together.

In terms of a formal assessment of her cognitive ability Barbara was of at least average intelligence. Using the Wechsler Intelligence Scale for Children she was significantly more able to cope with the practical tests than the tests requiring more abstract verbal reasoning. More informal though more real assessments based upon her work in the Centre indicated that she was capable of sensitive, articulate (though syntactically incorrect) written work and was capable of (though rarely achieved) accurate work appropriate for her age in mathematics. Barbara's problems at school could therefore not be accounted for in terms of formal or informal assessments of her cognitive abilities. They could, however, more reasonably be accounted for in terms of her behavioural responses — for example, she abreacted to male members of staff to such an extent that she was likely to escalate even a minor incident into a full-scale confrontation. Undoubtedly her behaviour was a result

of the stress to which she was subjected at home but in a comprehensive school (had she chosen to attend) she would have provided
and escalated confrontations to such an extent that she would have
been excluded or suspended.

Away from the Centre, Barbara had so few constraints placed
upon her that there was little to modify her 'flight or fight'
response. This aspect of Barbara's behaviour forced a very careful
consideration of the possibility of taking her into care.
Inappropriate provision would have led to her acting out in such a
way that progressively more custodial settings would have to have
been sought. Returning Barbara to a comprehensive school without
her care situation having been resolved would have led rapidly to
failure, but resolution of the care situation via the courts (for
example) would also have led to an unsatisfactory placement. An
alternative strategy had to be found. The strategy finally decided
upon was to consider voluntary care on the basis of an assessment
made at the Sheaf Centre with the full co-operation of the family
social worker, the Centre social worker and the Centre teaching
staff. It was hoped that this community-based assessment, as
opposed to an assessment centre, would lead to the most
appropriate care setting being selected at the most opportune
moment rather than one forced by a court decision or by
suspension from school.

John

John, like Barbara, was one of the first group of pupils to start at
the Centre. He arrived with his sister Gwen and brother Peter and
his difficulties need to be discussed in terms of the whole family
and the relationship between the siblings (see Figure 9.2).

John's parents were unhappily married with a large family —
eight children. They appeared to live separate lives under the same
roof. His mother frequently went out at night with a regular boyfriend, by whom she had had three children. Her boyfriend was
West Indian and despite these children obviously not being his own
John's father and the other children have accepted them into the
household. John's mother appeared in good health despite her
years of childbearing and very poor living conditions. She did,
however (but not surprisingly), give the impression of being
oppressed by her circumstances and saw herself as a martyr to her
family. John's father was a small, frail looking man who had only
worked sporadically. He continued to assert that he was seeking
employment but there seemed little hope of him ever getting a job.

Figure 9.2: John — A Summary of His Circumstances

		GRAVE RISK	CONSIDERABLE DISTRESS	SOME DISCOMFORT	LIMITED STRENGTHS	SUBSTANTIAL ASSETS
I N D I V I D U A L S	PARENTS AND ADULTS		▲ Father worked sporadically in the past but now unemployed. Dominant mother. Very unstable marriage.			
	CHILDREN			▲ Eight children, three youngest have West Indian father but are totally accepted into family. All attend school regularly.		
F A M I L Y	QUALITY OF CARE AND RELATIONSHIP			▲ Parents have caring attitude to children but are inept at providing a stable home.		
	HOME AND FINANCIAL CIRCUMSTANCES	▲ Heavily in debt, largely to Y.E.B. Electricity supply off at present - a common occurrence. House severely overcrowded and dirty.				
C O M M U N I T Y	SOCIAL NETWORK		▲ Very limited. Regular contact with mother's sister 16 year old girl has been living with the family for 8 months.			
	GENERAL ENVIRONMENTAL CONDITIONS			▲ Inner city, run down area. Shabby house in poor repair. Environment had little effect on family.		
S C H O O L	ACADEMIC ABILITY AND ATTAINMENTS	▲ Borderline E.S.N. Literacy and numeracy increased by more than three years in three terms. Still well below average and will have problems.				
	BEHAVIOUR AND ADJUSTMENT				▲ Immature but quiet and friendly. Makes satisfactory relationships with peers and adults.	

There was often friction between the parents and the results of this discord were manifested at the Centre. Gwen was usually the one who mentioned the problems at home but all three children would be subdued and generally depressed for a few days following any conflict. It was also noticeable that at times of stress the children were particularly supportive to each other and could be verbally aggressive in each other's defence.

Both parents, but especially mother, were co-operative with the Centre. They expressed relief and gratitude when their three children were admitted — circumstances at home being particularly fraught at that time. There had been occasions when Gwen and Peter would become hysterical and cling on to furniture when an education welfare officer had attempted to get them to comprehensive school. The very fact that the three children attended the Centre provided immediate relief to the domestic situation. The younger siblings also started to attend primary school more regularly leaving the parents some time and (psychological) space to recuperate. Both parents made frequent 'drop-in' visits to the Centre and they never hesitated to report the improvement in all-round development. Their mother had been astonished by their improving behaviour at home and the lessening of their anxiety and nervousness. When Peter was later successfully reintegrated into comprehensive school, his father said he was 'as proud as if Peter had won a scholarship'.

The Family — Quality of Care and Relationships. The lasting impression of this family is of its unity and cohesiveness, particularly with respect to the mother and children. It was an inward-looking family where the children had been kept indoors for much of the time. The parents used to accept large numbers of children into the family house in order to keep their children off the streets and out of trouble. This situation did seem to change and the children used to mention activities such as swimming, football and a local disco which obviously took place out of the home. It was still noticeable, however, that they took part in these activities with one or more of their siblings.

Their mother genuinely cared for the children and seemed to feel that she had sacrificed a great deal for them. She claimed that she would have left her husband years ago if it hadn't been for the children. As a result of her attitude towards her children, and despite advice to the contrary, she tended to keep her children close by her — although she realised that part of their difficulty in dealing with new situations and making friends was due to their lack of experience of the world outside the home.

When the children first attended the Centre it was extremely difficult to rid them of head lice and the boys especially smelled of stale urine. During their time at the Centre, however, their standard of dress and cleanliness improved considerably — although the wardrobe was obviously very limited and the children shared clothes, wearing whatever fitted them.

Home and Financial Circumstances. The family live in a terraced house (their fifth address in as many years) which is rented from a housing association. It is in a dilapidated condition and stands out in the block as being the most shabby and generally uncared for.

There are two rooms downstairs. There is a kitchen/dining room in which the family seem to spend most of their time — it is very dirty and usually very overcrowded. The other downstairs room showed many changes while the children were at the Centre. When the preliminary visit was made the room was empty of furniture but at the same time very dirty. Subsequently the room was decorated and furnished but on a further visit the furniture had disappeared. The last time the house was visited the room was once again furnished — but with different furniture.

Upstairs there were two bedrooms, one of which had been split to provide a bathroom. There was in addition an attic bedroom. In view of the age and sex distribution of the children the sleeping arrangements gave cause for concern. This problem was intensified by the family taking another 16-year-old girl into the home. This girl had experienced very difficult family problems and, despite the material and financial poverty of the household, received a great deal of care and support from John's mother.

On the broader financial situation a social inquiry report indicated:

This family has had severe and chronic financial problems over a period of years. The money has been owed for fuel and rent. The arrears were originally accrued during the period of 1974 to 1976 when the family moved house four times because of the Housing Association's need to improve the houses. By 1976 they owed more than £600 — principally to the Yorkshire Electricity Board. Social Workers have concentrated their efforts on trying to protect the family from eviction and from the disconnection of gas and electricity supplies. The parents have needed a great deal of support with their budgeting and at one time a social worker called at least once a week to collect money. The whole family have suffered considerable distress because of these debts. The installation of pre-payment meters in 1978 eased some of the pressure, but unfortunately father tampered with the electricity meter and the supply was cut off for about 18 months. The family then owed more than £1,000 to the electricity company. There was some evidence to suggest that mother is the better manager of money — father, it is alleged, drinks and gambles.

The main source of income is from the DHSS and family allowance, and the eldest son who has a job. Despite their obvious shortage of money and as an indication of her inability to budget carefully the mother bought a leather coat costing about £100. Obviously the coat was bought on credit but the repayments could not be kept up.

Social Networks. There was no evidence of any extensive social interactions outside the home and family. The family knew their immediate neighbours but claimed to have nothing to do with them — although there had been some obvious contact through the borrowing and lending of a television and furniture. The mother spent a great deal of time at her younger sister's house about half a mile away. This sister had a young child for whom John, Peter and Gwen frequently babysat. One sometimes got the impression that visits to the post office (to claim benefits) and the Centre were major expeditions into the outside world. This was certainly evident when the parents first visited the Centre; the mother in particular made frequent visits often bringing her younger sister as well.

However, despite the evident material impoverishment of the household, as has already been indicated the house and family do provide a refuge for other children experiencing problems in their own home. On most occasions when the house was visited there were other children there and other Centre pupils are regular visitors.

John himself was a very small, slightly-built boy who, when he first attended the Centre was shabbily dressed, dirty and smelled of stale urine. As a result of his elder sister's influence and her recent fashion-consciousness, John's appearance has improved — although he often seems to only wash the parts of his body which show; when revealed his feet and neck, for example, are usually dirty.

The most striking point about John was his sense of awe and wide-eyed wonder at new situations and places. In fact he became one of the yardsticks against which the success of visits and camps was judged. For example, the children returned from their first experience of hostelling by train. John had never previously been on a train and his white knuckles gave some indication of his apprehension as an elderly diesel rail-car rattled rather too fast through the countryside. No ghost trains, however, had such an effect as the railcar as it plunged into a long tunnel. Before they emerged John was almost paralysed with fear believing that he'd never come to the tunnel end.

When taken horseriding, John sat in the saddle with his jaw agape and his eyes almost popping out of his head. It quickly became clear that John (and Peter and Gwen) had an extremely limited range of experience. They had never left the immediate district where they lived, neither had they seen anything nor done anything. When they went to London on an exchange visit with a similar Centre they were but half-a-mile from the city centre when they asked if they were in London yet. And yet three hours later and 30 miles from London they asked if they were in Sheffield yet.

John was well-behaved and obedient but should he commit any minor misdemeanour he was immediately admonished by his elder sister. During his first few months at the Centre John was shy, timid and continually looked to his elder sister for guidance and approval — she usually responded in a motherly manner. When asked about friends, John actually said that he played with some boys at home. It became evident, however, that John's 'best friend' was actually the friend of his eldest brother. John had never really had any friends of his own because he had never been allowed out of the house to make his own friends. This situation changed while John was at the Centre, where he became quite capable of making his own friends and 'standing up for himself' should the need arise. He became quite a stable personality and much more friendly and outgoing. He was always popular with other pupils — even if this was initially in a negative way, in that he never posed any threat or showed any aggression to others.

When he started at the Centre John could read and write his own name and virtually nothing else; he could also recite the alphabet, the days of the week and some months of the year. By his own admission he had only copied writing from a book or blackboard and had never known what he was writing about. But even copying he would randomly jumble in capital letters, full stops, etc.

John had developed strategies for concealing from others and from himself the fact that he couldn't read. He was, however, by far the poorest academically and in the small groups in the Centre it was virtually impossible for him not to be aware of this — not surprisingly he was initially quite distressed when he realised that he really had to start at the beginning. It was undoubtedly fortunate for John that the Centre had the staff and material resources which he so desperately needed — much of the reading material which was necessary had to be made solely for him. He eventually became interested in books and in reading generally — his formal level of literacy was still low but he felt that he could and wanted to read.

Written English was a different matter — John continued to have great difficulty with any free or creative writing. The best that he could achieve was a series of short, probably factual, statements. He seemed to have a very limited imagination and was not really creative in any other sphere. Getting sentences together was a very gruelling exercise for John; he didn't appear to think in sentences. Even given stimulus, e.g. the previous day's trip to Manchester airport, he still had trouble and would respond by saying he couldn't think of anything to say or that he couldn't get it right.

On arrival John was marginally more numerate than literate. His mathematical ability stretched to the addition of whole numbers. Early attempts at subtraction showed total and utter confusion; he usually employed both decomposition and 'borrow and pay back' methods. Alternatively he would in each column take the smaller digit from the larger. And wherever a nought appeared he ignored it completely — as if he didn't know what to do with it. John had few basic number concepts, no understanding of place value or number patterns. He developed reasonable competence in the few rules but this needed considerable individual attention and carefully selected materials. Nevertheless he never really grasped any basic concepts and actually understood 'why?'

As part of the regular discussions it became clear that to teach John to understand was probably not viable. With the time available it seemed more efficient to fly educational theory in the face and to teach John algorithms so that he could at least get the right answer.

Return to Comprehensive School. John's level of social maturity increased tremendously during his period at the Centre. After an initial settling-in period he was able to cope quite well socially because he had developed the social skills to make satisfactory relationships with peers and adults. Academically, however, John had a struggle to keep up even in the extremely effective and sympathetic Special English department at his new school. The Centre staff had an established relationship with the Special English department where John was able to spend a large part of the week and were hence able to maintain regular contact over John's first term. He was also in the Remedial Maths class but he was in no way the least able in the group. In his last few weeks at the Centre, John was able to work from the maths text books which were in use in the comprehensive. All the other classes were mixed ability but many of the staff were very sympathetic towards poor achievers and catered very well for them.

John's elder brother, Peter, and a younger sister, Mary, had been at the comprehensive school for a term before he arrived, and apart from their near 100 per cent attendance the staff were also generally very pleased with their performance and adjustment. Although John did experience some difficulties academically and did require a great deal of support, on balance, it was felt that it was the optimum time for transfer back to mainstream education.

Explaining Non-attendance

Small-scale action-research projects like the Sheaf Centre can contribute to the process which elevates partial descriptions of a particular social phenomenon (in this case non-attendance) to the status of explanations. The population of children who were referred to and were subsequently investigated by the Centre made up a small but extreme sample of the school population. The extreme of that sample and the relative simplicity of the interpretative frameworks which are available to 'make sense' of a particular social phenomenon create the superficial impression that the children constitute a homogeneous group: an impression which is clearly non-substantiated by everyday, common-sense knowledge of the children as individuals. It is, however, the apparent homogeneity of the group and the apparent difference of that group from the population at large which is seen to 'explain' non-attendance.

There are clearly a number of theoretical frameworks which can provide a basis for describing children who refuse to attend school. The various aspects of non-attendance which these theoretical frameworks isolate are what subsequently come to be regarded as explanations. Each theoretical framework is, however, a reflection of a broader underlying social or educational ideology rather than an explanation of non-attendance.

It is, for example, possible to examine and discuss the family circumstances of the children who attended the Sheaf Centre in terms of indicators of social disadvantage — i.e. no indoor sanitation, single-parent families, multiple occupancy, ill-health, unemployment, etc. The majority (over 90 per cent) of the children who attended the Centre came from families which manifested five or more such indicators. Is it the case, therefore, that social disadvantage provides an explanation of poor attendance? Unfortunately the situation is not so simple. The problem of extrapolating from small samples can be represented as shown in Table 9.1.

With particular reference to the Sheaf Centre and the problems of non-attendance there was only information about the small sample of poor attenders, i.e. in the first column a, c and a + c. There was no similar information about the effect of social disadvantage on good attendance. All that was known was that there were children from equally disadvantaged homes who did not manifest problems of attendance at school. There was no systematic information about the total population. By using information from the reports produced by the Department of Planning and Design, and the Corporate Management Unit of Sheffield MDC, together with information from the Education Social Work Service, it is possible to produce a not unreasonable composite version of Table 9.1.

From Table 9.2 it can be seen that for the small group of poor attenders social disadvantage does appear to be an important factor (at the Sheaf Centre). When the total population is examined, however, the pattern is not so clear: the children coming from areas of social disadvantage are almost equally divided into poor attenders and good attenders. The relationship between social disadvantage and school attendance is of course theoretical: there is

Table 9.1: Interaction Between School Attendance and Social Disadvantage — A Diagrammatic Representation

	Poor School Attendance	Good School Attendance	
Social Disadvantage	a	b	a+b
No Social Disadvantage	c	d	c+b
	a+c	b+d	100%

little systematic information about the total population. It does, however, serve to illustrate the problems involved in extrapolating from small samples when the characteristics of the total population are unknown and, in terms of one of the factors, the sampling process is not random.

Being 'at risk' in terms of indication of social disadvantage was not the only characteristic of the children who came to the Sheaf Centre. There were a number of aspects of the children and their families, together with concomitant theoretical frameworks, which

Table 9.2: Interaction Between School Attendance and Social Disadvantage — Based on Data from Sheffield Agencies

	Poor Attendance	Good Attendance	
Social Disadvantage	9%	11%	20%
No Social Disadvantage	1%	79%	8o%
	10%	90%	100%

provide some description of their problems and can be used similarly to explain non-attendance. Each of these explanations, however, is, as has already been suggested, a reflection of some broader pre-existing ideology. Thus, for example,

(a) There has been some research evidence which indicates the importance of parents and parental attitudes in the education of their children. If one is committed, therefore, to the possibility of involving parents in schools and one examines the attitudes of the parents of the children at the Centre, then one can find superficial support for one's pre-existing ideology. The parents of the children rarely visited the comprehensive schools, they didn't know the name of the headteacher, had little idea of the school curriculum, etc. The Centre made enormous efforts to involve parents — they were invited to school, staff visited the homes, the Centre functioned as a 'drop-in centre' for mothers. This, however, was part of a wider ideology and commitment of the staff at the Centre. It did not constitute an explanation of non-attendance; it may have been no more than a description of one view of good practice.

(b) Similarly there are those within the educational community whose wider commitment is to curriculum reform. They would find 'evidence' to support their view in the curriculum needs of the children at the Centre. Even the bright children (in formal IQ terms) had a considerably restricted knowledge and incomplete understanding of the immediate world in which they lived. They did not understand and made little sense of a secondary school curriculum based upon the transition of knowledge. They lacked the assumed knowledge and experience upon which the success of such a curriculum is based.

However, children who do not attend school may not be the only children who understand little of what happens in the classroom; there is little real evidence of what children who *do* attend school understand. The appropriateness or inappropriateness of the secondary school curriculum cannot be seen as an explanation of poor attendance. All that could be said on the basis of working with children in the Centre was that the intensive monitoring of children's understanding which the teacher/pupil ratio facilitated led one to question a curriculum based upon the knowledge ideal. But it was the close monitoring of children's understanding (denied to the majority of teachers) which raised as problematic the relevance of the curriculum, not the phenomenon of non-attendance itself.

(c) An alternative perspective which might be seen to characterise the children at the Centre is concerned with the interpersonal relationships within their families. It becomes almost axiomatic to those interested in family dynamics that the relationships within a family are an important contributor to success or failure at school. Undoubtedly the interpersonal relationships within the families of children who attended the Centre gave great cause for concern. It is not possible, however, to conclude that there is a direct causal relationship between family dynamics and poor school attendance.

These three examples together with the earlier concern with social disadvantage serve to illustrate that there are aspects of the lives of children who absent themselves from school which can be seen from various theoretical standpoints to distinguish these children from the school population at large. These partial descriptions of the population of children who don't go to school cannot, however, be regarded as explanations of the problems of non-attendance.

What is clear is that if one has an ideological commitment to a particular theoretical interpretation then working with children who refuse to attend school will not challenge the ideology upon which the framework is grounded. It will, however, provide superficial evidence of the appropriateness of that theoretical framework for interpreting the problem of poor school attendance. In other words, if one has a social or educational axe to grind, or more appropriately a scythe to sharpen, one can sharpen it on children who refuse to attend school and end up with a Sheaf of corn.

10 'VANDALISM' IN SCHOOLS

Brian Harrison

Introduction

In mid-1979 the cost of vandalism to the schools in one northern city was just under £1,000 per week — £50,485 for the financial year 1978-9. This was an increase of more than £9,500 on the previous year. Figures for the number of recorded incidents showed a similarly steep rise — 401 cases in the year ending 1976, 606 cases by 1977 and 738 cases by 1978. Thus both the number of recorded incidents of vandalism, and the cost of making good the damage so caused, show an almost exponential increase over recent years. Whether we look at the increasing cost of vandalism or the increasing number of recorded incidents, the figures make depressing reading.

Problems of Definitions

But there is no crime of 'vandalism' as such, and the definition of it is notoriously difficult (see Clarke, 1978, p. 2; and Design Council, 1979, p. 20). Prosecutions for most of the acts of deliberate and malicious damage to property take place under Section 1 (1) of the Criminal Damage Act, 1971, which says:

A person who without lawful excuse destroys or damages any property belonging to another intending to destroy or damage any such property or being reckless as to whether such property would be destroyed or damaged shall be guilty of an offence.

Given that one of the difficulties in deriving any universally acceptable definition of vandalism is that the phenomenon 'gains its meaning from the situation in which it occurs' (Design Council, 1979, p. 20), these latter authors attempt a definition of it by saying what it is not: a rather easier task. The difficulties besetting this problem of definition may be best illustrated by taking a commonly occuring example of damage — a broken shop window — and, in considering the number of ways in which it could get broken, decide which ways are the result of vandalism and which are not.

It could be broken by a looter attempting to steal the goods on display. A penniless drunk may see the act as an easy way to get a night's free board and lodging at the local police station. Children may be the culprits, doing it either accidentally in the course of their play, or, more deliberately, as a result of a dare. An aggrieved customer may find breaking the window an easier method of obtaining personal satisfaction than seeking redress through the courts. A motive of jealousy may lie behind the act if it is performed by a less-successful competitor. It would doubtless be put down to 'horse-play' and 'youthful high spirits' if it was done in the course of a students' rag procession. Political considerations would appear to underlie the act if the victim of it had been selected on some racial or religious grounds. Thus one and the same act, the breaking of a shop window, may be done for a whole host of reasons, not all of which would be defined, unreservedly and without qualification, as vandalism by everyone.

And that raises a second problem in the matter of the definition of vandalism. By rendering the perpetrator liable to prosecution for criminal damage, it becomes a very covert act, like most crimes. In our example, the shopkeeper is left to reconstruct the circumstances of the 'crime' from the 'discovered damage' left behind. Clearly, the detective-work is made easier if goods are missing from the window display, or if a brick (or a football) is found among the broken glass. But, helpful as such 'clues' may be, the evidence they provide is only circumstantial and do not, in and of themselves, provide the necessary hard evidence of the motives of the window-breaker. To use a medical analogy, the breaking of the window may be merely the visible symptom of a condition which has subtle, perhaps multiple, underlying causation. If the aim is to try to avoid the phenomenon of symptom-substitution in this area of deviant behaviour, just as would be the case with other undesirable behaviours, one must try to determine the motives of the vandals and the meaning of their actions. To continue the medical analogy, the aim must be to determine and treat the cause of the malady, not just suppress the symptoms.

The foregoing notwithstanding, there is a degree of consensus among writers on the subject upon the necessary, if not the sufficient, conditions for an act resulting in damage to be defined as vandalism. Firstly, the damaged property must be *owned by 'someone'* at the time it sustains the damage. That is to say, it is impossible to vandalise, in the generally understood sense of the word, and perhaps in the strict legal sense of it, something which has been discarded as rubbish. (Consider, then, the situation of the damage done to a long-parked car by children playing in it because they *thought* it had been abandoned. Or, conversely, the damage done to a public telephone-box by young children who had an inadequate grasp of the concept of corporate ownership of such street furniture. They did not realise that the *community*, through the rates and taxes that they paid, *owned* the public amenity.)

Secondly, to constitute vandalism, the damaged property must belong to *someone else*. Ordinarily, of course, this poses no problems. Only the insane wilfully damage their own property. Or do they? Increasingly, since Ward wrote in 1973 (chapter on 'Planners as Vandals' in Ward, 1973), the owners of property, be they local authorities or unscrupulous and/or unthinking private individuals having responsibility for listed buildings, have been perceived to be committing acts of gross destruction and deface-ment with impunity — a form of legalised vandalism.

Thirdly, to justify the definition of vandalism, it must be the intention of the actor that the damaged property shall be repaired, or paid for, by someone else. If an act of retribution or recompense is intended, as might be the case with a students' rag or a party in the officers' mess, vandalism becomes impossible.

Recent Trends in Vandalism

Nevertheless, despite the difficulties of definition, we saw in the opening paragraph of this chapter how steeply both the number of recorded incidents of vandalism, and the cost of making good the damage, has risen in recent years. But does this apparently ever-steepening rise in the incidence of deliberate damage paint a true picture?

Ignoring for the moment the fact that changes in building design might, *ipso facto*, bring larger repair bills in their wake (e.g. large windows, the modern trend, still only require a single football to break them), other factors might be at work.

At the time of the introduction of the 1971 Criminal Damage Act, a Home Office directive to chief constables laid down that only those reported acts of 'vandalism' which resulted in a repair bill of £20 or more would be recorded and collected for statistical purposes. That figure of £20 has remained unchanged throughout the decade. But inflation over the same period has rarely been out of double figures and stood at one time at 23 per cent p.a.

A study in one large city which ran their apparently mounting costs of vandalism through a computer program which took account of the year-on-year effect of continuing inflation and adjusted the costs to 1971 'real' values, showed the 'true' shape of the curve of vandalism over the decade to be horizontal, not exponential — the apparent increase in the amount of vandalism seems to be an artefact of inflation.

The increasing size of the windows put into modern buildings, referred to earlier, is not the only change in modern building technique which may have served to increase the costs attributed to vandalism. As building materials, such as wood, and the labour to fashion them, have become more expensive over the years, so has there been a trend to stem the rising cost of school buildings by using flimsier materials and new designs. Solid pine doors, a standard feature of every Victorian school, are now a thing of the past. Modern school doors usually consist of two sheets of thin plywood covering a solid frame. The former were fit for their purpose, the latter rarely are. The caliper arms of a popular brand of door-returning spring used to be made of cast iron of a substantial thickness. The present-day equivalent has arms which are so thin that they vibrate like a tuning-fork when plucked by a playful child and break commensurately easily. Flat roofs, once known to the children only through pictures in a geography text-book of the lands with Mediteranean and desert climates, now abound in areas where the rainfall is measured in many tens of inches each year.

The system of local government budgeting controlled by the politicians, a proportion of whom are elected each year, militates against long-term planning to combat vandalism. Elected members could not be persuaded to build schools more robustly if so doing meant the possibility of a higher rate demand and the consequent risk of a loss of votes at the next election. Measures of short-term, but cheap, expediency rule the day. It would be no use spending large sums to build a damage-proof school only to see one's political adversaries reap the advantages, in terms of reduced repair bills, after the next election.

Just as political considerations surround the building of new schools, so do they affect the repair or maintenance of old ones. Writing in 1973, Leather and Matthews (in Ward, 1973) report:

It rapidly became apparent during our research, and was mentioned by many of those interviewed, that an increase in the incidence of vandalism occurs if an area is in any way dilapidated whereas generally when buildings and their surroundings are kept clean, tidy and in good repair they are relatively free from attack . . . It is important, therefore, that buildings and their surroundings should be as well maintained as possible (p. 166).

It may be that these well-meaning precepts are not followed by the local authority's direct works department in the period immediately prior to the local elections, when political intervention causes a change in departmental priorities. At such a time, it is not unusual for workmen to be unavailable to carry out repair work on public buildings because they are all fully employed working in the politically more sensitive area of council-owned dwelling-houses.

Finally in this section mention must be made of the opportunities created for vandalism during both repair work and new building projects. Building sites, with their piles of sand, dumps of hard-core infill, dumper trucks, cement-mixers and wheelbarrows, have an inherent, sometimes fatal, attraction for children. Scattered sand is an expensive waste; hard-core can become a missile with which to do more damage; equipment which has been stolen and plant which has become damaged through joy-riding all add to the overall cost of the work. Preventive measures, such as the securing of all materials and machinery with an impenetrable fence, will simultaneously reduce the opportunity for vandalism and repay the costs of doing so.

Types of Vandalism (see Figure 10.1)

1. *Acquisitive Vandalism*

This is damage done in the course of theft — i.e. the act of acquiring money and/or property belonging to another with the intention of permanently depriving the owner of it. In our context, it must be remembered that the acquisition of the property might be either the end in itself (e.g. the taking of crisps and sweets from the school tuck-shop in order to eat them, the taking of a cassette-recorder from the store room in order to play pop music), or items might be taken as a means to an end (e.g. to be sold for money; to fulfil a 'dare'; to 'buy' friendship by giving some or all of the stolen goods to peers; to 'add to the collection' of similar objects, such as door signs, laboratory and workshop furnishing, fittings and equipment).

Figure 10.1: Seven Types of Vandalism

An important consideration here is the distinction that must be made between the *intention* of the actor and the *effect* of the act. Thus just as when the lead is stripped from a church roof for the money that it can later realise and it is no part of the *intention* of the thief to do the untold damage to the interior structure, decoration and contents of the property that might occur as a consequence, so it is no part of the *intention* of the child, in kicking his way into a locked tuck-shop, to involve the school in a repair bill often many times the value of the food taken. The *intention* might be quite limited in extent, the unforeseen effect might be considerably in excess of what was intended.

2. *Tactical Vandalism*

'Throwing a spanner in the works', whether done literally or metaphorically, has for centuries been known as a way of achieving a particular end. It requires a belief, on the part of the 'spanner-thrower', that the particular end in mind is either not attainable by any other means, such as by negotiation, or that it will be attained more easily, more quickly or in a more desirable manner by 'throwing the spanner' than in more conventional, more legitimate ways. However, within schools, just as within automated car-plants (the stereotypical locus of 'spanner-throwing'), the problem is not so easy to define and explain as it first appears. A degree of tactical vandalism, wherever it may occur, is tacitly accepted by the 'Authority' side of the relationship, and for several reasons. It is only when the degree of tactical vandalism exceeds some hitherto unstated but formerly tolerated level that action is taken. Foremen and supervisors on the car assembly line may fear to take disciplinary action against an operative who deliberately sets fire to a waste paper basket and pushes the fire-bell in order to obtain an unscheduled tea-, toilet- or smoke-break, for fear of precipitating more serious industrial action, which may lead, in turn, to him being considered an incompetent line-manager by his superiors. Similarly a teacher may tolerate a degree of tactical vandalism in his classrooms because the cost to him, in all sorts of analogous terms, of doing anything about it might be judged too high a price to pay: impositions that are set have to be collected in and checked; detentions handed out have to be supervised and recorded, etc.

As with acquisitive vandals, the *intention* of the actors and the *effect* of their actions have to be clearly distinguished if one is to obtain a full understanding of the event. Setting fire to the old sweet papers found in the drawer of the chemistry laboratory may be intended to do no more than divert the attention of the class to the fire-raiser and annoy the disliked teacher who is conducting a boring lesson. It is only when the fire gets out of hand, by involving some nearby solvents for example, that the 'disruptive pupil' becomes an 'arsonist'.

3. *Play Vandalism*

Children have always incorporated aspects of their material environment into their creative, imaginative play. Newly-gathered sheaves of corn, when stood on their bases and propped one against the other, form a make-believe wigwam. Later the haystacks form effective trampolines and dens to jump on and hide in, respectively. The urban child is no less ingenious in his use of the modern artefacts he finds around him — supermarket trolleys become go-carts, partly-built or unoccupied and derelict houses serve as forts or hideaways, escalators make impromptu trains, lifts form gang headquarters and meeting places. The list is endless.

As with the two previous forms of vandalism, drawing the distinction between intention and effect is essential if effective means of prevention are to be introduced. But here the distinction applies *a fortiori*. In most of the examples given above, the continued correct functioning of the artefact is *absolutely essential* if the game is to continue at all. Supermarket trolleys with a wheel off make poor go-carts; stationary escalators become boring trains. How and why, then, does property get damaged during play? It is because the children are motivated by such feelings as curiosity, competitiveness, bravado or the display of skill and strength.

A complicated mechanism such as a watch which is taken apart 'to see how it works' will be left for 'broken' when it cannot be reassembled. A spirit of competition is invoked when someone in the group says, 'let's see how many of these windows we can break'. It was this motive, coupled with bravado, that led to a novel game being developed on a new housing estate in Barnsley. When the usual practice of throwing a stone from a safe distance at a newly-glazed window became mundane because it no longer provoked the expected hostile response from adults — 'It was too easy,' said one child, 'you could always get away by the time the brick had landed, you could be well away' — the 'dare' became to break the window with a clothed elbow. In quick succession, the game progressed through gloved fist and bare fist. The ultimate stage of this progression, indulged in only by the 'nutters' was to use the unprotected forehead. However, to break, by whatever means, a stationary window requires very little skill. Moving windows, such as on cars and trains, require considerably more skill, and, because the potential damage and penalty if caught are so much greater, more bravado. If the competition is in terms of skill and bravado, trainlines and motorways are the area for this symbolic action. In one school known to the author, a newly-fitted-out boys' toilet was effectively put out of action before it had been handed over to the LEA by the builders. The micro-bore piping to smart-looking swan-necked mixer taps had been wrenched bodily from its connections and the swan-necked faucets had been twisted against their retaining grub-screws so that the water could be directed over the side of the sink and on to the floor. Adolescent boys, conscious of their newly-emergent masculinity and strength, had been testing themselves against the washroom fittings.

4. *Vindictive Vandalism*

Many people feel ill-treated and despised in a society which they see as becoming bureaucratic and in which they have no effective voice. The stereotypical, headline-making example of this sort of vandalism is the person who returns at night to put a brick through the window of the social security office which refused him money earlier in the day. Prewer (1959) gives an 'insight' into the meaning to the perpetrator of this sort of act:

> . . . to break a man's window is a much safer way of paying him out than to punch him in the nose, for example. The victim is left with a cold draught, to be followed later by a glazier's bill; and he may remain in complete ignorance as to who had done the deed. The smash itself may be pleasurable, so that this form of revenge is often safe, usually certain and always sweet.

But if adults in our society can feel themselves to be weak and defenceless against what must seem to them to be the massed forces of a giant conspiracy bent on their humiliation and denigration, how much more must this seem to be the situation to at least a section of schoolchildren. If adults *feel* weak, children, by definition almost, *are* the weakest. And in many ways.

They are obviously the weakest physically. And the weak can always be hit, with impunity, by the strong. Even with the

increasing abolition by many LEAs of formal corporal punishment, i.e. that administered with a cane, entered in the punishment
book and witnessed by another member of staff, such edicts do
nothing to remove the teachers' rights, when acting *in loco
parentis*, to mete out such reasonable physical discipline as they
think fit. Some children know this, and most certainly resent the
ear-tweakings, pushings and shakings that they receive from their
teachers, but cannot repay in like manner.

Children are weak economically, too. Although they may
gradually obtain a degree of financial independence by taking a
paper-round or working at filling shelves in a supermarket, most
children get at least a degree of parental subsidy until the day they
leave home. The schoolchild, then, is usually unable to 'buy' the
friendship of the peers in his membership group or the attention
and adulation of those in his reference group. Most adults find
ways of fulfilling both these aims, and in socially-approved ways,
by virtue of their economic independence.

Many schools, particularly in the secondary sector, now have
school councils in which representatives from each year-group meet
with the staff to discuss the running of the school and to suggest
ways to alter and improve it. A further extension of this principle is
to allow older pupils to sit, with full speaking and voting rights, on
the board of governors. Laudable as such attempts to give schoolchildren a political voice may be, they may still fall short in the eyes
of some pupils. In short, and maybe of necessity, pupils may need
to be kept politically dependent because they are politically
immature, but such innovations in school management may do
little to increase children's feelings of control over aspects of their
daily lives and can, paradoxically, by heightening their awareness
of their political dependence, increase their frustration with their
lot.

One of the purposes of education is to increase a child's ability to
express his ideas, thoughts and beliefs by means of the (socially
approved, social-class determined) spoken word. In this respect, as
in most teaching situations, the teachers can perform better than
their pupils. When this ability is used properly and constructively,
all is well and good, and a lesson is well taught. But, for a whole
host of reasons, the adults' superior ability to manipulate their
more extensive vocabulary can be abused, to the detriment of the
child. Children treated in this way and feeling they have not had a
fair hearing, may attempt to redress the balance by reverting to

more primitive means of communication.

Children are required, by law, to attend school from their fifth until just after their sixteenth birthdays. Although teachers may be under contractual obligations to the school, staff can always choose when to give the required two/three months notice. This makes the children the only people on the school campus who have no legal voice in the decision as to where and how they will spend their term-time weekdays. This fact, coupled with the earlier mentioned one that whilst in school they may be legally beaten, leads to a great deal of frustration and resentment in some pupils. That they have no legitimate and approved means of redressing their grievances serves only to heighten these feelings. Vandalism may be seen by the pupils as one way of, literally and metaphorically, taking the law into their own hands in order to wrest some power back unto themselves.

If the academic selection procedures have worked correctly, all teachers should be more intelligent than at least a minority of their pupils. The intellectual weakness of some pupils, as with all other forms of weakness (physical, economic, political, verbal, and legal), does not necessarily mean that the children are automatically and inevitably wrong all of the time. Whether children are in the right, or even if they just feel that they are, they can usually recognise the exploitation by their intellectual superiors — and they resent it.

5. *Graffiti as a Form of Vandalism*

People express their personality and uniqueness to the rest of the world through their bodies and their possessions. We make 'statements' about ourselves to anyone who is prepared to 'listen' through our hairstyles, jewellery, adornments, clothes, cars, houses, gardens and the like. Self-evidently, some people have more possessions than others, and hence more opportunities for self-expression than others. Again, children as a group will feature towards the bottom of this particular 'league table', and those with fewer legitimate opportunities than others for self-expression may resort to defacement and graffiti in order to redress the balance in their favour. In the classic study of graffiti on the New York underground trains, filmed under the descriptive title 'Watching My Name Go By', the police described the boys who would sit for hours by the side of the railway lines watching for their, often elaborate, signatures to appear on the side of the carriages, as 'nobodies' trying to be 'somebodies' (Cook, 1977).

6. *Ideological Vandalism*

'Ban the Cane', scrawled in a childish hand on the school wall, is a particular form of graffiti which occurs with sufficient frequency to justify the creation of specific sub-set of the category, namely 'Ideological Vandalism'. Cohen (1973) defines ideological vandalism as that:

> category of property destruction which has either or both of the following characteristics:
> i. the rule is broken as a means towards some explicit and conscious ideological end.
> ii. there is no consensus over the content of the rule which is being broken and, more particularly, the content of the rule is being explicitly and consciously challenged.

Three important points need to be made about this form of property defacement:

(1) From the time of the first, invading Vandals, through the Peasants' Revolt and Luddite riots, to the present 'Troubles' in Northern Ireland, there has always been ideological vandalism — it is not a uniquely twentieth-century phenomenon. The fact that it is reported at all now, the way in which it is covered by the media (i.e. in using such beloved labels and phrases as 'mindless', 'wanton', 'heedless', 'orgy of destruction', 'wild rampage', etc.), and the fact that through modern telecommunications we can witness the 'race riots' in Alabama or the destruction of an embassy in the Far East within hours of its occurrence, only make it appear to be a new means of drawing attention to a grievance.

(2) In an age of increasing accountability and questioning, of and by each, to and of all (e.g. senior pupils now sit on many school governing bodies with full voting, speaking and questioning rights), ideological vandalism may well become more prevalent before it decreases in extent. Just as history teaches us that the uprising of the oppressed increases, not when the oppression is at its height, as might be expected, but when conditions are already beginning to improve (c.f. the situation in Spain in the few years before and after Franco's death), so might we expect an increase in

ideological vandalism as pupil representation on school councils and governing bodies becomes more widespread.

(3) That sub-category of ideological vandalism which may be described as ideological graffiti may be rendered easier to perform and longer-lasting in its effects through the invention and widespread, easy availability of the means to perform it. Felt-tip markers and, more particularly, aerosol spray-paint cans, are cheap and easy to buy. They are quick to use and require little or no skill in their application. The results, depending upon type of surface defaced, are fairly permanent and/or expensive to remove. Given that there is some evidence that the propellant in the spray-paint cans may be damaging the environment in other ways, perhaps the time has come to prohibit, by law, the production and retail of such products.

7. *Malicious Vandalism*

The image of the vandal as portrayed by the popular, tabloid press, is almost invariably one of a wanton hooligan hell-bent on an orgy of mindless property destruction. We have seen how, in the previous six categories of vandalism, this is far from the truth: the vandal has a *motive* for his or her action at the time of performing it and this act has a *meaning* to the youngster which may last long after it has been performed. Even if the act is later regretted, the stereotypical statement of the apprehended vandal — 'Well it seemed a good idea at the time' — may have some basis in truth.

But there still remains an amount of property destruction which does not fall easily or obviously into any of the categories of vandalism described earlier, so-called 'malicious vandalism'. In general terms, acts of malicious vandalism are 'neither, on the one hand, as specific as in vindictive, tactical or acquisitive vandalism, nor on the other, as differentiated, diffuse or arbitrary as terms like "wanton" imply' (Cohen, 1973). More specifically, acts of malicious vandalism may include instances where whole class-rooms, or even whole schools, have had desks overturned, furniture broken, paint thrown around, paper strewn all over and all normal academic activity rendered impossible. To employ the term 'malicious' to describe such acts is to imply that the act is not merely an expression of more or less generalised hatred towards whatever the damaged property is assumed to symbolise, but also to assume that the action is enjoyed for its own sake — perhaps for the amusement that it provides. If youths will pay to break crockery at a village fête, why should they not enjoy it as much, but without payment, in a school kitchen or staff room?

If the postulation of a hedonistic motive only partially explains the aetiology of malicious vandalism, from where does that component attributed to hatred derive? Throughout this section, great emphasis has been placed upon the subjective feelings of the vandal during the period surrounding the commission of the crime. A full exposition of all such feelings is beyond the scope of this present work. Suffice it to say that emotions such as frustration, boredom, hostility, despair, resentment, exasperation and failure are normal in the sense that we all experience them, to a greater or lesser extent, from time to time in our lives. Perhaps the difference between the law-abiding adult and the adolescent vandal is not so much that the former is sufficiently mature to curb the widest swings of these emotions, although that most certainly is true, but more that he or she can find socially-approved ways and means of both avoiding frustrating, and boring, etc., situations in the first place and of coping with them if they do occur. As we saw in our discussion of vindictive vandalism and graffiti, the range of such options is dramatically reduced for children and young people.

It is possible, however, to explain some acts of so-called malicious vandalism without needing to invoke notions such as 'hatred' at all. It is rarely the intention of the office practical joker to inflict extreme pain, cost, inconvenience, or injury upon his colleagues. And such is the office prankster's knowledge of the way the things work, the strength of the materials of which they are made, etc., that jokes can be designed to stop at the point at which they just remain what they were intended to be — a humorous experience for all concerned. The practical jokes of children, who are unlikely to have such knowledge, may fail to stop at this point. For example, the old 'stall-and-trough' urinals in the boys' toilets in one school were considered to be in need of replacement. In an attempt to improve both the sanitary and aesthetic aspects of the toilets, modern, individual, wall-mounted urinals were fitted. In accordance with current plumbing practice, the waste-outlets were made of plastic and fully exposed to view and touch. Being of plastic, as opposed to metal, the screwed unions were only hand-tight. It was not long before the boys realised that that which is screwed-up by hand can also be unscrewed by hand. And the only visible difference between a fully screwed-up union and a totally unscrewed one is about half an inch of thread — barely noticeable to a passing glance. A later reconstruction of events determined that it was considered quite a fun thing to do to unscrew a waste outlet after use, certain in the knowledge that the *next* user of that particular urinal would be the architect of his own downfall, as his warm, wet shoes would remind him, whilst the perpetrator would remain free from detection and hence punishment. Unfortunately, what the boys did not realise was that, as it had never been intended to have large amounts of *any sort* of water on the tiled floor, non-porous grout had not been specified. Furthermore, the floor levels had not been made to slope sufficiently towards the drainage grate. The result, therefore, and with hindsight not surprisingly, was that large amounts of static urine that lay on the floor slowly seeped into the grout, changing into ammonia as it did so, until the whole room became practically unbearable, particularly in summer. An expensive reversal to the more 'old-fashioned' but functional 'stall-and-trough' system has completely cured the problem. The point of this example is that it was almost certainly *not* the intention of the boys, individually or collectively, to involve the school in a great deal of extra expenditure, far less to make their own toilets such an unpleasant place in which to be. Rather, their intention had been to play a prank on a, possibly unknown, fellow-pupil. The eventual consequence derived directly from their ignorance.

Solutions and Problems

There is, fortunately for all concerned, a vast and ever-growing literature of specific remedial techniques (e.g. see Design Council, 1979; Ward, 1973; Stone and Taylor, 1977). The majority of the solutions recommended are to do with 'hardening the target', and there is no doubt, as we have seen earlier, that some 'targets' need to be 'hardened'. For example, damage that is discovered to have happened to a thin plywood-clad door and the associated return-spring may, in fact, be caused by 'fair wear and tear' rather than 'vandalism' in the generally accepted lay sense. Other remedies concern themselves less with equating the strength and design of the fixtures, fittings and furniture of the school with the purpose to which it is being put, but advocate a more global strategy. An example of such a recommended solution would be to alter either the design and layout of the building or the curriculum and timetable in such a way as to divert the pressure of (legitimate) use away from a hard-pressed area of the school and thereby bring about a more even distribution of wear all over the building.

However, in this area as in few others, the implementation of recommended solutions is notoriously prone to failure. Alterations, thought at the time to be improvements, serve merely either to displace the scene or type of damage from one place to another (Mayhew *et al.*, 1976), or to alter the nature of the expression of the dissatisfaction felt by the children so that redress of grievance is sought in ways other than damaging the fabric of their environment. Why should 'vandalism' be so difficult to eliminate?

The first reason has been alluded to earlier. We have seen how 'vandalism' is, almost uniquely, difficult to define because we are, by the very nature of the act, usually forced to try to reconstruct the meanings of the act, and the motives of the actor, from the damage that is discovered. Secondly, we have also seen earlier how party political pressures effectively conspire to prevent the introduction of a patently obvious solution of proven worth. But within-school political pressures may be equally effective in bringing about the same result. A large amount of capitation money spent on improving the decor in the English department will almost certainly mean less for all the other departments, and may, therefore, prove difficult to gain acceptance at a staff meeting. Extension of the space allocated to the Modern Language suite may be at the expense of the Geography department, and so on.

Finally, in this section, there are the administrative and bureaucratic (using the word in its literal, non-pejorative sense of office-procedural) obstacles to effective, preventive action. The discovery by a person of some authority, e.g. teacher, caretaker, etc., of a new piece of damage is the first step in a long chain of events which will eventually result in its rectification. Assuming that the discoverer of the damage does not have a vested interest in the concealment of the damage (as might be the case, for example, if some blame for it could be attached, through negligence, to the discoverer), and assuming the discoverer is sufficiently conscientious and industrious to bother reporting it, it still constitutes another chore for someone — the filling-in of a job requisition. The natural history of a typical such document is interesting to trace. It will usually be completed by someone fairly lowly-placed in the school hierarchy — probably the caretaker or office clerk. It will then progress upwards through this hierarchy, receiving an increasing degree of authorisation at each stage, until it arrives at the headteacher's desk to be sanctioned for onward transmission to the education office. Upon arrival at the education office it again ascends a hierarchical structure of variable length until it is passed by the appropriate education officer to his opposite number in the direct works department (assuming no authorisation is required from an elected member).

Within the Direct Works Department it descends a similar hierarchy until it becomes a job-sheet for the relevant tradesman. With the best of wills and the highest of intentions, the process is a lengthy, expensive and fallible one. And the end result of the delay inherent in the system is, at best, a decreased quality of working environment for teacher and pupil alike and, at worst, an open invitation and god-sent opportunity for more damage to be added to the original destruction.

What follows, then, is not so much a repetitive list of *ad hoc*, expedient, possibly short-term solutions but more an attempt to construct an 'Algorithm for Action Upon Discovering Damage in School'.

Adopt a Hypothetico-deductive Approach to the Problem

On every possible occasion when damage is discovered, attempt to discover *how* and *why* it came to be damaged. This is more important in the long term than discovering *who* broke it, although this might be a necessary first step in this process. It is emphasised, *attempt to understand the aetiology of the problem* and do not just apportion blame and improve sanctions. In practical terms this means, for example, considering whether the broken hinge was strong enough to withstand the amount of legitimate use to which it was put. Depending upon the answer to this implied question, the solution may be either to strengthen the replacement hinge or reduce by some means, such as rerouting the traffic, the amount of use the hinge gets.

Adopt a Small-scale Empirical Intervention Strategy

Once all that can reasonably be done to understand the true causes of the problem has been done, formulate a solution and adopt it on a small scale. In our previous example, if it is considered that the hinge broke under fair wear and tear, it might be decided to replace it with a strengthened one. All the hinges of similar design to the one which broke should not, at this stage at least, be replaced.

There are reasons for this recommendation. The diagnosis of the cause of the problem may be incorrect, and it is unlikely that a correct and final solution will emanate from a faulty understanding of the problem. Secondly, it may incur unnecessary expenditure — hinges of similar design elsewhere in the school may be subject to less use and therefore be adequate for the task they are being required to do. And thirdly, strengthening of the hinge may merely display the locus of the damage and the failure of the first hinge may simply be the early-warning sign, as it were, of something more serious. For instance, if the first hinge broke not through fair wear and tear but because the door was being repeatedly opened by a booted foot instead of by hand, strengthening of the hinge will allow this undesirable practice to continue, with possible detriment to the rest of the door, which will prove more expensive to replace than just the hinge.

Evaluate the Outcome of any Solution which is Adopted

Taking again the example of the broken hinge, the performance of the replacement item ought to be monitored and compared with that of a hinge of identical design to the former one which is in use in a similar location. In this way, two advantages will accrue. It is more likely that the *true* reason for the failure of the first hinge will be established and it will make the likelihood of the correct response to the breaking of subsequent hinges being adopted that much greater.

When the period of evaluation is judged to be complete, one of two strategies can be adopted depending upon the outcome. If the solution originally adopted is thought to be successful, it can be adopted wholesale — each subsequent hinge that breaks should be replaced by one of the new, improved, strengthened design. Fundamental and simple as this may sound, it is unlikely to happen if the decision as to choice of hinge is left to the joiner who came to fit it. Conversely, if the solution originally adopted is deemed to be wrong, there is no alternative but to return to Stage One of this algorithm and begin the process all over again.

Some guidelines for consideration when entering this algorithm would include, as a minimum, the following items:

Within School

(a) Basic design and layout of (i) the school building; (ii) the fixtures, fitting and furniture in use in the various parts of the school.

(b) Coupled with (a) above, the appropriateness of the strength of the materials in the school buildings, fixtures, fittings and furniture *for the use to which they are being put.*

(c) The 'fitness-of-design-for-its-purpose', e.g. what is the maximum throughput capacity of the corridors, toilets, changing rooms, showers, etc?

(d) The corollary of (c) above, the curricular/organisational goodness-of-it for the architecture.*

(e) Free-assembly time and free-assembly places, i.e. for how long and how often do the children have relatively unstructured and relatively unsupervised breaks such as 'playtime' and 'dinnertime'? Subsidiary questions to be asked here involve considerations as to whether the breaks are too long or too short, too many or too few, and what the children are required to do in the breaks, e.g. visit the toilet, collect dinner tickets, report to year- and form-tutors, attend music and sports practices, hand in completed work, etc.

Outside School, but on Campus

(a) Access to and from school buildings. Most external doors have their throughput capacities decreased by pupils trying to pass in both directions simultaneously. It might be worth considering if the throughput capacity could be increased by introducing an easily enforceable one-way system, i.e. 'enforceable' in this context means a one-way flow of traffic which is *encouraged* by the architecture — not one which is *demanded* by teachers acting as traffic wardens, as this latter solution might bring more problems than it solves. Alternatively, it might be asked if entry and departure times might be staggered in some way so as to reduce the pressure on doorways at peak times.

---

*Up to the 1960s, most children took all the subjects in their core curriculum (English, maths, history, geography, foreign languages and RE) in their own box classrooms and travelled to lessons only for such specialist subjects as PE, science, craft, etc. With the modern trend towards departmental suites of classrooms, brought about, it is argued, by an increasing application of expensive and heavy highly technological equipment, there is much more movement by the children between lessons. Thus whereas before the end-of-lesson bell signalled the movement of, perhaps, a quarter of the pupils and three-quarters of the staff, it is likely that in most schools this ratio is now reversed. Coincidentally, of course, this has led to a reduction in the unofficial 'policing' function which teachers formerly exercised by their mere presence on the corridors.

(b) The nature of the area immediately adjacent to a main entrance door ought to be considered. Ideally, it should be a large area of paving or tarmac but all too often such doors lead on to narrow, winding paths and the resulting overspill turns the edges of lawns and flowerbeds into areas of unsightly and dysfunctional baked clay or deep mud — depending upon the recent weather.

(c) The lines of external communication between either the various parts of the main building or those between the main building and the annexe(s) need special consideration. The natural tendency of humans, particularly young ones, to take the shortest route between two points — lawns, flowerbeds and weather conditions notwithstanding — is extremely strong. Paths which take the 'scenic' route will tend to be ignored in favour of the most direct one.*

(d) Far too little attention is usually given to the design of the playground in modern schools. A rectangle of tarmac, with a wall of glass windows down one side is not suitable as a play area. Ball games usually have to be forbidden — a travesty of natural justice in the eyes of the pupils. The unrelieved starkness of such playgrounds offers no opportunities for creative and imaginative games — or shelter from wind and rain. With respect to play areas, then, due consideration must be paid to:

(i) the age differences of the pupils;

(ii) the sex differences of the pupils;

(iii) the variety of ball games that might be played simultaneously;

(iv) the varying weather conditions — it should be possible to use a good playground in all but the most extreme of weather conditions;

(v) the fact that the quantity and perhaps quality of supervision may be dramatically reduced.

---

*One consequence of the move towards departmental suites of rooms, with the attendant increase in student mobility and decrease in staff mobility, is important to consider here. The end-of-lesson bell is also the beginning-of-next-lesson bell. Whereas before, when the staff did the majority of the moving between classrooms, children could count on a few minutes' break whilst the teacher collected the necessary books and arrived at the classroom, the situation is now reversed. It is the teacher, typically, who stays put and is ready, immediately after dismissing one class, to receive the next, and the children who have to 'work' under this pressure of what Rabinowitz has called 'zero time' (private communication), to get to their next lesson on time. It is this pressure which gives the pupils a vested interest in taking short-cuts across the lawn.

General Considerations

(a) Serious consideration should be given to the administrative/ bureaucratic infrastructure of the school (see above). Three aspects merit especial and separate attention. They are:

(i) repairs, e.g. mending a broken window;

(ii) minor new work, e.g. fitting a new sink in a laboratory;

(iii) major new work, e.g. building a new extension.

It is important to point out that items (i) and (ii) above, whilst involving perhaps a fraction of the cost of (iii) might actually be more disruptive to the life of the school than the latter one. For example, fitting a new sink in a laboratory, possibly a day's job, necessitates the whole room being out-of-bounds for the day and involves consequent re-timetabling. Whereas, on the principle that what you never had you never miss, the building of a new extension may be little more than a minor irritant.

The presence of workmen on a school campus is a matter of serious concern for the school, if for no other reason than that they are usually the only people allowed in a school campus over whom the headteacher has no *direct* control. The effects of their presence (hammering, sawing, drilling, shouting, whistling, singing, smoking and playing radios) on both staff (of both sexes) and on pupils (of both sexes) can be formidably disruptive to the smooth running of the school.

(b) Finally, in this chapter, some thought ought to be given to other, local, off-campus provision. Sufficient, and sufficiently attractive, local provision of youth clubs, scout troops, guide companies, etc., will serve to divert attention away from school buildings in the evenings and at weekends when they are most unsupervised and hence most vulnerable. It is always possible, of course, for the youth clubs, scouts, guides, etc., to meet in the school, thus increasing the amount of such supervision normally available.

It was stated earlier in this chapter that 'vandalism' is notoriously resistant to eradication. Why should this be so? Stopping short of psychoanalytic explanations of property destruction, which may or may not be valid, there are other, much more prosaic, reasons why the phenomenon persists. For example, it may be that the recommended 'solutions' just do not work, or work only for a short time. In one school an unused noticeboard had become an unofficial graffiti board. The remedy of painting it to become an elaborate mural was only partially successful in that, although it staved off all further writing for a year, it gradually crept back on again. Perhaps 12 months' respite is as long as could reasonably be expected for a measure such as this and an annual renewal is indicated?

Alternatively, it may be that the remedial measures do work, but bring other problems in their wake. The fence that was eventually put around the base of a mobile classroom to prevent footballs from going into the mud underneath it was of such a design as to dam up the draining surface water, causing partial flooding of the playground. The 'cure' was as bad as the original fault.

Preventive measures may be costly to implement, and, as we have seen, highly expensive preventive steps, however successful they may be in operation, are unlikely to be taken whilst even politicians are annually accountable for the expenditure they authorise. Poly carbonate sheeting is much stronger than glass as glazing material, but its present high cost means that it will not be used in other than the most vulnerable of situations.

Finally, it may be that schools have design faults built into them. That is, known preventive measures, of proven efficacy, are available but fail to be adopted for a variety of reasons. In his article on 'The weakness in current school design', P. M. Burns (1979), an HMI, cited what he considered to be the definitive list of those who had something of value to contribute to the process of school design. His list includes 'elected members, administrators, teachers, phase and subject advisers, adult, youth, and community specialists, architects, quantity surveyors, structural, mechanical and electrical engineers, town planners, landscape architects and environmental specialists, energy conservationists and parents'. Nowhere in that long list does he mention the police, in their crime prevention role, or the educational psychologist, the school's specialist in the behavioural sciences.

However, to end on a positive note, despite this dismaying catalogue of reasons why there will always be some vandalism in schools, the weight of the evidence is heavily in favour of concluding that this need not be so, providing the will to eradicate it exists.

11 THE 1981 EDUCATION ACT

Geoff Lindsay

The identification of special educational needs has for many years been subject to two processes. The first, an informal process, occurred when a teacher became concerned that a pupil needed some extra or different help within the ordinary school. The second, a formal process, was normally reserved for those children who were likely to require placement in a special school or unit (although the formal process was not meant to be for these children alone). The 1944 Education Act demanded that all children should be educated according to age, aptitude, and ability and Regulations published in 1945 defined the categories of children requiring special education, who had a 'disability of mind or body'. A special set of forms (the HP forms) were produced to aid the administration of this process.

Dissatisfaction with this arrangement increased steadily until in 1975 the Department of Education and Science produced a new circular (Circular 2/75) which redefined this formal assessment process, and proposed a new set of forms — the SE (special education) forms. The dissatisfactions had been several. First, the old procedure was ultimately in the hands of school medical officers who ascertained the child as requiring special education. The new procedure continued the slow progress since the end of the nineteenth century of taking special education out of medical hands, and into the educational domain. Under the new procedure it was a senior educational psychologist or adviser who should specify the special educational needs of a child, and how these should be met. This decision was based upon information from teacher(s) (SE1), a medical officer (SE2) and an educational psychologist (SE3). There was no specific input from parents, whose views were usually reported by others, particularly the psychologists. However, Circular 2/75 was for guidance and therefore non-mandatory, although most LEAs followed its recommendations (Cornwall and Spicer, 1982).

Although the SE procedure was generally considered better than its predecessor (except perhaps by medical officers whose power diminished) its use is now to be terminated. This arises as a result

231

of the comprehensive rethinking of special education during the 1970s. The Warnock Committee reported in 1978 and in 1980 a White Paper, *Special Needs in Education* (Cmnd. 7997) was published. Subsequently the 1981 Education Act was passed, replacing the sections of the 1944 Education Act which specified policy in special education. This came into operation on 1 April 1983.

During the next few years, there will be a transition period while the effects of that Act are felt. Along with new legislation on the definition of needs and how these should be met, Regulations are to be published which specify the operation of the new assessment process. This will also be a formal procedure, although specific forms like the SE and HP forms will not be used. It is hoped that the assessment of needs will integrate an informal and formal system in the manner advocated in the Warnock Committee's proposals, but this remains to be seen.

1981 Education Act

The 1981 Education Act lays a duty on LEAs to ensure that special educational provision is made for pupils who have special educational needs. Section 4 (1) states:

> It shall be the duty of every local education authority to exercise their powers under this Act with a view to securing that of the children for whom they are responsible, those with special educational needs which call for the local education authority to determine the special educational provision that should be made for them are identified by the authority.

The LEA has a duty to perform an assessment on a child to discover these educational needs. Before so doing, the parents must be informed of this proposal, of the procedure to be followed, the name of an officer of the authority from whom further information may be obtained, and their right to make representations and submit written evidence to the authority within a period of not less than 29 days from the time when the notice is served (Section 5).

Where an assessment has been made under this section, and the child is deemed to have special educational needs, the LEA shall make a statement of these special needs. Parents have the right to see a copy of the statement, which they may challenge. If this happens, the LEA must arrange meetings with appropriate officers to discuss differences of opinion, but if the problem is still not resolved, the parents may appeal against the statement to an Appeals Committee constituted in accordance with paragraph 1 of Part 1 of Schedule 2 of the 1980 Education Act. Finally a parent may appeal to the Secretary of State. In addition, parents have a right to request that an assessment of their child's educational needs is carried out by the LEA and this must be done, unless it is considered unreasonable.

The Regulations accompanying the Act (DES, 1983a) specify the professionals who must contribute to the assessment procedure. These comprise a medical officer, a teacher and an educational psychologist. In certain cases other professionals are also appropriate.

In the context of the present discussion it is necessary to note that this system, which pertains to an Act of Parliament, is of necessity rather formal. The Circular (*Assessments and Statements of Special Educational Needs*, DES, 1983b) does give useful advice on how this formality may be reduced, but the degree to which this can be done will be limited. Parents now have a right to request an assessment, and the LEA has to justify itself if it refuses. On the other hand, parents can challenge proposed statements about the children. Furthermore, they will be given copies of the statement which contains the reports of the professionals involved.

Each school must ensure that it has an appropriate system of identifying needs and involving outside professionals. Indeed there is a duty under the Act on the school itself, through its governing body:

It shall be the duty of the governors, in the case of a county or voluntary school, and of the local education authority by whom the school is maintained, in the case of a maintained nursery school —
a) to use their best endeavours, in exercising their functions in relation to the school, to secure that if any registered pupil has special educational needs the special educational provision that is required for him is made;
b) to secure that, where the responsible person has been informed by the local education authority that a registered pupil has special educational needs, those needs are made known to all who are likely to teach him; and

c) to secure that the teachers in the school are aware of the importance of identifying and providing for those registered pupils who have special educational needs. (1981 Education Act, Section 2(5))

This places responsibility directly on the school to identify needs, and to ensure that these needs are communicated to relevant teachers in order that they might be provided for.

Process of Assessment

The Regulations accompanying the Act stipulate the professionals who must be involved. However, unlike the two previous systems, no special forms are specified. This partly reflects a dissatisfaction with those forms which, particularly in the case of the SE2 (medical assessment), often contained little if any relevant information. Instead a checklist of suggested key areas is provided, but each LEA will be free to introduce its own forms, or not as it wishes.

Schools must institute a good system of identifying needs (see Chapter 2) and of deciding when to call for an assessment under the Act. Good practice, it is envisaged, will entail a series of preliminary assessments and discussion with parents and professionals before a decision to request an assessment under the Act is made. This follows advice in the Warnock Report, who proposed five stages of assessment, with more specialised professionals becoming involved at successive stages.

The Statement

The form and content of the statement are prescribed in the Education (Special Educational Needs) Regulations 1983 (DES, 1983a) although the design and production of the statement document will be a matter for individual LEAs. It will comprise an Introduction (Section I) and four main sections:

Special Educational Needs (Section II). The LEA must take into consideration any representations and evidence submitted by the child's parent, the advice the LEA has obtained from professional advisers, and any relevant information provided by the District Health Authority (DHA) or Social Services Department (SSD). Copies of these documents must be appended to the statement and, if the LEA accepts the advice of its advisers (which must take account of the views of parents) it can simply say so in this section.

Special Educational Provision (Section III). The LEA may discuss the provision to be made for the child with some or all of the professional advisers who reported in Section II. It must specify the special educational provision to be made for the child in terms of facilities and equipment, staffing arrangements, curriculum and other arrangements to be made to meet the child's special educational needs.

Appropriate School or other Arrangements (Section IV). The LEA must describe the type of school they consider appropriate for the child, and name the particular school if known. If the child is to be educated otherwise than at school (an apparently growing trend with parents of a broad range of children), this provision must also be described. Also, if the parents are meeting the cost of schooling, the name of the school is not required on the statement.

Additional and Non-Educational Provision (Section V). In this section the LEA must specify the details of provision which would be available for the child by a DHA or some other body in addition to the child's special educational provision. For example, the support of a speech therapist or psychiatrist would be stated here.

In addition to these Sections, it is expected that full copies of relevant documents be attached as appendices. A suggested format is provided in Appendix 2 of Circular 1/83. If this is followed a statement will also have the following additions:

Appendix A: Parental Representations. This will include both written representations (in full) and a summary of any oral recommendations made, which the parent agrees is accurate.

Appendix B: Parental Evidence. This might include additional evidence provided by the parent on the child's behalf, for example by a professional in private practice, or a worker from a voluntary body who is supporting the child and/or parent.

Appendix C: Educational Advice. In almost all cases of children of secondary school age this will be provided by the headteacher, in consultation with teachers who have actually taught the youngster. In addition if the pupil is deaf or partially hearing or blind or otherwise visually handicapped, the educational advice must be given following consultation with a person qualified as a teacher of the deaf or blind, respectively.

Appendix D: Medical Advice. This must be given by a registered medical practitioner who is designated by the DHA or nominated by them in the individual case. Normally this would be the person known as the 'school doctor'.

Appendix E: Psychological Advice. This must be provided by an educational psychologist either regularly employed by the LEA, or employed for the case in question. If another psychologist is involved, normally a clinical psychologist, the educational psychologist must consult with that colleague before providing the advice.

Appendix F: Other Advice Obtained by Education Authority. This might include advice from a previous LEA, or any other educational advice considered helpful.

Appendix G: Information Furnished by the District Health Authority or Social Services Authority. In this section reports by, for example, a psychiatrist, social worker, speech therapist or probation officer might be included.

In all cases there must be reports in Appendices C, D, and E but reports for Appendices A, B, F and G are optional. For example, a parent may not wish to make any representation. In all cases where no report is provided in these appendices, this must be stated as the case.

There are two important aspects of the statement. The first is that it makes a clear distinction between the assessment of needs and the allocation of resources to meet those needs. The reasons for this are given in Circular 1/83. Assessment should not simply be conducted with a view to available provision, although that knowledge is useful to the professional concerned. The effects of this distinction remain to be seen. Not only is there a tidier arrangement at an intellectual level, there is possibly a better basis for parents who may wish to take issue with the LEA. For example, a statement may say, in Section II, that the child's needs require that certain facilities be provided. If the LEA does not have these, and so fails to match Section II with Section III, the parents can use this evidence in their appeal.

The second point to make is that the procedure and the documentation must be more carefully considered than before. The procedure is derived from an Act, and the statement and accompanying reports can be viewed by an Appeals Committee in cases of dispute. What teachers and other professional write, therefore, could become open to much greater scrutiny.

Parents

The issue of the involvement of parents is a crucial one under the Act. For the first time they have a statutory basis for both demanding an assessment of their child, and for seeing the reports making up the statement. The appeals machinery is a further positive element in their favour, although its powers under the 1980 Education Act will be more limited than the comparable machinery for children in ordinary schools. On the other hand, critics of the Act point to the ultimate legal sanction of forcing children to be assessed even against their parents' wishes. Also, Tomlinson (1982) argues that the Appeals Committee, and recourse to the Secretary of State, will rarely be used:

> Parental rights, under the 1944 and the 1980 and 1981 Education Acts, amount to a grudging appeals system to which few parents will actually have recourse. (p. 108)

The issue of parental involvement actually incorporates several different components, each of which is contentious, and the several issues are often confounded.

Rights of the Parent. Here the issue is legal in nature, and incorporates concerns such as access to information and provision. It is certainly the case that the Act does extend parents' rights, at least in theory. Whether this extension is sufficient can be questioned. There is also the separate issue of whether parents are aware of their rights, and will fight accordingly. Hannon (1982) argues that before this Act, challenges in the courts were rare. However, it is possible that parents will become more aware of their rights and make use of the appeals and other machinery if they are dissatisfied. This was once largely a middle-class phenomenon, and could be exemplified by appeals of parents against placement of children in ESN(M) schools, which rarely happened with working-class parents. However, recent events have shown a greater, and increasing, political awareness of working-class parents. School closures are now being fought in working-class as well as in middle-class areas. For example, parents of children at Croxteth School, Liverpool refused to accept closure and occupied the premises during the summer of 1982.

Children's Rights. It is often very difficult to separate discussions of children's and parents' rights. However, this is an area which has come to recent prominence and clarification of some of the basic issues, at a legal level, has been made (e.g. see King, 1981; Morris *et al.*, 1980). Within the field of special education, children's rights have gradually improved. Severely mentally handicapped children, for example, were excluded from the education system until the passing of the 1970 Education (Handicapped Children) Act. Under the present Act, one of the main benefits will be from an extension of the LEA's responsibility to assess children even below the age of two years, if the parents request this.

Within the group of children under consideration here, i.e. secondary pupils, the main benefits in terms of rights are those which follow from a more complete and thorough system of assessment and, assuming this happens, provision. Thus pupils who are deemed to have special needs, as specified in the statement, will have a more sound basis for demanding better provision. A further element, which is not incorporated in the Act but was recommended for incorporation into the Circular and Regulations by the Division of Educational and Child Psychology of the British Psychological Society in its evidence, would be a separate element of the statement which contains the pupil's views.

Although there is no specific section for youngsters to make their own views known, Circular 1/83 states:

The feelings and perceptions of the child concerned should be taken into account, and the concept of partnership should wherever be possible be extended to older children and young persons.

The youngster's own views could probably be included in Appendix F of the statement.

Access to Reports. When the White Paper *Special Needs in Education* (DES, 1980), on which the 1981 Education Act was based, was being discussed there was much debate on access to reports. Some professionals argued strongly against this, while other organisations, particularly pressure groups, argued for greater access. This debate can be seen within the wider context of access to school reports (e.g. Newell, 1982) and indeed to reports in general (e.g. Cohen, 1982). The Warnock Report (DES, 1978) argued that 'parents too should be treated as partners in this process (of exchange of information) whenever possible . . . they should be able to see most of the factual information about their child' (p. 298). Under the 1981 Act parents must have a copy of the Statement, and so have copies of the professionals' reports.

Teachers, and particularly headteachers, therefore, must be aware that what they write will be seen by the parents. This applies equally to medical officers and educational psychologists, and the other professionals who may contribute to particular statements. For many professionals this is a cause of concern, and some practice in the writing of reports will clearly be required. There are two main issues here. One relates to *usefulness*, and is discussed in more detail below. The second concerns defensibility. Professionals often make assumptions about the capacity of other professionals to understand their arguments, and so do not justify all their comments in a report. This practice will need to be re-examined. Furthermore, some of the basic assumptions underlying ways of thinking, and recommendations, may need to be reconsidered as they could be challenged (e.g. see Sutton, 1981).

Working Together. A discussion of legal rights of parents and children, and even access to reports, often assumes a confrontationist attitude. There is an assumption that the parents and child are fighting a system which is trying to impose its will on an unwilling victim. Tomlinson's (1982) perspective on special education is very much of this kind and her analysis of the failings of the system to some extent justify this. There is some validity in the argument that the special education system is designed to solve the problems of the main system, rather than to help the children concerned. The past research on the effectiveness of special education has not been encouraging, particularly with the deaf (Conrad, 1979) and the ESN(M) (Galloway and Goodwin, 1979; Ghodsian and Calnan, 1977; see also Strain and Kerr, 1981, for a review if the effectiveness of work with educable mentally retarded children in the USA). Also, Tomlinson's study of children referred to ESN(M) schools indicates worrying aspects of the system (Tomlinson, 1981).

However, these arguments do not necessarily justify a view that assessing a child as having special educational needs is sinister and negative in its nature. Most parents, in my experience, are quite aware when their child has problems and, even if this is not the case initially, sensitive discussions and presentation of evidence can reveal this. At times this can be traumatic (e.g. in the diagnosis of profound deafness or mental handicap) but particularly in the case of secondary school pupils, parents are rarely unaware that there is a problem, and almost invariably are keen for something to be done to alleviate or solve it. Thus while rights are important, the issue of collaboration is also a major factor.

In the present case this must demand several components. First, parents must feel that they are treated as partners in the process. This requires early discussions when a teacher has a concern, or alternatively a sympathetic and positive response if the parent is worried. Second, they must be kept fully informed of what is happening and what the possibilities are. This may not always be possible, particularly when several hypotheses are being tested, or when very sensitive issues are being explored, but these should be the rare exceptions, and do not detract from the general principle.

Third, reports and information given to parents must be understood by them. Thus in addition to concerns about the defensibility of statements in reports (see above) professionals must also be aware of the need to avoid jargon, explain their meaning, and to provide useful advice. Similarly the parents' own views should be listened to and taken into account. Fourth, discussions of options must be held. If this includes transfer to a special school, the implications of this must be explored. A visit to the proposed school should also be arranged before a decision is made by the parents. It is rarely appropriate for this to be left to an administrator who has no contact with the family. Rather this task would normally be undertaken by the head, psychologist or education welfare officer.

Finally, professionals must be sensitive to their style of working. Are the parents being guided and helped to learn of the nature of their child's special needs, and the possibilities for assistance, or are they being manipulated into accepting the professionals' view of things? This is a very difficult issue as it strikes at the heart of each professional's self-awareness.

Provision

In some cases, an assessment will reveal no special needs, and so no extra provision will be required. In other cases, however, the LEA must state how it will meet the needs identified, in Section III of the statement.

Traditionally the use of special education procedures, using HP and later the SE forms, tended to be limited to children who required transfer to separate provision, i.e. special schools or units. In theory this was not intended to be the case, as the terms 'special education' and 'special educational treatment' were supposed to include any child requiring special help, e.g. in a remedial department. Under the 1981 Act this point is again emphasised, although it remains to be seen to what degree it will materialise.

Circular 1/83 suggests that:

Formal procedures should be initiated where there are prima facie grounds to suggest that a child's needs are such as to require provision additional to, or otherwise different from, the facilities and resources generally available in ordinary schools in the area under normal circumstances. (para. 13)

It goes on to suggest that these pupils will have 'severe or complex learning difficulties which require the provision, of extra resources in ordinary schools' (para 14), in addition to those youngsters in special schools and units. However, the Circular specifically exempts pupils for whom

schools provide special educational provision from their own resources in the form of additional tuition and remedial provision, or, in normal circumstances, where the child attends a reading centre or unit for disruptive children. (para. 15)

It is clear that the intention is to restrict statements to a very small number of pupils, and these sound suspiciously like those that presently attend special provision. It must be remembered that the Circular does not have the force of law — interpretation of the Act is for the courts — but what will this mean in practice? If schools successfully integrate pupils, with the help of their own remedial provision, will that render those pupils ineligible for a statement? Surely the Circular cannot be reinforcing the old idea of medically defined conditions? What of pupils with specific learning difficulties — will they be excluded from the benefits of a statement? Are statements to be confined to the 2 per cent or all the 20 per cent suggested by the Warnock Committee?

There is clearly difficulty here. At the conceptual level there is some confusion over who has special needs, and whether there are, or are not, different groups of children. At the practical level there is the issue of which children should be the subject of statements. The Act and accompanying Circular clearly have in mind a small number, i.e. about 2 per cent, who represent those children presently within the special education system. There is, therefore, a danger of simply perpetuating a system whereby special education is seen as a segregated system. Avoidance of this will depend on the policies of LEAs in making provision to meet the needs identified, and on the results of appeals by parents against LEAs who, they believe, are not making the appropriate provision. Pressure will almost certainly come from a number of groups.

First, parents who want their child integrated into the ordinary school system, and demand extra resources to enable this to happen. This is already happening but in a random way, resulting in individual children being integrated in odd schools and little overall planning of resource allocation. Section 2(2) of the Act specifies that the child must be 'educated in an ordinary school' but, under Section 2(3) there are three let-out clauses. This education must be compatible with:

(a) his receiving the special educational provision that he requires;
(b) the provision of efficient education for the children with whom he will be educated; and
(c) the efficient use of resources.

Second, parents of children in the so-called 18 per cent, who are regarded as having special needs, but about whom the LEA may be reluctant to make a statement. The main population here will be those pupils with reading difficulties, particularly those who may be called 'dyslexic'. Given the problem over definitions (see Chapter 4) it is questionable whether it is possible to decide on psychoeducational grounds whether many such children should be the subject of statements or not. It remains to be seen whether LEAs adopt loose or rigid approaches to this issue.

Third, there are pressure groups, whether of parents or combinations of parents and others, who object to the type of provision made. In the 1970s the West Indian community particularly took great exception to the apparent over-representation of their children in ESN(M) schools (Rampton Report, Cmnd. 8273, 1981). Recently concern had been expressed about the growth of units for children considered to have behavioural problems. Again, the West

Indian community had been particularly affected. The argument here, therefore, is not whether provision should be made, but its type. Unlike the pressure groups discussed above who *want* their children recognised as having special needs, the groups under consideration here would challenge this concept, arguing that their children are normal, but are subjected to inappropriate curricula, and in the case of some ethnic minority groups, racism.

Conclusions

The 1981 Education Act has been seen by different people in quite different ways. Some argue that it perpetuates a legal framework which is against the interests of children. Others would suggest that it does not go far enough in protecting children. There are many issues to be resolved, which can only be worked out in practice. There are ambiguities, but that is in the nature of the issue. Once it is accepted that children cannot be easily, and justly, classified, it becomes very difficult to produce a precise framework which applies only to a defined population.

It is important, therefore, to return to the issue of motivation. If the ideas behind the Warnock Report are accepted then we should be producing a system which aims to identify needs and then make suitable provision to meet those needs. Parents are seen as partners and the process is viewed as a collaborative venture to ensure the best outcome for the child. This will depend on the needs specified and may range from appliances to help the child in the ordinary classroom to transfer to a separate school.

However, this view can be said to be too rosy. At a time of stringent cutbacks in the education service, resources are being reduced. Provision, therefore, may be made which is a very loose approximation to a 'good fit'. Similarly schools, under increasing pressure, may be more keen to define a pupil as having special educational needs resulting from patterns of behaviour, more for the sake of the school than the benefit of the individual child.

Clearly these issues range beyond the educational, into the legal and political arenas. Professionals must be aware of these perspectives, as must parents. However, I would contend that it is important to discriminate between the legal-political and educational issues, and this should be possible under the Act. If professionals really are working with parents, for the children, the assessment part of the process is the place to make a clear statement of the young person's needs. The provision to meet those needs is, as has been stated above, a quite different issue. It is here that the main debates should be held, and battles fought.

12 SUPPORT SERVICES

Geoff Lindsay

In the previous chapter the implications of the 1981 Education Act were discussed, with the main emphasis on its formal aspects. As part of the requirement of this Act, educational psychologists and medical officers as well as teachers must be involved in the process of assessing special educational needs. Other professionals, social workers for example, will also be involved in particular cases (*Education (Special Educational Needs) Regulations 1983*, DES, 1983a). These professionals could act with very little discussion or collaboration.

Circular 1/83, *Assessment and Statements of Special Educational Needs* (DES, 1983b) devotes a section to co-operation. It is suggested that a sequence of reports may be sensible (as with the previous SE procedure) with educational advice being followed by medical and then psychological advice. However, it also states that professional advisers could submit reports separately to the LEA, although each professional should have a copy of other available reports. In some instances a case conference might be useful.

At this basic level there is an issue only of sharing knowledge in the most efficient way. However, the concern here is also one of efficacy and it will be argued that this is improved by setting up informal, though efficient, systems of collaboration between schools and support agencies. To this end the suggestion in the Warnock Report of five stages of assessment, at each of which a more specialised person is brought in, will be challenged.

Who are the Main Outside Professionals?

In order for teachers in schools to have a realistic appraisal of what the support services can provide, it is important to have some basic knowledge about them. All the major services have undergone changes of various kinds in the past 15 years. The number of professions and the number of members of each profession have increased during the past 20 years. In many cases there have also been major changes in roles of these professionals and publications

245

which describe these which are more than a few years old are likely to be out of date. For example, Ince (1974) describes the School Psychological Service as 'another important aspect of medical help' (p. 174).

Educational Psychologists

There are at present just over 1,000 educational psychologists in England and Wales, an increase from 326 in 1965. This increase followed the publication of the Summerfield Report in 1968 which argued for an expansion of training courses to meet the demand. Every LEA now has a psychological service, although the level of staffing is variable across the country. The Warnock Report recommended that there should be one educational psychologist for every 5,000 children and young people of 0 to 19 years. If this aim were to be met, two to three times as many psychologists would be required. Although a number of LEAs have recently expanded to meet the demands of the 1981 Education Act, there is no immediate likelihood of this ratio being achieved.

Educational psychologists have a training in both psychology and education. The normal pattern now is for a person to take a first degree in psychology and then undertake postgraduate training as a teacher. At least two years teaching will then be undertaken, preferably in a range of schools, before postgraduate training in educational psychology. Some, however, train initially as teachers and later gain a first degree in psychology or a Master of Education with an approved amount of psychology, after many years teaching, before undertaking the postgraduate training. Some will have been senior teachers, including heads, of schools. The situation in Scotland is different where a shorter period of training is possible, and teaching is not necessarily expected.

The role of educational psychologists has expanded greatly over the past 10 to 15 years. At one time much of the work was in a child guidance clinic, together with a child psychiatrist and psychiatric social worker, where a major task was assessing children on a variety of tests. During the 1970s a major challenge to this role was made. The reasons for this were varied, including the major influx of new psychologists entering the profession, and reorganisation of local government; education and health services being presented with new demands (e.g. raising of school leaving age and LEAs acquiring responsibility for mentally handicapped youngsters); and studies which examined the effectiveness of current practice. A survey of the work of educational psychologists at the end of the decade revealed involvement in a vast range of activities in many different settings and with many different client groups (Wedell and Lambourne, 1980). Teachers and other professionals are not always aware of these facts. For example, a typical educational psychologist might have 30 to 40 ordinary schools plus special schools and units. In some county areas, or places with inferior provision, this might rise to 60 to 70. Work with individual youngsters might include severely handicapped pre-school children, toddlers with behaviour problems at home, a junior pupil with a specific learning difficulty, and a 15-year-old who is about to be excluded or suspended from school. In addition to their work with individual children educational psychologists work with parents and teachers. They also contribute to in-service training, particularly of teachers, and to the policy-making of LEAs.

The amount of time currently spent with pupils subject to the SE procedure is certainly a minority. Wedell and Lambourne report that about 40 per cent of time was spent on *all* assessment work, much of which would not be part of the formal SE procedure. The 1981 Education Act may, however, result in the need to allocate more time to the formal assessment procedure and unless staffing ratios are improved in line with the Warnock recommendations, other important work will suffer.

In a minority of cases, clinical psychologists employed by the health service might also be involved in the assessment process. These are people with first degrees in psychology and a post-graduate qualification in clinical psychology. They are usually hospital-based, although there is a movement to increase community-based work. It is estimated that about 300 clinical psychologists work at least part of their time with children and young people (Lindsay and Cogill, in press) but this includes many who work with only specific groups (e.g. mentally handicapped) or in certain units (e.g. adolescent psychiatric units). As far as the assessment process is concerned, it is advocated by the DES that an educational psychologist is *always* involved, but that in some cases he or she should co-ordinate the contribution of a psychologist colleague. How frequently this occurs will depend on local provision — in many places there will be no relevant clinical psychologists, while in London, with its large numbers of hospitals cutting across LEA boundaries, the situation can be more complicated.

Over the past 10 to 15 years, therefore, educational psychologists have increased in number but their workload has also expanded. In addition, their *style* of working has also changed. It will be argued below that there are great benefits from a greater use of the informal assessment procedures. But this requires educational psychologists to be available for fequent visits to secondary schools, normally at least once every two to three weeks. Criticisms of the involvement of psychologists in the previous HP and SE procedures usually pertained to either a delay in responding, or the inappropriateness of the assessment. Increases in personnel and changes in practice have helped to reduce these complaints. The need for assessment over time, and the limited appropriateness of the 'one-off' assessment, demand closer collaboration with teachers, parents and other workers. In many areas this is already happening and it is to be hoped that the existing good practices can easily be accommodated to the demands of the new Act. This will require agreed methods of collaboration in schools, which are normally aided by a time-contracting system of organisation, whereby the psychologist allocates a set time for visits according to the needs of the pupils in that school, and other commitments (Forrester, 1981). However, it must also be remembered that the educational psychologist is independent of the school, and in some cases parents must feel confident of this, particularly if they are in dispute with the school.

Teachers

Within a secondary school it is now common for a number of teachers to have posts of responsibility in the area of pastoral care. In the case of a pupil who has special educational needs, the school should have a system for identifying those needs (see Chapter 2). In addition there must be a way for outside professionals to be involved in an efficient manner. This requires one or two key people to act at this interface. They must organise and be responsible for the system of surveillance and ensure that information is passed to appropriate people — far from easy tasks in a large secondary school. There are also teachers who will be providing for the needs identified.

In most schools the responsibility for the organisation of pastoral care will be taken by an assistant headteacher. Discovery of and action for learning problems will be part of the brief of the remedial teacher, while the comparable processes for emotional and behavioural problems will be the responsibility of form tutors and year tutors (or housemasters/mistresses).

If an assessment under Section 5 of the 1981 Education Act is requested, which requires completion of a statement, the school must have a coherent system for gathering the relevant data and making its thoughts known. Unlike a primary school where the educational part of the statement will probably be completed by the classteacher and head, the secondary school must in some way produce a combined educational input, as perhaps 12 or more teachers will have an appropriate comment. In some cases this can be left to one or two specialists (e.g. remedial teacher, year tutor) but this will often be insufficient. Particularly in cases of emotional and behavioural difficulties, the effects of situations may be highly relevant, so demanding information from different teachers. Thus the final educational report will be an amalgam of several teachers' perspectives.

But increasingly there are other teachers available to schools, though not on their own staff. Many LEAs have for some time employed peripatetic remedial teachers, but some have now followed the recommendations of the Warnock Report and appointed advisory teachers and peripatetic specialist teachers. Some may be attached to existing special schools; in other cases they exist as a separate, centrally organised service. Such teachers can have much to offer both on the level of advice and direct teaching. However, this service must fit in with the schools and other services and there needs to be a coherent system of collaboration if duplication of effort or confusion is not to occur. Unfortunately some services have been set up without such careful planning.

When teachers from such a Special Education Advisory and Support Service (to use Warnock's phrase) are available, their views must also often be incorporated into the educational component of the statement. This is particularly necessary if such a teacher has actually been teaching the youngster.

Medical Officers

Traditionally the medical assessment of children considered to need special education was provided by school medical officers, employed by the LEA. With reorganisation in 1974, responsibility for the renamed clinical medical officers was transferred to the Area Health Authority. Following the latest health service reorganisation, in 1982, this responsibility transfers to the District

Health Authority. Such doctors require no special training in either paediatrics or educational medicine to enable them to practise, although only those who had undertaken a 3 to 4 week approved course were allowed to ascertain pupils as educationally subnormal and requiring special education. The school health service was for long regarded as unattractive by doctors, having a poor career structure and low status. The Court Report on child health services (DHSS, 1976), criticised the lack of co-ordination between school doctors and general practitioners, and recommended an integrated service — a suggestion which was not accepted by the medical profession. The Committee also recommended that adolescents should have access to a doctor for at least one confidential interview at about 13 years to discuss personal matters, and that each school should have: 'a doctor and nurse nominated as their school doctor and school nurse who are suitably qualified and knowledgeable about educational medicine and nursing.' (DHSS 1976, para. 10.10)

The present position, however, is little changed from pre-Court days. Many areas do now have named doctors for schools but as the service continues to have low status it is often regarded as short-term employment, so leading to a lack of continuity. There is still very little training in educational medicine and often poor integration of the service with the hospital and general practitioner services. In seeking medical advice, which forms part of the statement, the LEA should, according to the Education (Special Educational Needs) Regulation 1983, obtain this advice from 'a fully registered medical practitioner who is either designated for the purposes of this Regulation by the district health authority or is nominated by them in the case in question. This will usually be a clinical medical officer.'

Experience of working in the previous SE system has revealed that in most cases the clinical medical officer has only a limited contribution — it was not unknown for the relevant form, SE2, to be almost blank apart from the child's personal details (name, address, etc.). In cases of severe handicap, hospital consultants will be involved; in certain cases of emotional or behavioural problems, psychiatrists will be the most relevant; while in the majority of cases no significant medical information will be relevant. It is certainly necessary that an assessment of a child is made to rule out medical factors contributing to a problem of development, but the system is still far short of the comprehensive and integrated service advocated by the Court Committee. The danger is that, as some-times happens, doctors make *educational* assessments and recom-mendations, rather than limit themselves to indicating the *possible* educational *implications* of medical factors.

However, in some areas doctors are working more productively with schools and other professionals in a way similar to that recommended by Court. Where this happens benefits to both pupils and staff, who have regular access to the school doctor, are apparent. This seems to depend on two factors: first, good working relationships where each professional respects the limits of his or her expertise, and second where involvement is at a school level and seen to be effective. Such doctors, if they are attached to a par-ticular school for a period of time, can build up a good picture of need and local characteristics, and become familiar and less threatening to pupils.

Education Welfare Officers

Education Welfare Officers (EWOs) are another group whose role has changed, or perhaps begun to change. Traditionally they were the 'truant catchers' or 'school bobbies', but their role has expanded into several areas of welfare (e.g. providing information on entitlement to free school meals and educational maintenance allowances). A survey by MacMillan (1977) found that most were involved with children with special needs at some time, if only the escorting of pupils to residential schools. In some cases they were the first professional to identify a pre-school child with special educational needs.

During the 1970s, as a result of recommendations of the Ralphs Committee (Local Government Training Board, 1975), there was an increase in formal training of EWOs, many of whom took the Certificate of Qualification in Social Work, as part of a move to develop an education social work agency. However, this step was taken by very few LEAs, and most EWOs remain without a formal social work training.

In many schools the EWO is limited in function to ensuring attendance, yet many are able to contribute a great deal to the identification of children with special needs and to help alleviate these. Some EWOs who have worked in one area for many years become well known to families, who respect their help and advice. In some cases they are the first to hear about sensitive problems. For example, one highly respected female EWO, well known in the area in which she both lived and worked, was informed of such delicate matters as schoolgirl pregnancy and incest. Such a person is able to not only support the family in times of stress, but advise them of how to make best use of other services — a far cry from the image of the truant catcher (although this particular EWO also carries out that function with great efficiency).

It is not clear how the role of EWOs will change during the next decade. Some wish to apply the casework approaches of social work, rather than be concerned with welfare rights. Some LEAs have appointed Education Social Workers to specific schools, to act as social workers from a school base. But whatever route is taken, EWOs or ESWs provide a valuable resource. Although the statement does not require a contribution from them, this can often be a very useful addition when a school and the EWO or ESW have a concept of the role which includes close working with parents and youngsters with difficulties.

Social Workers

Most social workers who are relevant to this discussion are employed by the local authority's Social Services Departments, or by a few bodies such as the National Society for the Prevention of Cruelty to Children. There are many reasons why a youngster with difficulty may have contact with social workers. This might be specific to the young person when, for example, he or she is subject to a care order. In other cases it will be another member of the family who is the client, and the social worker is aware of the pupil in question by contact with the family. In some cases of multiple and complex difficulties it might be the whole family that is receiving help from the social services department.

Social workers are often criticised by teachers and indeed by many members of the public. Well-publicised errors of judgement, particularly those involving abuse of young children and babies, resulted in an enquiry into the role and tasks of social workers — the Barclay Report (National Institute for Social Work, 1982). This provides a comprehensive account of the work of social workers, although it has itself been subject to criticism in the profession's journal, *Social Work Today*, following its publication. The Barclay Report states that in 1980 there were approximately 15,700 field social workers engaged in frontline social work, a further 5,000 who were team leaders or area or divisional managers, and 4,000 in headquarters or advisory posts. Over 70 per cent of the frontline workers were qualified, and the profession was growing at a very fast rate: 3,500 people per year were receiving qualifications. Although only about 3 per cent of field social workers were below 25 years of age, 65 per cent were between 25 and 45 years. The profession is, therefore, quite young, though the Report states that: 'The conventional view that most field social workers are very young and inexperienced is not, therefore, supported by this evidence' (p. 25—6).

Excluding management staff there was one local authority field social worker for every 3,200 of the population (of whom about 600 to 700 would be of school age). The Report also estimates that for every 10,000 population, served by three social workers, a team leader and social work assistant, a typical year would bring the following: 25 divorces, affecting up to 30 children; 150 single parent families, with up to 350 children; 2 adoptions; 150 children displaying moderate to severe behaviour problems; one case of child abuse and several children on the 'at risk' register. Twenty children will be in the care of the local authority at any one time, and 10 or 11 will be received into care in a year. (N.B. Social workers also deal with many other client groups including the elderly and mentally handicapped.)

A large number of pupils at secondary school with emotional and behavioural problems will be known to social workers, but there is a history of poor communication between social workers and teachers. Some of this is based on a lack of awareness of the other profession's work — the constraints, workload and required duties. For example, teachers often think a youngster should be taken into care when they are aware of an apparently damaging family background, but the social worker may not have the power to do this, or the resources to use even if this were possible. Other problems are a result of different philosophies. The stereotyped teacher is authoritarian, making the youngster fit a 'bad' system, while the equivalent stereotyped social worker is young, inexperienced and too easily manipulated by the young person to adopt only his or her perspective. Some attempts have been made recently to overcome these problems, an example being a project jointly funded by the DES and DHSS, Working Together for Children in Sheffield. Apart from producing practical suggestions, one aim was that the actual working together by teachers, social workers and many other professionals would enable attitudes to be revealed and examined.

The Regulations recommend that where relevant the social services authority should provide evidence. This would form part of Section II of the statement but would be produced in full as part of Appendix G. In order for this to be effective it is necessary, as with other professionals, for the social worker to have a positive working relationship with the school. This does not necessarily imply collusion, but that the child's educational and social needs can be fully explored, from different perspectives, finally providing a coherent picture. This is especially important when residential placement is concerned — should this be in a residential special school or a children's home?

Collaboration

One theme running through the previous section was the need for collaboration among professionals. There are two main reasons for this. First, negative attitudes among professionals towards each other's worth or practice can interfere with the optimal delivery of a service to children. Justified criticism and examination of working practices are necessary, but are best done in a positive manner. Second, the need to consider a youngster within a context has increasingly been recognised. For young people the main contexts are the family, the school and the peer group. Each professional has a particular perspective which can lead to erroneous assumptions if taken alone. However, when several are combined, a comprehensive picture can be built up of the youngster's needs.

Collaboration is not always easy. Tomlinson (1981) reports a study of the assessment process in one city for children entering ESN(M) schools, and reveals an unhealthy lack of respect and competitiveness. She relates this to the emerging power of educational psychologists and other educationalists (e.g. advisers and education officers) while the medical officers were gradually losing their influence. Of course all groups of people have problems of status, personal relationships and working together and it would be naive to expect that this would happen easily across professional bodies. But the optimal delivery of the services demands that attempts be made to ensure that good practice is developed.

There are also practical difficulties, even assuming good will. The data on numbers of professionals reveal that they are relatively few in number. For example, a secondary school might have the equivalent of 50 per cent of an education welfare officer, and 5 to 10 per cent of an educational psychologist. Demands on social workers and others will also be such that little time is available for any one school. The difference in boundaries (they are rarely co-terminous between professions) reduces the degree of time overlap still further. However, outside professionals can optimise their availability to the school. Psychologists commonly see pupils from a specific group of schools rather than in clinics, so increasing availability. School doctors and EWOs are also usually allocated to specific schools. When this occurs, each professional can build up a view of the school context in which the pupil operates. Also meetings can be held at school which enable the teacher to meet and discuss pupils' problems informally. Such discussions were advocated in Chapter 2 when the new entrants had settled in and teachers had had a chance to notice problems of adjustment. Regular, though not frequent, meetings for other year groups can also be useful. At these meetings information collected by teachers can be considered and the advice of other professionals be solicited. As a result, it might be decided that a fuller investigation by a psychologist, medical officer or other specialist is required.

One criticism of this approach is the charge that it leads to collusion. There can be a healthy aspect to different professionals challenging each other's practice. In a particular case perhaps the teachers are overreacting to a problem so causing it to magnify, or the psychologist is not sufficiently sympathetic to the needs of the teachers and peers, in addition to those of the pupil in question. Working together, therefore, should not become too cosy with each professional simply bolstering the self-image of colleagues. It must be remembered that the reason for their being there is the well-being of the young person.

Another potential difficulty is choosing the time to involve parents. The argument presented here is that parents are highly important in this process, not simply from a position of their rights but because their active involvement is usually in the best interests of the pupil. Hopefully parents will have been involved in discussions with teachers before other professionals are brought in, but on occasion teachers will wish to discuss a child whose parents have not been informed: perhaps a worrying incident had occurred just prior to the psychologist's visit. It is rare for doctors and psychologists to see a young person below 16 years when the parents have not been informed and given their consent but a discussion of whether there is a need to involve such a professional is a slightly different matter. This should happen rarely if a school has developed a close relationship with its parents.

Collaboration between teachers and other professionals, and with parents, does pose difficulties, but is necessary if the pupil's needs are to be properly identified and met. This requires sensitive approaches by each person to the others, and parents and professionals are respected for their particular contribution. But beyond these interpersonal skills there is a need for an efficient, well-conceived system. Information gathering must be relevant and presented in a way understood by others involved, while discussions should be well organised with a clear focus not on raising one's own status, or denigrating that of another, but on ensuring that the youngster's special needs are identified and that provision to meet those needs made.

NOTES ON CONTRIBUTORS

Phil Budgell, Educational Psychologist, City of Sheffield Education Department, Psychological Service; former head of Sheaf Centre, Sheffield.

Kathleen Cox, Senior Educational Psychologist, City of Sheffield Education Department, Psychological Service.

Martin Desforges, Educational Psychologist, City of Sheffield Education Department, Psychological Service.

Eileen Gledhill, Headteacher, Bradfield School, Sheffield.

Brian Harrison, Senior Educational Psychologist, City of Sheffield Education Department, Psychological Service.

Geoff Lindsay, Senior Educational Psychologist, City of Sheffield Education Department, Psychological Service; and Honorary Lecturer, Division and Institute of Education, University of Sheffield.

Mike Pomerantz, Senior Educational Psychologist, Psychological Service, Derbyshire; and Honorary Lecturer, Division and Institute of Education, University of Sheffield.

BIBLIOGRAPHY

Advisory Centre for Education (1980) 'Disruptive units', *Where*, 158, 15−16

Ainscow, M. and Tweddle, D. (1979) *Preventing Classroom Failure: An Objectives Approach*, Wiley, Chichester

Ashton, P., Kneen, P., Davies, F. and Holley, B. (1975) *The Aims of Primary Education: A Study of Teachers' Opinion*, Macmillan, Basingstoke

Athey, L. (1978) 'Current provision for remedial education in Welsh secondary schools', *Remedial Education*, 13, 123−8

Axline, V. (1971) *Dibs: In Search of Self*, Penguin, Harmondsworth

Bailey, T. J. (1979) 'Arithmetical difficulties of less able pupils in the secondary school — some thoughts on assessment and remediation', *Remedial Education*, 14, 204−10

Baldwin, J. and Wells, H. (1979) *Active Tutorial Work*, Blackwell, Oxford

Ball, S. (1981) *Beachside Comprehensive*, Cambridge University Press, Cambridge

Becker, W. C., Engelmann, S., Carnine, D. W. and Rhine, R. (1981) 'Direct Instruction Model', in R. Rhine (ed.), *Making Schools More Effective*, Academic Press, London

Berg, I. (1980a) 'School refusal in early adolescence', in L. Hersov and I. Berg (eds.), *Out of School*, Wiley, Chichester

——— (1980b) 'Absence from school and the Law', in L. Hersov and I. Berg (eds.), *Out of School*, Wiley, Chichester

Bernstein, A. (1976) 'How to tell children about sex', *Psychology Today*, 2(12), 46−51

Best, R., Jarvis, C. and Ribbins, P. (eds.) (1980) *Perspectives on Pastoral Care*, Heinemann, London

Bird, C., Chessum, R., Furlong, J. and Johnson, D. (1980) *Disaffected Pupils*, Brunel University, Educational Studies Unit

Blume, J. (1980) *Are You There God? It's Me Margaret*, Piccolo, Basingstoke

Brennan, W. (1979) *Curricular Needs of Slow Learners*, Evans/Methuen, London

Brown, R. T. (1980) 'A closer examination of the Education for all handicapped children Act: A guide for the 1980s', *Psychology in the Schools*, 17, 355−60

Budgell, P. W. (1982) 'Working with the parents of pupils who refuse to attend school', *Occasional Papers of the Division of Educational and Child Psychology*, 6(1), 65−72

Burns, P. M. (1979) 'The Weakness in Current School Design', *Education*, 31 August, 213−15

Byrne, D., Williamson, B. and Fletcher, B. (1975) *The Poverty of Education*, Martin Robertson, London

Chazan, M. (1962) 'School Phobia', *British Journal of Educational Psychology*, 32, 209−17

——— Cox, T., Jackson, S. and Laing, A. (1977) *Deprivation and Development.* Schools Council, London

Clarke, A. D. B. (1978) 'Predicting human behaviour: Problems, evidence, implications', *Bulletin of the British Psychological Society*, 31, 249−58

Clarke, R. V. G. (ed.) (1978) *Tackling Vandalism*, HMSO, London

Clift, P., Weiner, G. and Wilson, E. (1981) *Record-keeping in the primary school*. Macmillan, Basingstoke

Cohen, R. N. (1982) *Whose file is it anyway?*, National Council for Civil Liberties, London

Cohen, S. (1973) 'Property destruction: Motives and meanings', in C. Ward (ed.), *Vandalism*, Architectural Press, London

Cole, M. (1973) *What about a new approach to sex education?*, available from 38 School Lane, Birmingham

Conrad, R. (1979) *The Deaf School Child*. Harper & Row, London

Cook, B. (1977) *A look at vandalism in the United States of America*. Central Office of Information, London

Cooper, J. (1981) *The British in Love*, Penguin, Harmondsworth

Cope, C. and Anderson, E. (1977) *Special Units in Ordinary Schools*, University of London Institute of Education, London

Cornwall, K. and Spicer, J. (1982) 'DECP enquiry: the role of the educational psychologist in the discovery and assessment of children requiring special education', *Division of Education and Child Psychology Occasional Papers*, 6(2), 3–30

Cox, K. (1981) 'Experiential learning for teachers in sex education', *Occasional Papers of the Division of Educational and Child Psychology*, 5(3)

—— and Lavelle, M. (1982) 'The role and contribution of the visitor', *Interface*, Sheffield Local Education Authority, Sheffield

Cox, T. (1978) 'Children's Adjustment to school over six years', *Journal of Child Psychology and Psychiatry*, 19, 363–71

Crampton-Smith, G. (1977) *Too Great a Risk*, Family Planning Association, London

Crisp, A. H., Palmer, R. L. and Kalucy, R. S. (1976) 'How common is anorexia nervosa? A prevalence study', *British Journal of Psychiatry*, 128, 549–54

Dallas, D. (1972) *Sex Education in School and Society*, National Foundation for Educational Research, Windsor

Dalton, K. (1979) *Once a Month*, Fontana, London

Davie, R. (1982) 'Child development in context', *Education Section Review*, 6(1), 4–12, British Psychological Society, Leicester.

—— Butler, N. and Goldenstein, H. (1972) *From Birth to Seven,* Longmans, London

Dawson, R. (1980) *Special Provision for Disturbed Pupils: A Survey*, Macmillan, Basingstoke

Department of Education and Science (1968) *Psychologists in the Education Services*, HMSO, London

—— (1971) *Slow Learners in Secondary Schools* (Education Survey, Number 15), HMSO, London

—— (1975) *A Language for Life* (Bullock Report), HMSO, London

—— (1977) *Education in Schools — a Consultative Document*, Cmnd. 6869, HMSO, London

—— (1978a) *Special Educational Needs* (Warnock Report), HMSO, London

—— (1978b) *Behavioural Units: A Survey of Special Units for Pupils with Behavioural Problems*, Department of Education and Science, London

—— (1980) *Special Needs in Education*, Cmnd. 7996, HMSO, London

—— (1981) Circular 8/81, *The Education Act 1981*, HMSO, London

—— (1983a) *Education (Special Educational Needs) Regulations 1983*, HMSO, London

—— (1983b) *Assessments and Statements of Special Educational Needs*, Circular 1/83, HMSO, London

Department of Health and Social Security (1974) *One Parent Families* (Finer Report), Cmnd. 5629, HMSO, London

—— (1976) *Fit for the Future* (Court Report), Cmnd. 6684, HMSO, London

Design Council (1979) *Designing Against Vandalism*, Heinemann, London

Dorn, N. (1981) 'Social analysis of drugs in health education and the media', in G. Edwards and C. Busch (eds.), *Drug Problems in Britain: A Review of Ten Years*, Academic Press, London

—— and Thompson, A. (1976) 'Decision-making skills: a possible goal for drug education?' *Health Service Journal*, 35, 248–57.

Dowling, J. R. (1980) 'Adjustment from primary to secondary school: A one year follow-up', *British Journal of Educational Psychology*, 50, 26–32

Edwards, G. (1981) 'The Background', in G. Edwards and C. Busch (eds.), *Drug Problems in Britain: A Review of Ten Years*, Academic Press, London

Elder, F. (1980) 'Adolescence in historical perspective', in J. Adelson (ed.), *Handbook of Adolescent Psychology*, Wiley, Chichester

Emerson, S. (1982) 'Slush Money', *Sunday Express Magazine*, 29 August, 14

Equal Opportunities Commission (1982) 'Gender and the Secondary School Curriculum', *Research Bulletin number 6*, Equal Opportunities Commission, Manchester

Erikson, E. (1965) *Childhood and Society*, Penguin, Harmondsworth

Farrell, C. (1978) *My Mother Said*, Routledge & Kegan Paul, London

Farrington, D. P. (1978) 'The family background of aggressive youths', in L. Hersov, M. Berger and D. Shaffer (eds.), *Aggression and Anti-Social Behaviour in Childhood and Adolescence*, Pergamon, Oxford

Ferguson, N. and Adams, M. (1982) 'Assessing the advantages of team-teaching in remedial education: the remedial teacher's role', *Remedial Education*, 17, 24–31

Fogelman, K. (1976) *Britain's Sixteen Year Olds*, National Children's Bureau, London

Forrester, A. (1981) 'Reactions to a system of contract-based school work', *Association of Educational Psychologists Journal*, 5(5), 26–32

Gains, C. W. (1980) 'Remedial Education in the 1980s', *Remedial Education*, 15, 5–10

Galletley, I. (1976) 'How to do away with yourself', *Remedial Education*, 11, 149–51

Galloway, D. M. (1976) 'Size of school, socio-economic hardship, suspension rates and persistent unjustified absence from schools', *British Journal of Educational Psychology*, 46, 40–7

—— (1980) 'Problems of assessment and management of persistent absenteeism from school', in L. Hersov and I. Berg (eds.), *Out of School*, Wiley, Chichester

—— (1982) 'A study of persistent absentees and their families', *British Journal of Educational Psychology*, 52, 317–30

—— and Goodwin, C. (1979) *Educating Slow-Learning and Maladjusted Children — Integration or Segregation*, Longman, London

—— Ball, T., Blomfield, D. and Seyd, R. (1982) *Schools and Disruptive Pupils*, Longman, London

Geddes, A. and Crone, R. (1978) 'A programme for literacy in the mixed ability context', *Remedial Education*, 13, 182−7

Ghodse, H. (1981) 'Morbidity and mortality', in G. Edwards and C. Busch (eds.) *Drug Problems in Britain: A Review of Ten Years*, Academic Press, London

Ghodsian, M. and Calnan, M. (1977) 'A comparative longitudinal analysis of special education groups', *British Journal of Educational Psychology*, 47, 162−74

Gill, C. (1982) 'Integration for the deaf: a most restrictive environment', M.Sc. dissertation, University of Sheffield Institute of Education, Sheffield

Gillham, B. (ed.) (1981) *Problem Behaviour in the Secondary School*, Croom Helm, London

Goldman, R. and Goldman, J. (1982) *Children's Sexual Thinking*, Routledge & Kegan Paul, London

Graham, P. and Rutter, M. (1977) 'Adolescent disorders', in M. Rutter and L. Hersov (eds.), *Child Psychiatry: Modern Approaches*, Blackwell, Oxford

Gray, J. (1981) 'School effectiveness research: key issues', *Educational Research*, 24, 49−54

Gregory, R. P., Hackney, C. and Gregory, N. M. (1982), 'Corrective reading programmes: An evaluation', *British Journal of Educational Psychology*, 52, 33−50

Hallahan, D. P. and Cruickshank, W. M. (1973) *Psychoeducational Foundations of Learning Disabilities*, Prentice Hall, London

Hamblin, D. H. (1974) *The Teacher and Counselling*, Blackwell, Oxford

Hannon, V. (1982) 'The Education Act 1981: New rights and duties in special education', *Journal of Social Welfare Law*, 275−84

Hargreaves, D. H. (1967) *Social Relationships in a Secondary School*, Routledge & Kegan Paul, London

—— (1982) *The Challenge for the Comprehensive*, Routledge & Kegan Paul, London

—— Hestor, S. and Mellor, F. J. (1975) *Deviance in Classrooms*, Routledge & Kegan Paul, London

Haring, N., Lovitt, T., Eaton, M. and Hansen, C. (1978) *The Fourth R: Research in the Classroom*, Merrill, Columbus

Harms, E. (1965) *Drug Addiction in Youth*, Pergamon, Oxford

Harrison, C. (1980) *Readability in the Classroom*, Cambridge University Press, Cambridge

Hastings, J. (1981) 'One school's experience', in B. Gillham (ed.), *Problem Behaviour in the Secondary School*, Croom Helm, London

Hawton, K. (1982) 'Attempted suicide in children and adolescents', *Journal of Child Psychology and Psychiatry*, 23, 497−503

Hayman, S. (1977) *Advertising and Contraceptives*, Birth Control Trust and Brook Advisory Centre, London

Hegarty, S. and Pocklington, K. (1981) *Educating Pupils with Special Needs in the Ordinary School*, NFER-Nelson, Windsor

—— (1982) *Integration in Action*, NFER-Nelson, Windsor

Herbert, M. (1978) *Conduct Disorders of Childhood and Adolescence*, Wiley, Chichester

Heron, A. (1963) *A Quaker View of Sex*, Friends House Service Committee, London

Hindley, C. B. and Owen, C. F. (1978) 'The extent of individual changes in I.Q.

for ages between 6 months and 17 years in a British longitudinal sample', *Journal of Child Psychology and Psychiatry*, 19, 329–50

Hobbs, N. and Robinson, S. (1982) 'Adolescent development and public policy', *American Psychologist*, 37, 212–23

Hoghughi, M. (1978) *Troubled and Troublesome*, Burnett Books, London

Hollingshead, A. (1949) *Elmstown's Youth*, Wiley, New York

Hornsby, B. and Miles, T. (1980) 'The effects of a dyslexia-centred teaching programme', *British Journal of Educational Psychology*, 50, 236–42

Ince, D. (1974) 'The supporting services', in M. Marland (ed.), *Pastoral Care*, Heinemann, London

Kamin, L. (1974) *The Science and Politics of I.Q.*, Wiley, Chichester

Keddie, N. (1973) *Tinker Taylor — The Myth of Cultural Deprivation*, Penguin, Harmondsworth

Kennedy, I. (1981) *The Unmasking of Medicine*, Allen & Unwin, London

King, M. (1981) *Childhood, Welfare and Justice*, Batsford, London

Leverhulme Trust (1978) *Health Education Project*, Nottingham University, Nottingham

Lewis, D. G. and Pumfrey, P. D. (1978) *Manual for the Lewis Counselling Inventory*, NFER, Windsor

Lindsay, G. A. (1980) 'Monitoring children's learning: an in-service approach', *British Journal of In-Service Education*, 6, 189–91

——— (1981a) 'Getting it out of your system', *Association of Educational Psycholgists Journal*, 5, 33–6.

——— (1981b) *The Infant Rating Scale*, Hodder & Stoughton, Sevenoaks

——— and Cogill, S. (in press) 'Psychological Services for children: A survey', *Bulletin of the British Psychological Society*

——— and Cox, K. (1982) 'Schoolgirl pregnancies', in SERCH, 3, University of Sheffield Institute of Education, Sheffield

——— and Pearson, L. S. (198!) *Identification and Intervention: School-based Approaches*, TRC, Oxford

Local Government Training Board (1975) *The Role and Training of Welfare Officers: Report of the Working Party*, Local Government Training Board, Luton

Lonton, A. (1979) 'The relationship between intellectual skills and the computerised axial tomograms of children with spina bifida and hydrocephalus', *Zeitschrift fur Kinderchirugie un Grenzgebiete*, 28, 368–74

McDermott, P. A. (1980) 'Principal components analysis of the revised Bristol Social Adjustment Guides', *British Journal of Educational Psychology*, 50, 223–8

Macey, M. (1978) 'Record cards — Education's best-kept secret', *Where*, 138, 139–42

MacMillan, K. (1977) *Education Welfare: Strategy and Structure*, Longman, London

Marks, I. M. and Gelder, M. G. (1966) 'Different ages of onset in varieties of phobia', *American Journal of Psychiatry*, 123, 218–21

Marland, M. (1974) *Pastoral Care*, Heinemann, London

Maslow, A. H. (1966) *The Psychology of Science: A Reconnaissance*, Harper & Row, New York

Masters, W. H. and Johnson, V. E. (1970) *Human Sexual Inadequacy*, Churchill,

London

Mayhew, P., Clarke, R. V. G., Sturman, A. and Hough, J. M. (1976) *Crime As Opportunity*, HMSO, London

Mayle, P. (1978) *Will I Like It?*, W. H. Allen, London

Miles, M. (1979) *Pregnant at School*, One Parent Families Association, London

Miller, L. C., Barrett, C. L. and Hampe, E. (1974) 'Phobias of childhood in a pre-scientific era', in A. Davids (ed.), *Child Personality and Psychopathology, Volume 1*, Wiley, New York

Morris, A., Giller, H., Szweld, E. and Geach, H. (1980) *Justice for Children*, Macmillan, Basingstoke

Moseley, D. (1975) *Special Provision for Reading*, NFER, Windsor

National Children's Bureau (1982) *Child Sexual Abuse and Incest*, Highlight Number 50, National Children's Bureau, London

National Institute for Social Work (1982) *Social Workers: Their Role and Tasks*, Bedford Square Press, London

Nelson-Jones, R. (1982) *The Theory and Practice of Counselling Pychology*, Holt, Reinhart & Winston, London

Newell, P. (1982) 'Private Lives?', *Times Educational Supplement*, 23 April, 18–19

Newman, L. (1982) 'Sex — Results of a nationwide survey', *19*, May/June

Palmer, R. L. (1980) *Anorexia Nervosa*, Penguin, Harmondsworth

Parish, P. (1980) *Medicines: A Guide for Everybody*, Penguin, Harmondsworth

Pavlidis, G. and Miles, T. (1981) *Dyslexia Research and its Application to Education*, Wiley, London

Pecherek, A. (1982) 'Do teachers give more attention to boys than they do to girls?', unpublished M.Sc. dissertation, Sheffield University Institute of Education, Sheffield

Pocs, O., Godow, A., Tolone, W. and Walsh, R. (1977) 'Can you imagine your parents' sex lives?', *Psychology Today*, October, 25–8

Preston, K. and Lindsay, G. A. (1976) 'Schoolgirl Mothers', *New Society*, 14 October, 76

Prewer, R. (1959) 'Some observations on window smashing', *British Journal of Delinquency*, 10

Pumfrey, P. D. (1976) *Reading: Tests and Assessment Techniques*, Hodder & Stoughton, London

——— (1981) 'The educational psychologist and the school counsellor', *Occasional Papers of the Division of Educational and Child Psychology*, 5(3), 15–21

——— and Ward, J. (1976) 'Adjustment from Primary to Secondary School', *Educational Research*, 19, 25–34

Reid, D. (1982) 'School sex education and the causes of unintended pregnancies — a review', *Health Education Journal*, 41, 4

Reid, K. and Kendall, L. (1982) 'A review of some recent research into persistent school absenteeism', *British Journal of Educational Studies*, 30, 295–312

Renvoize, J. (1982) *Incest: A family Pattern*, Routledge & Kegan Paul, London

Reynolds, D., Jones, D., St. Leger, S. and Murgatroyd, S. (1980) 'School factors and truancy', in Hersov, L. and Berg, I. (eds.) *Out of School*, Wiley, Chichester

Rice, B. (1980) *Young People on Drugs*, Teachers Advisory Council on Alcohol and Drug Education, Manchester

Roberts, R. (1976) *A Ragged Schooling*, Manchester University Press, Manchester

Robins, L. (1978) 'A study of childhood predictors of adult anti-social behaviour: replications from longitudinal studies', *Psychological Medicine*, 8, 611–22

Rogers, C. (1951) *Client Centred Therapy*, Houghton Mifflin, Boston

—— (1961) *On Becoming a Person*, Houghton Mifflin, Boston

Rutter, M. (1967) 'A children's behaviour questionnaire for completion by teachers: Preliminary findings', *Journal of Child Psychology and Psychiatry*, 8, 1–11

—— (1975) *Troubled Children*, Penguin, Harmondsworth

—— (1977) 'Classification', in M. Rutter and L. Hersov (eds.), *Child Psychiatry: Modern Approaches*, Blackwell, Oxford

—— (1979) *Changing Youth in a Changing Society*, Nuffield Provincial Hospitals Trust, London

—— and Hersov, L. (eds.) (1977) *Child Psychiatry: Modern Approaches*, Blackwell, Oxford

—— Tizard, J. and Whitmore, K. (1970) *Education, Health and Behaviour*, Longman, London

—— Graham, P., Chadwick, O. F. D. and Yule, W. (1976) 'Adolescent turmoil: fact or fiction?', *Journal of Child Psychology and Psychiatry*, 17, 35–56

—— Maughan, B., Mortimore, P. and Ouston, J. (1980) *Fifteen Thousand Hours*, Open Books, London

Sampson, O. (1980) *Child Guidance: Its History, Provenance and Future*, British Psychological Society, Leicester

—— and Pumfrey, P. D. (1970) 'A study of remedial education in the secondary stage of schooling', *Remedial Education*, 5, 102–11

Schacher, R., Rutter, M. and Smith, A. (1981) 'The characteristics of situationally pervasively hyperactive children: implications for syndrome definition', *Journal of Child Psychology and Psychiatry*, 22, 375–92

Schaffer, D., Pettigrew, A., Wolkind, S. and Jadijee, E. (1978) 'Psychiatric aspects of pregnancy in schoolgirls', *Psychological Medicine*, 8, 119–30

Schofield, M. (1965) *The Sexual Behaviour of Young People*, Penguin, Harmondsworth

—— (1973) 'V.D. and the Young', *New Society*, 18 October

Senior, P. H. (1979) 'Science for slow learners: some personal observations', *Remedial Education*, 14, 121–4

Sexual Problems of the Disabled (1978) advisory leaflet, from 49 Victoria Street, London SW1

Shaffer, D. (1974) 'Suicide in childhood and adolescence', *Journal of Child Psychology and Psychiatry*, 15, 275–91

Sheffield Metropolitan District Council (1978) *The Inner City*, Department of Planning and Design

—— (1978) *Sheffield Housing Survey*, Corporate Management Unit

Shepherd, M., Oppenheim, B. and Mitchell, S. (1971) *Childhood Behaviour and Mental Health*, University Press, London

Smith, F. (1978) *Reading*, Cambridge University Press, Cambridge

Spender, D. (1980) *Man Made Language*, Routledge & Kegan Paul, London

—— (1982) *Invisible Women: The Schooling Scandal*, Writers and Readers, London

Stepney, R. (1981) 'Habits and Addictions', *Bulletin of the British Psychological Society*, 34, 233–5

Stimson, J. (1981) 'Epidemiological research on drug use in general populations', in G. Edwards and C. Busch (eds.), *Drug Problems in Britain: A Review of Ten Years*, Academic Press, London

Stone, J. and Taylor, F. (eds.) (1977) *Vandalism in Schools*, Save The Children Fund, London

Stott, D. H. (1974) *Manual to the Bristol Social Adjustment Guides*, Hodder & Stoughton, London

Strain, P. S. and Kerr, M. M. (1981) *Mainstreaming of Children in Schools*, Academic Press, London

Sutherland, M. (1981) *Sex Bias in Education*, Blackwell, Oxford

Sutton, A. (1981) 'Science in court', in M. King (ed.), *Childhood, Welfare and Justice*, Batsford, London

Tansley, P. and Panckhurst, J. (1981) *Children with Specific Learning Difficulties*, NFER-Nelson, Windsor

Teachers Advisory Council on Alcohol and Drug Education (1981) *Free to Choose*, Manchester

Tizard, J. (1973) 'Maladjusted children and the child guidance service', *London Educational Review*, 2(2), 22–37

Toffler, A. (1971) *Future Shock*, Pan, London

Tomlinson, S. (1981) *Educational Subnormality: A Study in Decision-Making*, Routledge & Kegan Paul, London

——— (1982) *A Sociology of Special Education*, Routledge & Kegan Paul, London

Topping, K. (1983) *Educational Systems for Disruptive Adolescents*, Croom Helm, Beckenham

Truax, C. B. and Carkhuff, R. R. (1967) *Towards Effective Counselling and Psychotherapy*, Aldine, Chicago

Upton, G. and Gobell, A. (eds.) (1980) *Behaviour Problems in the Comprehensive School*, University College, Cardiff, Faculty of Education

Wall, J. and Cederblad, M. L. (1982) *Video and schoolchildren*, paper presented to the 5th International School Psychology Colloquium, Stockholm

Ward, C. (ed.) (1973) *Vandalism*, Architectural Press, London

Watson, J. M. (1979) 'Solvent Abuse: A retrospective study', *Community Medicine*, 1, 153–6

Wedell, K. (1960) 'The visual perception of cerebral palsied children', *Journal of Child Psychology and Psychiatry*, 1, 217–27

——— (1973) *Learning and Perceptuo-motor disabilities in Children,* Wiley, Chichester

——— and Lambourne, R. (1980) 'Psychological services for children in England and Wales', *Occasional Papers of the Division of Educational and Child Psychology*, 4 (1 and 2)

Wedge, P. and Prosser, N. (1973) *Born to Fail?*, Arrow, London

West, D. J. and Farrington, D. P. (1977) *The Delinquent Way of Life*, Heinemann, London

White, M. and Kidd, J. (1976) *Sound Sex Education*, Order of Christian Unity, London

Willis, J. (1973) *Addicts: Drugs and Alcohol Re-examined*, Pitman, London

Wilson, J. (1970) *Moral Thinking*, Heinemann, London

Woods, D. (1979) *The Divided School*, Routledge & Kegan Paul, London

266   *Bibliography*

Wright, J. D. and Pearl, L. (1981) 'Knowledge and experience of young people regarding drug abuse between 1969 and 1979', *British Medical Journal*, 282, 793–6

Yule, W. (1972) 'Differential prognosis of reading backwardness and specific reading retardation', *British Journal of Educational Psychology*, 43, 244–8

——— (1977) 'Behavioural approaches', in M. Rutter and L. Hersov (eds.), *Child Psychiatry: Modern Approaches*, Blackwell, Oxford

——— Hersov, L. and Treseder, J. (1980) 'Behavioural treatment of school refusal', in L. Hersov and I. Berg (eds.), *Out of School*, Wiley, Chichester

INDEX

adolescence, changing aspects of 6–9
  time of turmoil? 85–7
assessment 40–61
  academic 44
  continuous 46–7
  emphasis of 40–1
  personal development 44
  pupil profiles 48–61 *passim*
  setting up a school-based system
    41–7 *passim*
  see also identification of problems

bereavement 98–9
behaviour problems 104–25
  causes of 113–18; family 116–17;
    genetic 113–14; inner conflicts
    114–15; limited range of
    responses 117–18; school 106–8
  classification 87–8
  difficulties with definition 105–6
  difficulties with referral 104–5
  incidence 86–7
  intervention 107–9, 118–25;
    analysis of classroom
    environment 122–4; role-playing
    118–20; teacher support
    111–13; *see also* counselling
  persistence 106–7
Bullock Report 20

Child Guidance Clinics 66–7
counselling 90, 112, 120–2, 144–5,
  181
Court Report 250–1
curriculum
  review 50, 57–8
  sex education 150–7; aims 150–2;
    content 126, 130–1; organisa-
    tion 152–7; teaching methods
    157–8
  see also special educational needs,
    curriculum

Disadvantage 69–70, 205–7
Divorce 99–100
  effects 99–100
  incidence 8, 99
drugs 161–81

adult reactions 174–6
definitions 161–3
dependence 163
factors affecting use 171–4
incidence of use 168–71
intervention 176–80
types 164–7; deliriants 167;
  hallucinogens 167; sedatives
  164–6
dyslexia 67, 82

Education Act (1981) 2, 10, 231–44
  parents 237
  provision 240–3
  statements 13, 234–6
  see also rights,children; rights,
    parents
emotional problems 85–104
  classification 87–8
  incidence 86–7
  types: anorexia nervosa 102–4;
    anxiety 88–91; phobias 91–4;
    school refusal (school phobia)
    94–7; suicide and parasuicide
    100–2; unhappiness 97–8
  see also bereavement, divorce

glue sniffing *see* drugs, types,
  deliriants

identification of problems 20–39
  academic 24–6, 35–9
  content 24–7, 29–30
  pastoral 26–7, 35–9
  problems of prediction 21–2
  timing 28–9
integration 9–13, 17

learning difficulties 62–84
  causes of 65–71; constitutional
    67–9; emotional 66–7;
    environmental 69–70; general
    intelligence 65–6
  provision for 71–84; across the
    curriculum 74–5; effectiveness
    72–3; special class 71;
    withdrawal groups 75–8